CROSSING THE BARRIERS

The
Paralympic
Legends
of India

CROSSING THE BARRIERS

Abhishek Dubey with **Mahavir Rawat**

KONARK

Konark Publishers Pvt. Ltd
206, First Floor,
Peacock Lane, Shahpur Jat,
New Delhi - 110 049
+91-11-4105 5065
india@konarkpublishers.com, us@konarkpublishers.com
www.konarkpublishers.com

ISBN: 978-81-963629-9-7

Edited by Preeta Priyamvada
Jacket design by Rohit Kathuria
Images for front jacket, endpapers and inserts© Paralympic Committee of India
Icons © Shutterstock
Typeset by Saanvi Graphics, Noida
Printed and bound at Saurabh Printers Pvt. Ltd, Greater Noida

Dedicated to

Maa
*(My nani Chameli Devi—though she has
passed away, she remains with me always)*

and

Mummy
*(My mother Ms Mridula Dubey—the pillar of
my life, whose constant support has been the anchor
to my life)*

CONTENT

Yogi Adityanath

**CHIEF MINISTER
UTTAR PRADESH**

Lok Bhawan,
Lucknow - 226001

Date : 2 1 DEC 2023

Foreword

The Olympics are where heroes are created; the Paralympics are where heroes come. This succinctly describes the incredible achievements of Indians at the Paralympics. They are the real-life heroes of the country. Against innumerable odds and insurmountable problems, these champions have conquered them all. Winners on the field, they are true champions in real life—an ideal inspiration for "New India", the true forebears of Naya Bharat.

Hon'ble Prime Minister Shri Narendra Modi ji, while hosting the Indian contingent that participated in the Tokyo 2020 Paralympics Games, said: "I draw inspiration and motivation from you all. You have defeated a defeatist mindset with your achievements. This is a big thing."

Inspired by the Hon'ble Prime Minister's words, Shri Abhishek Dubey, along with co-author Shri Mahavir Rawat, has come forward to write a book on this subject. The book, Crossing the Barriers: The Paralympic Legends of India, beautifully narrates the life journeys and accomplishments of all the Indians who have won medals for the country in the Paralympics.

This book chronicles the individual journeys of the medal winners. I am confident that each of these stories will inspire the youth of the country to navigate through crises in their own lives and excel in their chosen fields.

(Yogi Adityanath)

MESSAGE

The NAAD Wellness family extends its heartfelt congratulations to esteemed author and sports journalist, Abhishek Dubey, and to renowned publisher, Konark Publishers Pvt. Ltd, for bringing out this remarkable book titled *Crossing the Barriers: The Paralympic Legends of India*. This literary gem meticulously chronicles the triumph over adversities in the lives of the real heroes of our nation. It stands as a pioneer in literature, presenting the life lessons of all our Paralympic medal winners through eloquent storytelling, aiming to inspire the youth of our country.

We at NAAD family are honoured to have contributed to this endeavour, aligning with the vision of our esteemed Prime Minister Shri Narendra Modi *ji* to elevate the sports events of the differently abled to the same pedestal as for other sportspersons, fostering the vision of a truly developed global sporting nation. We are also delighted that the foreword to this book has been written by Shri Yogi Adityanath, the Honourable Chief Minister of Uttar Pradesh, whose administration includes a Paralympic medal winner among its ablest bureaucrats. Shri Adityanath *ji* is known for his commitment and proactive measures to propel Uttar Pradesh as the growth engine of the country.

As we delve into the profound life lessons of the remarkable athletes featured in the book, we recognise a common thread:

the importance of embracing healthy living and lifestyles across all age groups. These Paralympic athletes exemplify that a robust and healthy body fosters a resilient mind, which is a formidable weapon against adversity. Many of these differently-abled athletes began their pursuit at such stages in life when many would consider giving up. NAAD Wellness echoes this philosophy, emphasising that it's never too late to embark on a journey towards healthier bodies for stronger minds.

Situated within Delhi NCR, NAAD offers 39 rooms and a curated array of preventive and curative experiences, aimed at healing and guiding individuals towards holistic well-being. Like 'New India' takes pride in our roots, NAAD Wellness is rooted in the ancient principles of Ayurveda, yoga and naturopathy.

At NAAD, each of our experiences has been created around this ancient ethos and overseen by our resident physicians and experts. We strive to restore the balance of the five elements of nature within the body through Ayurvedic treatments, naturopathic therapies, yoga, and *sattvic* food. We help you to tune yourself into a "sound you". Our wellness centre provides a variety of experiences ranging from 3–28 nights and includes a blend of both experiential and medical packages tailored to individual needs, such as detoxification, stress management, diabetes management, PCOS (Polycystic Ovary Syndrome) management, spine care, and sports injury management.

Each experience begins with a personalised one-on-one consultation with our resident Ayurvedic or naturopathic physician, who designs an itinerary comprising therapies, yoga, *kriyas,* and nutrition, in order to address the root cause of any imbalance. Our goal is to facilitate healing the body, mind, and spirit from within, offering long-term solutions rather than quick fixes. This philosophy mirrors the profound approach taken by the Paralympic legends featured in the book. They sought long-term tangible solutions by delving into the root causes of their imbalances, instead of through a piecemeal approach.

As the NAAD Wellness team constantly embarks on a journey towards excellence in promoting healthy and holistic lifestyles to prepare individuals for life's toughest challenges, we extend our best wishes for the success of the book, *Crossing the Barriers: The Paralympic Legends of India*, to its author Abhishek Dubey and to publisher Konark. Having been acquainted with Abhishek Dubey as a passionate sports professional for several years, we are witness to his dedication and expertise shining throughout this book. May the book inspire individuals to navigate life's challenges with resilience and well-being.

Sonipat

Ramesh Kumar

Co-Founder

NAAD Wellness, Sonipat, Haryana

PRAISE FOR THE BOOK

My heartfelt congratulations to Abhishek Dubey and Mahavir Rawat for their outstanding efforts in bringing out a pioneering book that unveils the extraordinary journeys of India's Paralympic medal winners. As a badminton player who has experienced the highs and lows of the sporting world, I understand the dedication and sacrifice required to achieve greatness.

In their coverage of para sports, seasoned sports journalist Abhishek Dubey and trailblazer Mahavir Rawat illuminate the often overlooked stories of our Paralympic champions. Their commitment to bringing these stories to the forefront is not only commendable but also essential in reshaping the narrative around disability and sports in our country.

The Paralympic Movement in India has seen tremendous growth, and the athletes featured in this book exemplify the true spirit of resilience and determination. This collection celebrates the indomitable spirit that drives these athletes to achieve greatness despite facing numerous challenges. Their stories serve as a source of inspiration for aspiring athletes, reminding the world that ability knows no bounds.

Abhishek and Mahavir have meticulously interwoven narratives of triumph and tenacity, offering a fresh perspective and a deeper understanding of the incredible feats accomplished by our para athletes.

As we celebrate the accomplishments of these remarkable individuals, let us also acknowledge the authors for their dedication to telling these stories with sensitivity and authenticity. Through their work, they have given voice to the often unheard tales of perseverance and victory that define the Paralympic landscape in India.

Manjusha Kanwar

Commonwealth Games Medal Winner; Recipient of Dhyanchand Award for Lifetime Achievement

* * *

I was part of the 1983 World Cup-winning team, and later served as Chief Selector for the team that won the 2011 World Cup. Nothing can beat the feeling of being a part of your country's victorious team, witnessing the national anthem being played, and our Tricolour held up with pride. As a sportsperson, it's heartening to see our country excelling in Paralympic and Olympic sports. The medal winners in these multi-sporting global events are genuine heroes who inspire countless others to follow in their footsteps. I congratulate Abhishek Dubey, whom I have known for years, for bringing out a timely and relevant book on the Paralympic heroes of our country. This book, featuring the stories of India's Paralympic medal winners, is a first of its kind. I am confident that this book will inspire many to remain focused on their goals, fight hard, and ultimately triumph in life's battles.

K. Srikkanth

Former Captain & Chief Selector of the Indian Cricket Team

* * *

The Paralympic heroes of our country are the true heroes, both on and off the field. Their stories are waiting to be told and will serve as real inspiration and role models for the youth of our nation. Having known Abhishek Dubey as a sports journalist, writer, and broadcaster for years, I believe he is the right person to put in words the life and times of these remarkable achievers in the world of sports. The inclusion of stories about past Paralympic medal winners, alongside present ones, adds authenticity to the account. Abhishek brings his diverse sports experience to the forefront while narrating the tales of these champions. I extend my gratitude to Konark Publishers for bringing this book to fruition, as it will undoubtedly be a treasure trove for generations to come.

Maninder Singh

Former India Player & Cricket Expert

* * *

India aspires to become a global sporting powerhouse. Prime Minister Narendra Modi declared at the Indian Olympic Committee Mumbai Convention that the country aims to host the 2036 Olympics. In recent years, India has taken rapid strides on different multi-sporting global platforms. It is the ideal time to share the real-life stories of our sporting heroes, which will, in turn, inspire many more to pursue their dreams and become tomorrow's champions. India's phenomenal success in the Tokyo Paralympics and the Hangzhou Asian Para Games has propelled the Paralympic sports into the mainstream.

I am delighted that Abhishek Dubey, a writer and sports broadcast professional with nearly 25 years of experience, has penned this book on the Paralympic heroes of our nation. I am confident that the book will serve as a source for many films, web series, and articles in the coming years. Every chapter of the book touches the life of an Indian Paralympic icon, imparting invaluable life lessons and motivating us to never ever give up in life. This book, published by Konark Publishers, is a must-read.

Kiran More
Former India Cricketer & Chief Selector

* * *

Abhishek Dubey's unwavering dedication to illuminating diverse subjects radiates brilliantly through this insightful book. Through his exploration of the inspiring realm of para sports, Abhishek not only showcases his prowess as an author but also amplifies awareness and appreciation for athletes who redefine possibilities. This remarkable contribution underscores Abhishek's resolute commitment to nurturing understanding, respect, and admiration for the extraordinary achievements within the para sports community. We extend our heartfelt gratitude to Abhishek for his steadfast support to Samarthanam Trust and the Cricket Association for the Blind in India.

Mahantesh G. Kivadasannavar
Founder of Samarthanam Trust and Chairman of the Cricket Association for Blind in India

* * *

Crossing the Barriers: The Paralympic Legends of India offers a seamless narrative exploration into the unique journeys and valuable life lessons of several Paralympic medal winners from our country. Thanks to the vision of our Prime Minister Narendra Modi, the status of differently-abled sports has today been greatly elevated. I, for one, can deeply empathise with some of the highly taxing, challenging, and difficult struggles that each of these Paralympic stars must have had to undergo while building their careers. Hats off to Abhishek Dubey for bringing in all of the knowledge and resources that he gathered over the years as a sports journalist!

Rani Rampal

Former Indian women's hockey team captain

* * *

Crossing the Barriers is a timely and pertinent publication that chronicles the life journeys and lessons of India's Paralympic medallists. This book, first of its kind in the country, is inspired by the vision of Shri Narendra Modi, the Honourable Prime Minister of India, who aims to elevate the status of differently-abled sports to the level of able-bodied sports and propel our nation towards becoming a global sports power.

Being a world champion, I have a firsthand understanding of the level of dedication required to achieve such a prestigious title. The incredible journeys of India's Paralympic legends featured in this book, overcoming so many obstacles before emerging as champions, truly solidify their status as real-life heroes of extraordinary calibre. Authored by Abhishek Dubey, a prominent Indian sports journalist and expert, aptly showcases his professional acumen and experience through its narrative.

Anju Bobby George

Olympian, Indian Long Jumper and Vice President, Athletics Federation of India

* * *

Inclusivity is ingrained and deep-rooted in the culture of Bharat. A nation becomes truly great only when its values are based on inclusivity and when it starts identifying and celebrating its real heroes. It is in this context that the book on the Paralympic legends of India is timely and topical. Authored by Abhishek Dubey, who has been a keen observer of Indian sports for many years, the book *Crossing the Barriers* is a highly engrossing and informative read for readers across all sections.

Prafulla Ketkar
Editor, Organiser

* * *

We have much to learn from the lives of differently-abled individuals—how to maintain a positive outlook and stay focused on one's objectives despite setbacks and obstacles. To emulate their resilience, one must train hard, make bold decisions, strive continuously, and never succumb to defeat. These qualities are integral to the lexicon of every differently-abled achiever's life, serving as the key life lessons for us to embrace and emulate.

I became involved with the Paralympics after witnessing the challenges these athletes face. God has given us everything, yet we crib. Observing the Paralympians fills us with gratitude and motivates us to contribute positively to society in whatever way we can.

Honourable Prime Minister Narendra Modi, a visionary global leader, has integrated sports for differently-abled persons into the national mainstream. During his tenure as Chief Minister of Gujarat, he ensured that sports for the differently abled were a central aspect of the *Khel Mahakumbh*. Modi *ji*'s introduction of the term *Divyang* for differently-abled people exemplifies his forward-thinking leadership.

My best wishes to Abhishek Dubey and the publisher for their initiative in showcasing the lives, struggles, and triumphs of India's Paralympic heroes, who stand tall as real heroes of our time, inspiring us all.

Dr Mallika Nadda

President, Special Olympics Bharat

* * *

India is on the cusp of a Paralympic sports revolution. The Tokyo Paralympics marked the beginning of India's aspiration to be the leading para sports power, and, from this point forward, our ascent will only continue until we reach our ultimate goal. We are delighted that, inspired by the call of Honourable Prime Minister Narendra Modi to chronicle the real-life stories of our para sports heroes, Abhishek Dubey, a seasoned sports journalist with over 25 years of experience, has decided to come up with this book. He has been a keen observer of the evolution of para sports and this is evident in the diverse chapters of this book. We extend our best wishes to Abhishek for his efforts in sharing the stories of these true achievers in our society.

Gurucharan Singh

Former Secretary General, Paralympic Committee of India

* * *

Prime Minister Narendra Modi has played a defining role in promoting equal opportunity and respect to the differently-abled community through his policies. He has consistently advocated for providing financial assistance to those who need it the most. I recall that during his tenure as Chief Minister of Gujarat, Modi *ji* announced a prize of Rs 5 lakh for Sachin Tendulkar, despite facing criticism from a section of the intelligentsia. However, Modi *ji* was clear in what he was doing and has always believed in allocating public funds based on individual need. During the same period, he also announced a grant of Rs 3.5 lakh for girls participating in the *Khel Mahakumbh*, demonstrating his commitment to supporting diverse talent.

In addition to financial support, Modi *ji* envisions a society where differently-abled individuals are treated with dignity and respect, just like everyone else. They should possess self-confidence, pride, and faith in society, and it is imperative for society to take tangible measures to uphold these values for them. They ought to feel emotionally connected to society and understand that they are an intrinsic part of the national mainstream.

I am happy to see Abhishek Dubey, a seasoned sports media professional, shedding light on the achievements of Indian Paralympic medallists in his book, *Crossing the Barriers: The Paralympic Legends of India*. My heartfelt wishes go out to him for the successful publication of this inspiring work.

Uday Mahurkar

Former Information Commissioner, Writer & Expert on Modi Model of Governance

* * *

Arthritis paralysed me at the age of three, confining me to a wheelchair for the next eight years. Though people ridiculed my dream of becoming a professional wrestler, I was not willing to give up. I came from a humble background, and my mother was there for me with her rock-solid support. I began with small steps, moving my feet, gradually standing up, undergoing rigorous therapy sessions at home, and finally stepping into the arena to fight. I have had a tough life, but I am happy that I faced my battles head-on.

I have known Abhishek Dubey for over a decade; he is a wonderful storyteller. I am thrilled that he has chosen to pen a book based on the lives of real achievers who have overcome adversity. My heartfelt salute goes out to India's inspirational Paralympic heroes and I extend my best wishes to Abhishek for his book which will undoubtedly inspire many. Life sets up tough question papers, but by embracing the lessons learnt from the journeys of the Paralympic champions, one can solve every one of those tough questions with distinction.

Sangram Singh
Wrestler and Actor

* * *

Becoming a successful athlete is a lifelong struggle, and for Paralympians, it's an even greater challenge. But what about the unbelievable odds these Paralympians face all the way through their careers long after the arc lights have dimmed on their manifold glorious achievements? Abhishek Dubey and Mahavir Rawat have delved into one of the most difficult aspects of sports storytelling, coming up with this masterly volume that is nothing but a stark examination of the arduous journeys these extraordinary athletes endure in their relentless pursuit of excellence. Through a brutally honest, no-holds-barred narrative style, the authors reveal the humanity in these super men and women, unveiling the beauty within sports' most formidable quest.

Sanjeeb Mukherjea
Sportscaster & Author

INTRODUCTION

Act as if what you do makes a difference. It does.

—**William James**

We all aspire to make a difference, and the above quote by the great American philosopher, William James, serves as a reminder on how we are indeed making a difference, even if it may not seem as significant as we desire. But when we strive to do our best, our impact tends to grow over a period of time, however small our actions may have initially seemed.

If this book is able to make a difference to the lives of those who are currently feeling down and out after a setback—or those who happen to be depressed and lonely, or those feeling less motivated to do things—its objective will be achieved. After contracting COVID-19, I too experienced depression, but the stories of real-life heroes and their incredible journeys helped me overcome it. Based on my personal experience, I can confidently say that these stories have the potential to impact many others.

This book is a collection of stories about real-life heroes from the world of sports. What sets them apart as heroes is not only their achievements but also the adversities they faced, including various physical limitations they endured to pursue their goals. They have triumphed in personal battles and overcame hurdles in order to find a purpose. These

inspiring individuals participated in the Paralympics and won medals for their country. If they can achieve such feats, so can we.

In ancient times, tribal members would huddle around communal fireplaces at the end of the day for warmth and protection. These gatherings would give rise to the art of storytelling. Those who emerged as storytellers during these gatherings soon realised that tales of heroes and their heroic actions captivated listeners the most. Audiences found inspiration and fascination in such narratives. Reflecting on this often reminds me of my own childhood, when both of my grandmothers, affectionately called *nani* and *dadi*, would gather us around a fire pot—a type of brazier—during winters. They shared stories of heroes and their courageous acts, many drawn from epics and mythologies.

The art of storytelling is as ancient as human civilisation itself. But why do tales featuring heroes and their heroic deeds resonate with us so deeply? How do they possess the power to heal, transform, and connect with us on a profound level?

First, heroes and heroic actions evoke a unique emotional response in us. One of America's leading social psychologists, Jonathan Haidt, describes this connection with heroic characters in stories as a form of "elevation". Haidt borrowed this term from US President Thomas Jefferson, who used "moral elevation" to describe the euphoric feeling experienced after reading great literature. In the words of Haidt, elevation is "elicited by acts of virtue or moral beauty; it causes warm, open feelings in the chest". This is why we love stories of heroes and their noble actions; they elevate us and evoke that warm and open feeling within us.

Secondly, heroes heal our psychological wounds. They calm our fears, uplift our spirits, nourish our hopes, and foster values such as strength and resilience. We are drawn to stories of "good heroes" because they heal and comfort us.

Thirdly, storytelling is one of the most powerful community-building activities. The sense of family, group, or community has always been central to human emotional well-being. This is where our heroes fit in perfectly. The stories of our heroes create a strong sense of human identity. Their actions exemplify and affirm the most cherished values of our communities. They become our role models, and their behaviour reinforces our treasured values and connections with others.

Fourthly, heroes show us how to transform our lives. They undergo significant transformation in their own life journeys too. As they progress through different stages, they gain self-confidence and humility, and find their true purpose in life. Every hero's journey tells a story of personal transformation.

Lastly, heroes inspire us to become heroes ourselves. Real heroes are those who use the power of transformation not only to change themselves for the better but also to transform the world. These are the five points that make stories about heroes and heroic actions so intriguing and desirable.

The heroes featured in this book inspired me for these very reasons. They had a positive impact on my life. The storyteller in me got convinced that sharing these heroic stories of our role models can impact many other lives too. But what prompted me to share their stories now?

The Evolution of Youth

Despite a multitude of challenges and adversities, India's progress over the past 75 years since gaining independence can be attributed to the optimism of its youth. "*Koi baat nahin, kar lenge* (no worries, we will manage)" has been the mantra of Indian youth. Their morale has remained high despite grappling with scarcity of basic amenities and constrained resources. They have advanced despite harsh economic conditions, challenges in the labour market, and uncertainties due to global terrorism and climate change. There has been an inherent and consistent belief among the younger generation in India that their future is brighter and better than that of the previous generation. However, there has been a disturbing trend in recent times.

According to data shared at the *India Today* 2019 Mumbai Conclave, more than 40,000 students have reportedly committed suicide in India between 2014 and 2018. On average, one student commits suicide every hour in the country. These numbers are staggering, but they fail to capture the full extent of the suffering experienced by the younger generation. We often perceive these issues as affecting someone else, but they are occurring within our schools, homes, offices, canteens, and playgrounds. Why are the youth suffering? The reasons may vary, including relationship issues with friends and family, academic pressures, and bullying. Among the youth, there is a sense of loneliness and disconnection—a feeling of not being accepted, being judged, and being on the outside. The irony is that, despite appearing highly connected through social media and the internet, they still experience a profound sense of disconnection.

Another concern among today's youth is a lack of purpose or meaning. Young people often ask, "What am I doing here?

Why do you do what you do?" In a changing world, there is pressure to be perfect, leading to high societal expectations regarding academics, values, and co-curricular activities. While these issues may seem trivial at first glance, they have a profound impact on the mental well-being of adolescents. Regrettably, we often blame teenagers themselves, labelling them as attention-seekers, weaklings, or fragile individuals. It is imperative for us to introspect and ask pertinent questions: Are we spending enough time with our children? Are we fostering meaningful engagement with them? Are we imparting valuable life lessons through storytelling? In most cases, the answer will be "no".

American singer and songwriter Pete Seeger once remarked, "The key to the future of the world is finding the optimistic stories and letting them be known." This book is replete with such optimistic stories that are waiting to be told. Each tale within these pages imparts valuable life lessons. The younger generation will be able to relate to these heroes, the challenges they confronted and the manner in which they overcame them. As we go through each of the individual stories, an inner voice will emerge, proclaiming, "If they can do it, so can we!" So, who are these real heroes, and why are their stories waiting to be told?

Breaking into the Mainstream

These real heroes are the Paralympians of our country. The Paralympics are often referred to as the place where heroes participate, while the Olympics are where heroes are made. Though India's attention turned to the Paralympics during the 13 days between 24 August and 5 September 2021—during the 2020 Summer Paralympics in Tokyo—many of the participants had long been heroes in their own lives long before participating in these games.

India made its Paralympic debut in 1968, competed again in 1972, and then was absent until the 1984 Games. Since then, the country has maintained a consistent presence. However, it was during the Tokyo 2020 Games that the Indian contingent made a lasting impact, both in terms of performance and by receiving extensive coverage from mainstream media outlets.

How did I become acquainted with the Paralympic heroes? After serving in leadership roles at various private media organisations across the country for around 15 years, my association with Prasar Bharti, the public broadcaster of India, began in 2014. It was during my time with them at Doordarshan that I became closer to many differently-abled sportspersons and their federation officials, allowing me to get to know them better. I got many opportunities to produce and telecast their events on the DD Sports channel. What appealed to me most about these individuals was their attitude of never giving up and of fighting till the end. A defining moment was when the Indian national blind cricket team, victorious in the T20 World Cup for the Blind, shared their triumph with us, bringing me further closer to their stories.

As the Tokyo 2020 Paralympic Games drew near, senior officials from the Paralympic Committee of India approached us to discuss broadcasting possibilities on DD Sports. When the agreement was finalised, we learnt that India would be sending its largest-ever contingent to the games, with officials expressing confidence in achieving the best-ever performance this time. Beyond mere numbers, my colleagues and I were drawn to the human stories behind the statistics. Mahavir Rawat, my former colleague from *NDTV*, had become associated with the Paralympic Committee of India and was acquainted with many current athletes. Joining forces, Mahavir and I embarked on uncovering the personal stories of these Paralympic heroes and their heroic actions.

As the Tokyo 2020 Paralympics started, the Doordarshan telecast ensured that the games received the highest viewership. When the participants left for Tokyo, the popular perception was that they would merely get a few more medals than last time. However, their performance exceeded all expectations.

Another noteworthy feature of the games was in the way in which the Narendra Modi government engaged with differently-abled athletes and treated them on a par with other able-bodied athletes. Prime Minister Modi himself led from the front, engaging with them before, during, and after the games. A member of the Indian contingent shared how he had overheard athletes from other countries say, "You people are lucky; your Prime Minister directly communicates with you and supports you in your victories and defeats". Another member described the Prime Minister as a philosopher, mentor and guide to the Indian Paralympic athletes. In the years to come, this will be remembered as one of the major legacies of Prime Minister Narendra Modi in the field of sports. In a nutshell, the Indian contingent's participation in the Tokyo Paralympic event created history. The athletes have now reached a take-off stage, from where they could aim and soar even higher.

India's Paralympic journey began in 1968, marking its debut in the games. From 1968 to 2016, India had won 12 medals. However, the Tokyo 2020 Games proved to be India's best-ever Paralympics, with a total of 19 medals—five gold, eight silver, and six bronze. This remarkable achievement surpassed India's previous medal counts combined, marking an increase of seven medals. Having transitioned from a modest presence in earlier editions to a strong force, Indian athletes are now at a point where they can establish a formidable presence in future editions. In Tokyo, India secured the 24th position out of 162 participating nations in the medals tally and attained the 20th rank in terms of the total number of medals (19) won. With this momentum, India has the potential to secure a top-five position within the next decade. A closer look at these figures provides even greater hope for the future.

The five Indian Paralympic gold medallists, along with their respective disciplines, were Avani Lekhara (women's 10m air rifle-standing SH1 category), Pramod Bhagat (men's singles SL3 badminton category), Krishna Nagar (men's singles SH6 badminton category), Sumit Antil (men's javelin throw F46 category) and Manish Narwal (mixed 50-metre pistol SH1 category).

The eight silver-medal winners and their disciplines were Bhavinaben Patel in the women's singles class-4 table tennis category, Singharaj Adhana in the mixed 50-metre pistol SH1 category, Yogesh Kathuniya in the men's discus throw F56 category, Nishad Kumar in the men's high jump T47 category, Mariyappan Thangavelu in the men's high jump T63 category, Praveen Kumar in the men's high jump T64 category, Devendra Jhajharia in the men's javelin F46 category and Suhas L.Y. in the men's singles badminton category.

The six bronze medallists and their respective disciplines were Avani Lekhara in the women's 50-metre rifle-3 position

SH1 category, Harvinder Singh in the men's individual recurve archery category, Sharad Kumar in the men's high jump T63 category, Sunder Singh in the men's javelin throw F46 category, Manoj Sarkar in the men's singles badminton SL3 category, and Singhraj Adhana in the men's 10m air pistol SH1 category. Avani Lekhara and Singhraj Adhana both secured two medals each. In total, 17 athletes grabbed 19 medals for the country. In the process, several new records were set.

Sumit Antil set a new world record in the F64 men's javelin category. Avani Lekhara equalled the world record and set a new Paralympic record in the R2 women's 10m air-standing SH1 category. Nishad Kumar set an Asian record in the men's high jump T47 category, and Praveen Kumar set an Asian record in the men's high jump T64 category.

India had sent 54 para athletes to compete in the Tokyo 2020 Paralympic Games across nine sporting disciplines. Badminton and taekwondo made their debut in the games, and Indian players participated in both of them. Many athletes narrowly missed the podium—such as Swaroop Unhalkar and Rahul Jakhar in para shooting, Sandeep Chaudhary, Soman Rana, Navdeep, Ram Pal and Amit Saroha in para athletics, Tarun Dhillon in para badminton, and Sakina Khatun in para powerlifting. Many of the stories in this book are about the medal winners of the Tokyo 2020 Games.

However, India's history of Paralympic sports goes back a long way, much before its participation in Tokyo 2020 Games. What about the heroes who emerged in those games? Their stories are relatively difficult to come across, but they were the ones who initially inspired and instilled confidence in the heroes of the Tokyo 2020 Paralympics, making them strive for greater glory. The book commences with stories from the examples of many of those unsung heroes as well.

In the 1974 Paralympic Games, Murlikant Petkar had won a gold medal for swimming. Petkar had achieved a world record time of 37.331 seconds in the 50-metre freestyle event. In the 1984 Paralympic Games, Joginder Singh Bedi won a silver medal in the men's shot put category and followed it up with bronze medals in discus and javelin throws. He became the first Indian to win multiple medals in a single Paralympic event. Even after Tokyo 2020, Joginder Singh Bedi remains the only Indian to have achieved a hat-trick of medals in a single Paralympic Games. In the 1984 Paralympics, alongside Joginder Singh Bedi, Bhim Rao Kesarkar featured in the medals' column, winning a silver medal in javelin. Following the 1984 Paralympics, India's medal column remained blank until the Athens 2004 Paralympics.

In the 2004 Games, Devendra Jhajharia won a gold medal in javelin throw, and Rajinder Singh Rahelu secured a bronze medal in the 56-kg category of powerlifting. In the subsequent two Paralympics, Devendra was unable to compete, as his event was not included. Such a setback could have discouraged even the most seasoned campaigners from continuing in sports. However, this modern-day warrior from Rajasthan patiently waited for his opportunity and reclaimed a medal when his event was reintroduced in the Rio 2016 Paralympics. At the Tokyo 2020 Games, he won the silver medal. History is not about "ifs" and "buts", but one often wonders what Jhajharia's total medal count would have been if his event had been part of the 2008 and 2012 Games.

The Indian contingent had returned without any medal from the Beijing 2008 Paralympics. In the London 2012 Paralympics,

Girisha Nagarajegowda won a silver medal in the athletics men's high jump F42 category. When Girisha returned as the sole saviour with the medal, he raised a pertinent question, "When I went to participate in the games, differently-abled athletes from other countries repeatedly asked me one question: 'Yours is such a large country with the second largest population in the world. But still, why is your contingent so small?' I had no answer."

To be a strong nation in the Paralympics and Olympics, India needs to find an answer to this pertinent question. Has India been able to find an answer to this? The book briefly covers this aspect as well. In the Rio 2016 Paralympics, four Indians made their mark in the medal column. Devendra Jhajharia won a gold medal in F46 javelin throw category, Mariyappan Thangavelu won a gold medal in men's high jump 42 category, Deepa Malik earned a silver medal in the women's shot put F53 category, and Varun Singh Bhati won a bronze medal in the men's high jump F42 category. For the connoisseurs of inspiring stories, each of these four individuals holds many life lessons within their personal journeys. This book shares some of the major life lessons gleaned from the journeys of these emerging Indian greats.

Finding Recognition

There was a time when the achievements of the Indian Paralympians were mostly overlooked by mainstream media. At most, their accomplishments would get only single-column coverage, buried deep in the inner pages of newspapers. Today, however, their feats are prominently featured in headlines and receive significant coverage in national dailies and magazines. Indian Paralympians are often invited as star guests on popular

Indian television shows. Many of them endorse brands and serve as ambassadors for major public campaigns. Moreover, filmmakers have started producing biopics inspired by their compelling life stories.

Devendra Jhajharia, for instance, has experienced both phases in his journey from Athens 2004 to Tokyo 2020. This book attempts to unravel this seminal change through the lenses of Devendra and other athletes. Today, the Indian Paralympic journey has covered a long distance from where it started, and the future looks promising. However, it still has miles to go from here before it can reach the finishing line.

The marathon journey and its ultimate culmination each tell unique stories.

The first marathon race represents the incredible journey of India's Paralympic heroes. Each of them had made valuable contributions in their time and passed the baton onto future generations. This marathon journey will attain culmination when India becomes one of the top three nations or one of the top five nations in the medals tally.

The second marathon race involves the entire differently-abled community spread across the country as participants. They also aspire to touch the finishing line, which, for them, signifies a truly inclusive society where they will have access to public and private spaces and equal opportunities to compete and excel in various fields. Like the Paralympic heroes, the participants in the second marathon race have the potential to be equal stakeholders in nation-building. Changing our mindsets is essential for this to become a reality. If this book can contribute even a little in that direction, its objective will be achieved.

The book unveils the life and times of Paralympic heroes, one after another. The first hero featured in the series is Murlikant Petkar. But before we delve into his story, we begin with the origin and evolution of the Paralympic Games. Once upon a time...

New Delhi   **Abhishek Dubey**

ONCE UPON A TIME

"A journey of a thousand miles begins with a single step."

—Chinese proverb

(This saying is attributed to Lao Tzu, an illustrious Chinese philosopher, and finds its origins in the Chinese classic text Tao Te Ching. The original text in Chinese says: "A journey of a thousand li starts beneath one's feet." Here, "*li*" signifies a unit of distance.)

The beauty of this Chinese proverb lies in the paradoxical combination of "thousand miles" and a "single step". While this book is about the "thousand miles" that the Paralympic Movement in general and the Indian achievers in particular have covered, this chapter focuses on the significance of taking that very first "single step" towards one's journey.

Similar to many other incredible journeys in life, it is uncertain when and where differently-abled individuals first began playing organised sports. Although there have been several instances of disabled individuals being depicted sensitively in ancient Greek and Roman cultures, there are very few historical references that celebrate the physical achievements of injured war heroes from Greek mythology who may be celebrated as icons of physical achievement despite their disabilities. In ancient Indian folklore

too, there are accounts of disabled individuals who excelled in diverse fields, but there is no specific reference found to any differently-abled sporting genius.

The history of disabled sports does not span more than 150 years. There is evidence, for instance, that deaf clubs existed in Berlin (Germany) way back in 1888. So, the participation of disabled persons in organised sports is a contribution of the modern world, and one of its most beautiful manifestations is the Paralympic Games. However, questions still remain: When, where and how did the journey of the Paralympics begin? Who was its founder? And what were the different stages of its evolution?

The Paralympic Movement emerged out of a crisis, and turning such a crisis into an opportunity often requires a new perspective. The Second World War, which concluded on 2 September 1945, is widely regarded by historians as the most destructive war in human history, resulting in the loss of thousands of lives. The aftermath of the war left numerous war veterans and civilians injured during the conflict.

In such circumstances, the British government approached the German-British neurologist Dr Ludwig Guttmann with a proposal to launch a spinal injuries centre at the Stoke Mandeville Hospital, on the borders of Aylesbury and Stoke Mandeville, Buckinghamshire, England. The primary objective behind starting this hospital was to provide treatment to war veterans and injured civilians.

Before we delve further into the story, we need to understand who Dr Ludwig Guttmann was and how he became the founder of the Paralympic Games.

The Incredible Journey of Dr Ludwig Guttmann

Dr Guttmann, the eldest of four children, was born on 3 July 1899 as the son of Dorothy Guttmann and Bernard Guttmann (a distiller). Born in Tost, Prussia, which was then a part of the German empire and is currently located at Toszeg in Poland, the young Ludwig was raised in Jewish faith. Tragically, during the Second World War, his father, elder sister, and her husband, all perished in Auschwitz, a Nazi concentration camp situated in Germany-occupied Poland. Guttmann's maternal and paternal grandparents were farmers. In his formative years, he spent his holidays in the countryside, observing it with curiosity as his grandmother administered herbal remedies to the villagers.

When Guttmann was 17 years old, he became an orderly at the local resident hospital. An incident during this time left a deep impact on him and played an important role in shaping his future: a miner was brought to the hospital with a broken back and several deformities, which were reduced through extension and direct pressure. Guttmann was instructed not to write any case notes, as the authorities felt that the miner would anyway be dead in a few days. This defeatist attitude left a lasting impression on him.

During those days, Guttmann developed a severe throat infection, which led to further complications. In 1917, when he was called up for a test in the military, he was rejected due to still having an abscess drainage tube in place. Perhaps, it was destiny's way of guiding him toward the profession where he would bring about significant changes in the lives of many people in the years to come. After being rejected by the military, he began his medical studies at Breslau. Subsequently, in 1919, he was transferred to the University of Freiburg, where he obtained his Doctorate of Medicine in 1924.

In 1933, Guttmann started working as a neurosurgeon at Breslau and began giving lectures at the university. During his early career, he was mentored by the pioneer of neurosurgery, Otfrid Foerster. However, as his career started picking up, an unpredictable turn of events occurred. In 1933, under the implementation of the racist and anti-Semitic Nuremberg law, enacted during the Nazi regime, he was expelled from his university job. His title was downgraded from a prestigious position of professor and doctor to that of someone who simply treated the sick. After the Nazis came to power, Jews were prohibited from practicing medicine professionally.

Guttmann was assigned to work at the Breslau Jewish Hospital, where he eventually became the medical director in 1937. One day in November 1938, during the violent attacks on Jewish people and properties, Guttmann instructed his staff to admit every patient without carrying out any formalities. The next day, he was compelled to justify each admission to the Gestapo, a secret police organisation known for employing underhand and terrorist methods against suspected dissidents. Guttmann, however, managed to save 60 out of the 64 admitted patients from arrest and deportation to concentration camps. This courageous act came to light when his daughter Eva Loeffler recalled the episode in an interview with the Mandeville Legacy project.

Loeffler said: "He took the Gestapo officers from bed to bed, justifying each man's medical condition. He pulled faces and grimaced at the patients from behind their back, signalling to them to pull the same expression, and then he'd say, 'look at this man, he's having a fit!'"[1]

However, the increasing incidents of anti-Semitism started to affect Guttmann's mental well-being, as he felt suffocated and disgusted by the Nazi prosecution of Jews. This prompted him to search for an opportunity to leave the country. His chance came when the Nazis issued him a visa, instructing him to travel to Portugal to treat a friend of the Portuguese dictator. On his return to Germany via London, the Council for Assisting Refugee Academics (CARA) arranged for him to remain in the United Kingdom. Together with his wife, Else Samuel Guttmann, and their two children, Dennis and Eva, Guttmann arrived in Oxford, England, on 14 March 1939. Later on, this pivotal event was to play a decisive role in the origin and evolution of the Paralympic Movement.

A Lasting Contribution

In September 1943, the British government asked Guttmann to establish the National Spinal Injuries Centre at Stoke Mandeville Hospital in Buckinghamshire. The decision was part of an initiative by the Royal Air Force to ensure treatment and rehabilitation of pilots with spinal injuries. On 1 February 1944, the centre was inaugurated, and Guttmann was offered the post of the director. Guttmann accepted the offer on one condition: he would treat patients in his own way without any outside interference. Guttmann held onto the position of the director of the institute until 1966.

During his tenure, he created the template for the treatment and rehabilitation of paraplegics who had no further scope for improvement in the years ahead. Most importantly, it was during this phase that he laid down some solid groundwork for the launch of the Paralympic Movement. In these years, he implemented his own theories on how best to treat patients with paraplegia, which involved the use of rehabilitation through sport. For this, he started organising sports competitions within the hospital, which subsequently led to national competitions, followed by the international Stoke Mandeville Games and finally culminating into the Paralympic Games.

Today, when we see the grandeur and the sheer scale of the Paralympic Games and its gigantic multi-sporting stadiums with thousands cheering the para athletes, it's hard to believe that it all started out of a small hospital ward—with its patients as competitors and the hospital staff and its attendants as spectators. But before we go deeper into the different stages of the Paralympic evolution, it's pertinent to understand the philosophy and methodology of Dr Ludwig Guttmann, who is the founding father of the Paralympic Games.

What were the core elements of Guttmann's philosophy? In one straight and simple sentence, it was the total refusal to accept that a spinal injury was fatal or that it was a death sentence. Within this broader construct, Guttman advanced the treatment of paraplegia to a revolutionary level, setting a template that was followed worldwide.

Guttmann taught his methodology to a whole generation of physicians across the globe and influenced them, leading to the establishment of similar centres in Barcelona, Heidelberg and Israel. Professor Wagih El-Masri, who trained under him, said, "His philosophy of dedicated management for spinal injury patients from injury to the grave is credible even today and has whenever possible been adapted throughout the world ... Guttmann made Stoke Mandeville Hospital a successful model for others to copy."[2]

Guttmann's methodology focused on a total control over the minutest of details within treatment and care. Dr John Silver, who worked with him in Stoke Mandeville, observed:

Essentially, if spinal injury patients went anywhere else for care, they died. So, he exerted a total and obsessive control over all aspects of care at the hospital, whether it was him coming for rounds at the middle of the night to ensure that the nurses had not turned into patients or checking on the quality of the cleaners' work and the food served in the wards. Everything was his responsibility, in sharp contrast with other hospitals.[3]

Dr Allison Graham, one of the directors at Stoke Mandeville, summed it up succinctly, saying: "Sir Ludwig Guttmann's lasting legacy is that you must always ask yourself 'What needs to be done now?' That is the challenge he has handed down to each of his successors."[4] There could not be a better remark than that; it underscored the essence and potency of Guttmann's methodology.

So how did Guttmann's methodology and philosophy lay the foundation for the Paralympic Games? Bob Paterson, honorary treasurer of the International Wheelchair and Amputee Sports Federation, said: "After injury, Guttmann focused an individual's mind on what they can do, rather than regretting on what they can no longer do. Through sports, Guttmann gave that person back the will to live a full life with pride and self-respect."[5] Over the years, in our conversations with sportspersons and sports psychologists, these have been the two crucial points that have been repeatedly emphasised.

One of the essentials of Guttmann's treatment was to ensure that patients maintained hope in terms of making progress and regaining their previous way of life. As part of the process, patients engage in various activities to stay active and ensure their social and medical rehabilitation. Sporting activities held a prominent place in Guttmann's approach, with wheelchair polo using walking sticks and a puck being the first sport held, later replaced by wheelchair basketball. Soon, archery, which was the first sport introduced in the Stoke Mandeville Games in 1948, became the most popular sport among the disabled, relying on upper body strength and providing the paraplegics the necessary drive to compete with their non-disabled counterparts.

The Unlikely Beginning of a Legacy at Stoke Mandeville

Every beautiful idea evolves with time. As often seen in human history, there tends to be a particular date linked with a specific idea. In terms of the Paralympic Games, that date was 29 July 1948. It was on this day that Guttmann organised an archery competition at the hospital, aligning with the London 1948 Olympic Games. A total of 16 patients—out of which fourteen were male and two were female, from Stoke Mandeville and the Royal Star and Garter Home for injured war veterans—competed for the Challenge Shield.

The success of the games and the response it received motivated Dr Guttmann to take it further and establish paraplegic sport as an annual festival, thus giving birth to the Stoke Mandeville Games. Later on, these games became the Paralympic Games as we know them today. It's a different matter that even Dr Guttmann, the lead protagonist of the games, could not have foreseen that the Challenge Shield would eventually pave the way for the Stoke Mandeville Games—ultimately becoming the precursor to the Paralympic Games. Thus, as we move ahead, the journey that began on 29 July 1948 will be both interesting as well as absorbing.

In 1949, six teams competed, and a "wheelchair netball" category was added. Joan Newton was amongst one of the first nurses at the Stoke Mandeville Hospital. Later on, she got married to one of the patients she had nursed. Describing the build of the wheelchairs in those days, she says:

I remember the earliest self-propelled carts that the patients were using at Stoke Mandeville. They were the precursor to the wheelchairs that you could get yourself about in. They were just going out of use when I started at Stoke in 1948. We called them push-pulls; they were low four-wheeled carts that the patients could sit themselves in, and they had two levers on each side which they could move backwards and forwards to propel themselves along.[6]

The make and build of the wheelchairs evolved over the years, and so did the journey of the Paralympic Games from 1948 to 2020. Like the wheelchairs, most of the features related to the games were crude and fascinating in the initial years. The games were small scale and had a home-spun quality to them. Margaret Maughan, a patient in the initial years at the hospital who later became a lead athlete, said:

Every June, the national games would take place at the hospital; competitors would come from other spinal units, the Star and Garter homes and disabled sports clubs from around the country. They would empty out one or two wards for the other competitors to stay in and also put them up in some of the huts at the back of the hospital. I first saw the 1959 Games when I was still at the hospital; one of the nurses took me out to watch.[7]

The best professionals are now engaged in ensuring a smooth conduct of the games. But who ran the show back then? Most of the events were organised by the nurses and physiotherapists whom Guttmann selected to perform different duties related to the games. The participating athletes were fed and looked after by the volunteers from Aylesbury and surrounding villages. Friends and relatives of those taking part in the event (along with the hospital staff) used to be present in the audience.

During the 1950s, two striking features began to emerge. First, National Games were organised in July and attended by teams from different spinal units and disabled sports groups from around the country. These were followed by international games in the summer, where national teams from various countries participated. Secondly, as the Para Games spread its wings, awareness about paraplegic treatments also began to spread beyond the borders of Great Britain. Ida Bromley, a leading physiotherapist, explained,

> By the 1950s physios were coming from around the world to train here and Guttmann had introduced an educational programme for the doctors accompanying the teams running parallel to the Games. In 1950 several members of the French team that came to the Games at Stoke all had pressure sores; they hadn't yet learnt the importance of treating these; but after French doctors saw the British team then they were able to learn from that and treat accordingly.[8]

On 26 July 1952, a small team from the military rehabilitation centre at Aardenburg, near Doorn in the Netherlands, competed against the British teams. In 1956, for the first time, 18 countries, including Australia, Israel, the USA, South Africa, and Malaya, participated in the games. In that very year, the International Olympics Committee presented the Fearnley Cup to the Stoke Mandeville Games for its outstanding contribution to the "Olympics ideal".

Dr Guttmann considered this recognition as an acceptance of these games into the Olympics family. However, the games had to wait for another three decades to be formally accepted into the Olympics fold. In 1957, for the first time, countries from all five continents participated in the games. From 1958 onwards, the British team started holding national games before the Stoke Mandeville Games. This worked as the selection trial for the Great Britain team. In a way, the 1950s saw the games crossing the British frontier and becoming international. However, to become a global brand, it had to be organised in different countries across the globe and not restricted to Britain only. This became possible after Dr Guttmann partnered with another doctor, Dr Antonio Maglio, to make the games an international brand. Before elaborating further on this partnership, we need to briefly know about Dr Antonio Maglio.

Dr Antonia Maglio

Much like Dr Ludwig Guttmann, the thinking and line of action of Dr Antonia Maglio was also shaped by the Second World War. After the War, Maglio began working for the Italian National Institute for Insurance against Accidents at Work. As part of his role, he implemented a multi-sports programme which included track and field, swimming, basketball, fencing, table tennis, and archery. The primary objective of this programme was to reduce mortality and alleviate depression in patients.

In 1956, as a part of his programme, Dr Maglio took his athletes to participate in the Stoke Mandeville Games. The following year, he organised a wheelchair-fencing competition at an institute in Ostia, Italy, where he was the director. Dr Maglio had invited Dr Guttmann for this event and many valuable insights from the Stoke Mandeville Games were put into action. By then, the partnership between the two doctors had reached a level from where it was all set to alter the course of the Paralympic Movement.

Maglio had gained the patronage of Carla Gronchi, the wife of Italian President Giovanni Gronchi. Maglio used his proximity to the First Lady to convince the Italian sports administrators to host the Stoke Mandeville Games using the same facilities and residences planned for the 1960 Olympics Games. After getting positive responses from the administrators, Maglio approached Guttmann in 1958 with the proposal. During the closing ceremony of the 1958 Games, Maglio made the announcement that the 1960 Stoke Mandeville Games would be held in Italy. Thus, the stage was set for the games to gain global recognition.

On 18 September 1960, the games were inaugurated by Italy's Health Minister, Camillo Giardina. Carla Gronchi and representatives from the embassies of the participating countries graced the event. Athletes from all participating countries paraded behind their flags, and around 5000 spectators witnessed this historic occasion. Great Britain, acknowledged as the founding country of the games, led the parade, followed by other countries in alphabetical order. Italy, being the host nation, was the last contingent and they closed the parade.

Dr Guttmann emphasised the significance of the games when in his speech, he said: "The meaning of the games cannot be measured in terms of athletic performance. This sport movement has a greater meaning: it is a source of hope for thousands of people whose life has been shaken by illness and injuries."[9] The participation of the athletes in the games provided valuable insights into the atmosphere of the event.

Margaret Maughan, one of the early legends, who participated in the 1960 Games, said:

Getting to Rome in 1960! First of all we were put on a coach to go to the airport; we all had to be carried on and our wheelchairs folded and loaded. Then at Heathrow the same thing was done in reverse. It took hours! Then to get us onto the plane they had to use fork lift with four of us at a time in our chairs on a platform being lifted up onto the plane. Then we had to be lifted into our seats and our chairs folded and put as baggage. At the other end it all took hours more; if you were the last off the plane you were sitting waiting for two hours. But back then, that was part of your life; and you just had to accept it.[10]

The games left a lasting legacy in several ways. Dr Maglio invented several tools for disabled athletes but deliberately chose not to patent them as he wanted to keep their prices affordable for those in need. One of his notable inventions was a bus with an electric platform, making it easy for wheelchairs to access and disembark from the bus. The games came to an end on 25 September 1960, with a memorable closing ceremony held at the Palazzetto dello Sport within the Olympic Village in Rome.

Guttmann, in his closing remarks, said: "The vast majority of the competitors and escorts have fully understood the meaning of the Rome Games as a new pattern of the reintegration of the paralysed into the society as well as the world of sport."[11] The Rome Games, thus, marked the beginning of a global revolution for the integration of disabled individuals into society and raised worldwide awareness about the cause. In the formal chronology of the Paralympic Games, the Rome Games in 1960 are considered the first one.

As the games made significant strides on a global scale, they had to face new challenges. Two major challenges emerged in the 1970s. First, disagreements over the use of the name "Olympics" started between Guttmann and the International Olympics Committee. Secondly, individual wheelchair sports began setting up their own governing bodies and championships. These various entities had to be reconciled within the broader canvas of the games. Following the 1960 Games, a broader trend emerged wherein the Olympics took place every four years, while Stoke Mandeville continued organising the international games during the intervening three years. Another major development was that the facilities at Stoke Mandeville attained international-level status. The sports hall opened in 1969, and the Indoor Bowl Centre and the Olympic Village started functioning in the 1970s.

The 1972 Olympics were held in Munich, while the Paralympic Games took place in nearby Heidelberg. The official reason cited for not organising the Paralympic Games in Munich was the lack of sufficient accommodation facilities for the athletes. However, many felt this decision was more due to a lack of genuine intent rather than a true scarcity of resources. In these games, 92 athletes from 42 countries competed in 10 different sports.

In 1976, the first winter games were held in Örnsköldsvik, Sweden, under the title "Winter Olympics for the Disabled". These games were open to individuals, who were blind, partially sighted, or amputees, and not just paraplegics. The event featured Nordic and Alpine skiing competitions.

The Toronto 1976 Games were the first to use the title "Olympiad for Physically Disabled". The International Stoke Mandeville Games Federation and the International Sports Organisation for the Disabled had come together to create a unified international event. In these games, for the first time, the athletes who were blind, partially sighted, or amputees participated along with those who used wheelchairs. In total, 1271 athletes from 41 countries competed in 447 events in 13 sports.

With the dawn of the 1980s, new challenges arose at frequent intervals. However, the roots of the games had penetrated so deep that they could withstand any crisis. By the 1970s, it was broadly established that the host country of the Olympics would also be able to host the Paralympic Games, though host cities may vary. For instance, the 1972 Olympics took place in Munich whereas Heidelberg hosted the Paralympics. Similarly, the 1976 Montreal Olympics was followed by the Paralympics in Toronto. However, this trend faced a major challenge in 1980 when the Olympic Games host nation, Russia, refused to hold the Paralympics. As a result, the games were organised in Arnhem, the Netherlands.

In 1984, the USA, as the Olympic Games host nation, was initially set to organise the Paralympic wheelchair games at Champaign, Illinois. However, just four months before the games, the organiser, University of Illinois, pulled out, citing financial constraints. To salvage the situation, Stoke Mandeville offered to host the games. Additionally, in 1984, South Africa, which had been expelled from the games in 1964 due to apartheid, made a comeback in Stoke Mandeville.

As the decade was coming to a close, on 18 March 1980, Dr Ludwig Guttmann breathed his last. Ironically, after the death of the founder of the Paralympic Games, both the Olympics and the Paralympics started to come closer.

The 1988 Summer Olympics in Seoul proved to be a major turning point as it also hosted the Paralympic Summer Games immediately after. Not only did both events share the same host city, but a majority of the venues and facilities were also identical. This trend continued in 1992, in 1996, and in the 2000 Games as well. In 2001, the union between the two events was formalised through an agreement between the International Paralympic Committee (IPC) and the International Olympics Committee (IOC). This agreement ensured that the staging of the Paralympic Games was included in the bid for the Olympic Games. On 10 March 2018, the two committees further extended their contract to 2032. Over the years, the Paralympic Games have evolved into one of the most popular and significant multi-sporting global events. Every four years, they take place at the same venue where the Olympics are held, using almost similar facilities.

The Paralympic Games have come a long way, but when did India take its first step on this historic Paralympic journey? Who was the first Indian to take that "one step" which led the movement and brought it to the stage where it stands today? The remarkable real-life story of Murlikant Petkar in the first chapter is what will inspire generations to come.

Notes

1. National Paralympic Heritage Trust, https://www.paralympicheritage.org.uk/professor-sir-ludwig-guttmann
2. Ibid.
3. Ibid.
4. Ibid.
5. Ibid.
6. National Paralympic Heritage Trust, https://www.paralympicheritage.org.uk/joan-newton
7. National Paralympic Heritage Trust, https://www.paralympicheritage.org.uk/1950s-the-first-international-games
8. Ibid.
9. National Paralympic Heritage Trust, https://www.paralympicheritage.org.uk/rome-1960-paralympic-summer-games
10. Ibid.
11. Ibid.

MURLIKANT PETKAR

From War Hero to Paralympic Star

"Bad things do happen; how I respond to them defines my character and the quality of my life. I can choose to sit in perpetual sadness, immobilised by the gravity of my loss, or I can choose to rise from the pain and treasure the most precious gift I have—life itself."

—Walter Anderson

In addition to being celebrated for his visual genius, the famous American artist Walter Anderson is also known for his exceptional words of wisdom. One person who can be characterised by his above quote is Murlikant Petkar.

Bharat, our country, is a land of warriors. It has also produced sports champions for years. Murlikant Petkar is one such son of Bharat who stands out as a rare combination of both, warrior and champion. During the 1965 war against Pakistan, an army man sustained severe bullet injuries and narrowly escaped death. The injuries left him more than 90 percent paraplegic and caused significant memory loss. Before his injury, he was known for his deadly punches as a boxer, but afterward, he had to switch his sport. That man is Murlikant Rajaram Petkar.

In the 1968 Paralympic Games, Murlikant represented the country in table tennis and progressed through the first

round. Later, in the 1972 Paralympic Games, he competed in swimming and returned triumphantly with a gold medal. Remarkably, 36 years before Abhinav Bindra won the country's first individual gold medal in the Olympics, this former army man had achieved a similar feat in the Paralympics. Murlikant won an individual gold medal in the 1972 Summer Paralympics in Heidelberg, Germany.

India has dedicated its biggest sporting award, the Khel Ratna, to the memory of the tallest hockey player to have walked on the globe—Major Dhyanchand. The country celebrates his birth anniversary every year as the National Sports Day. India has conferred the Bharat Ratna to its once-in-a-generation cricketer, Sachin Tendulkar. The country has talked about the unforgettable "so near but yet so far" Olympics moments of Milkha Singh in the Rome 1960 Olympics and P.T. Usha in the Los Angeles 1984 Olympics a number of times. India has celebrated and towering world champions like Anju Bobby George, P.V. Sindhu, and Neeraj Chopra. Now, it is high time the world knew the story of this Indo-Pakistan war hero, the first person to win a Paralympic medal for India.

The Kolhapur-Sangli region in Maharashtra figures prominently in the wrestling map of India. Kolhapur is known as a city of wrestlers, with several historical rulers from the area being accomplished wrestlers themselves. In January 2018, wrestler Maruti Jadhav organised a bout inside a wrestling cage in Sangli to mark the launch of Pahalwan Premi Sanghatana. The organisers asserted that this style of wrestling was common in the region during the pre-Independence period and was revived in 2018 after a long hiatus.

Murlikant's journey starts from the Peth Islampur region of Sangli, where he was born on 1 November 1947. Like many other kids from the region, Murlikant had a natural attraction to wrestling and wrestlers. He said: "I had a special fondness for the fresh *thandai* (a refreshing drink with cooling effects) prepared at the local *akhadas* (the wrestling ground). The drink used to fill out my emaciated body as we trained hard under the local wrestler Ganpat Khedkar." However, Murlikant came from a family of tailors in a low-income group, with only one earning member responsible for six children. Sports and wrestling were luxuries for them as they struggled to meet their daily needs. "I used to help local wrestlers in their practice and training. I prepared *thandai* and occasionally offered *malish* (massage). In return, they shared ghee, dry fruits, and other foods with me. But more than the food, it gave me an opportunity to watch them closely and pick the nuances of the sport," said Murlikant. It was this love for wrestling that eventually led him to leave his village forever.

When Murlikant was 12 years old, his village organised a wrestling competition. Wrestlers from different villages participated in the event. As Murlikant was only 12 at that time, he could not take part in the competition; however, he got an opportunity to be part of a friendly match, where he was up against the son of the headman of the nearby village, Kanderi. He says: "As the right arm was raised, signalling the start of the bout, there was a massive roar. During those days, we used to get *batasa* (a kind of a sugar candy) and coconut as prizes for winning. But the stakes were higher in this match. As the match progressed, villagers started throwing coins on the cloth which was specifically kept there for this purpose." Murlikant won the bout, but the people of Kanderi took this as an insult. Knives were drawn, and somehow Murlikant managed to save his life and run away from there. Fortunately, he had the winner's cash in his pocket. He got into a truck, which took him to Pune.

After reaching Pune, Murlikant had to struggle for basic necessities. It was the first time the young boy had been out of his village. Even managing a square meal was a major challenge for him. There were many days when he had to sleep on an empty stomach. It was then that one of his relatives informed him about the army recruitment rally which was taking place there. The army had a boys' division, and recruitment for this division was going on. "As I was strong and well-built, I got selected. In a week's time, along with the other boys who were selected, I was on the train to Bangalore," he said.

Murlikant's life changed for the better after he came to Bengaluru (formerly known as Bangalore) and joined the Indian Army. He trained with other boys, had proper meals and a bed to sleep on. But more importantly, he gained access to facilities for playing multiple sports. From his early childhood days, nothing gave him more happiness and satisfaction than playing sports. Initially, he concentrated on hockey and started training hard in the sport. However, as he began rising in the ranks, his hockey career took a sudden break. "I was not selected for the Karnataka team as I was a Marathi. This was disappointing for me. I got so disheartened that I left hockey and started focusing on boxing," shared Murlikant.

Murlikant made an instant name in boxing as well. He became a star army boxer and was nicknamed "Chhotu Tiger". He won many medals and trophies in the sport, particularly in the army competitions. In 1964, he got an opportunity to travel overseas for the first time in his life. In Tokyo, Japan, the International Services Meet was taking place. "I still remember, when I was about to board a flight for the first time, I was so scared that I wanted to run away. Somehow, I held my nerves. I reached Tokyo along with others, and this was a different and a new experience for me," he says. Murlikant represented the Indian Army in the games and won his first international medal. "Impressed with my performance, my commanding officer asked me: 'Murlikant, what do you want?' I immediately replied: 'Sir, I would love to go to Kashmir. I have never been there.' Soon, I was in Kashmir, exploring the serene beauty of Shikara rides and the tranquil landscapes of Pahalgam."

It was the land of Kashmir where his life changed forever. In 1965, a war started between India and Pakistan. The Gurkha regiment, where Murlikant was engaged, was deputed in the border area of Kashmir to take on the Pakistani soldiers.

Murlikant was a craftsman-ranked soldier in the Corps of Electronics and Mechanical Engineers, stationed in the Sialkot sector. Around 4 p.m., their position was attacked by a Pakistani bomber. Murlikant recalls: "As far as I can remember, we were resting after lunch when the Havaldar Major suddenly came shouting. Some of us were half-asleep. When the afternoon whistle blew to signal an aerial attack, we mistook it for a call for a tea break. Being a sportsman, I did not drink tea, but I went outside. As I tried to return to my room, the firing had already begun."

As his army camp came under aerial firing from the Pakistani troops, Murlikant took nine bullets; one of them is still lodged in his backbone. He got hit in his skull, spine, cheek and thighs. Such was the impact of the bullets that he rolled down and was run over by an army vehicle. Murlikant started bleeding profusely and lost consciousness. He couldn't even remember his name. He became almost 95 per cent paraplegic and lost all movement in his legs.

This could have been the end of the road for many. But when such bad things happen to people like Murlikant, it's then that the real character of their personality gets defined. The manner in which he regained consciousness seems to be a plot taken straight out of a Bollywood movie.

One fine morning, the hospital general was inspecting the military hospital where Murlikant was being treated. As the general's inspection happened to be an unexpected visit, there was chaos and confusion all around. In the midst of this confusion, Murlikant got hit and fell from his bed. As he got hit on his head, he regained consciousness. Murlikant looked around, thinking that he had been captured by an enemy soldier and was in a hospital in Pakistan. He got up and tightly grabbed the general's neck, shocking people around him. One of the soldiers had to show him his identity card to convince him that he was being treated in an Indian hospital. However, after regaining consciousness, he realised that he had become physically disabled. It was hard for him to digest the fact that he would be dependent on others for the rest of his life and would not be able to play sports. "For me, nothing could be worse than this," he reminisces.

Despite this difficult situation, some of his friends kept him motivated and helped him shift to INHS Asvini, the naval hospital in Bombay. It was in this hospital where his immediate family members could come to meet him for the first time after the accident. When they met him, they said something that hurt him so much that he started thinking of ending his life. "We will not be able to look after you and take you home in this condition. You cannot move, and you don't have any control over your urine or bowel movement," they told him. A person is not defeated when he loses the battles of his life. Rather, he's defeated when he loses hope. This was that one rare moment in his life when he lost hope and started working on a plan to end his life. However, destiny had other plans.

As Murlikant sat, preparing to kill himself at INHS Asvini in 1967, a sweeper came rushing. He asked him for Rs 10 for *matka* (a form of street gambling). Murlikant had planned to commit suicide by gulping down 30 sleeping pills with alcohol. He handed over Rs 100 to the sweeper. After taking the money, the sweeper suggested that he place a bet as well. Murlikant gave him another hundred rupees note and asked him to bet on the number whose last digit should be one unit higher than what the sweeper chose for himself. Having done this, he went ahead with his plan. After gulping the pills along with liquor, he went to sleep. However, miraculously, everything started changing. His body refused to accept the pills and the alcohol, and he vomited them all. But more importantly, his body felt the need to urinate for the first time after the fateful afternoon in 1965 when he was badly injured. By then, the sweeper had also informed him that he had won the lottery. Perhaps, on realising that he had won a lottery of Rs 40,000, his bladders also woke up. "Destiny has been both cruel and kind to me. But this was the real turning point in my life," he says.

Murlikant realised that he could have lost his life in the war or when he was run over by the vehicle. But he had survived. He had lost his consciousness but miraculously recovered. He thought of committing suicide, but the plan failed. "I felt that despite one bad thing after another happening in my life, if I had still survived, there would have been a strong enough reason behind this," he said. He realised that he had got no right to end his life and the time had come to love the most precious gift of his life, i.e., life itself. Once he was convinced of this, he started finding a new purpose and meaning in life. It had to be sports, once again.

Meanwhile, the physiotherapists at INHS Asvini advised him to do swimming for better recovery. Murlikant says: "Swimming gave a new meaning to my life. I trained harder and started doing well at the national level." He began using the power in his upper body to excel in other sports as well. With this, the second innings of his life started. Like his first innings, his second innings also had its share of challenges, though entirely different in nature.

Murlikant was part of the 1960s and 1970s generation, a time when sportspersons received minimal support in terms of infrastructure and facilities. International exposure was too limited, if, at all, it existed. The conditions for the differently-abled athletes were even worse. There was almost negligible awareness regarding the inclusion of disabled individuals in society. Murlikant says: "I feel so good when I see our para-athletes getting so much support and encouragement now. It was not the case then. We had to struggle for funds and even basic facilities. We used to play and train on public grounds. And even there, we got our chance when the able-bodied athletes were done with their practice sessions." He further adds, "While preparing for the Paralympics, we had to make do with worn-out infrastructure, home-made contraptions which served as our equipment, and only coaches as our support staff."

In fact, Murlikant's first genuine exposure to international-class facilities for the differently-abled athletes was when he visited London just before the Tel Aviv Paralympics. "The facilities in London were unbelievable. It was for the first time that we saw international-class infrastructure and arrangements for differently-abled sportspersons. Till then, we had only heard about the facilities there and occasionally seen them on television. They had world-class infrastructure, separate tennis facilities, volleyball courts, dedicated coaches, trainers, and support staff. It was the first time that we realised how facilities for differently-abled athletes are different from those for able-bodied athletes. Their wheelchairs were made of metal and are very sturdy and smooth. On the other hand, we had three-wheeled wooden contraptions," he recalled.

However, the lack of facilities and resources was more than compensated by the strong determination, willpower, and support from many invisible and unexpected hands at crucial moments.

Murlikant said, "The doctors at INHS Asvini were of great help, and so was our commandant, who always backed me. They were with me when I needed them the most, encouraged me to give my best and excel in my chosen field." Before he was discharged from the military services in 1969, Murlikant participated in the Maharashtra State Athletics Meet in 1967. He became the state champion in shot put, discus throw, javelin throw, table tennis and archery.

This was the time when the Tatas were coming forward to help maimed soldiers. But Murlikant, a recipient of the Raksha medal in 1965, refused to accept any monetary help and instead asked for work. "They were pleasantly surprised and offered me a job. I joined Telco in Pune, where I worked for 30 years," he added. There was support from others as well. Former Indian cricket captain Vijay Merchant was a part of the NGO which supported disabled persons. This NGO sponsored tickets for his participation in the games. Murlikant, thus, moved ahead in his life.

Murlikant represented India in the 1968 Summer Paralympics in the table tennis event. He cleared the first round, but his campaign ended there. After the 1968 Paralympic Games, he started concentrating on swimming. In the 1972 Paralympic

Games, he won the gold medal in the 50-metre freestyle swimming category. His finishing time of 37.33 seconds was a world record then. He thus became the first Indian to win a medal in the Paralympic Games. It took India another 32 years to win its second gold medal in the games, when Devendra Jhajharia grabbed the gold medal in javelin in the Athens 2004 Games.

Murlikant won the General Championship Cup for five years, from 1969 to 1973. In the third Commonwealth Paraplegic Games in Edinburgh, Scotland, he won a gold medal in the 50-metre-freestyle swimming category, a silver in javelin throw, and a bronze in shot put. In the International FESPIC Games [Far East and South Pacific Games for the Disabled] in Hong Kong in 1982, he set another world record in the 50-metre swimming event. "I feel I could have won many more medals for the country if I had better facilities. It's this aspect where India has changed, and I am sure with the facilities and encouragement we have now, our para athletes will win many more medals in the years ahead," he said. The man who was the first to rise from amongst billions is confident about India's bright future in the Paralympics.

On 25 March 2018, President Ramnath Kovind conferred the Padma Shri upon Murlikant Petkar, one of the greatest sons of Mother India, at the Rashtrapati Bhavan. Though the clutches tied to his forearms prevented him from offering a crisp salute to the Supreme Commander of India's armed forces, his chest swelled with pride. His memories went back to 1982, when the government had rejected his claim for the Arjuna Award. In his customary style, Murlikant says, "I felt disheartened when I was denied an Arjuna Award on the grounds that I was a disabled person. I made a bundle of all my certificates and medals and stashed them. I made a resolve not to apply for any award again. On 25 January 2018, I got a call from the government that I had been shortlisted for the Padma Shri. I have put the past behind me. I am glad that the government finally recognised my achievements."

Murlikant stands as a war hero and one of India's most illustrious sportspersons. As the nation commemorates 75 years of Independence, a new India is emerging, one that acknowledges true heroes like Murlikant. A telling indicator of this shift can be observed when comparing the profiles of individuals conferred with prestigious civilian awards in the past eight years with those recognised before that era.

Kabir Khan's film *Chandu Champion*, starring Kartik Aaryan, vividly brings to life the remarkable story of Murlikant. The biopic premiered in theatres on 14 June 2024. Many may not know that Sushant Singh Rajput was originally set to bring Petkar's untold story to the screen. However, the project was halted after his tragic death. Interestingly, the film was released on the fourth anniversary of Sushant's passing.

Despite facing numerous adversities in life, Murlikant Petkar chose not to sit in perpetual sadness, immobilised by the gravity of his losses. Instead, he decided to rise above his pain, and cherish the most precious gift he possessed—life itself. In this series, our next real-life hero is Joginder Singh Bedi, the Maratha Sardar, who achieved the remarkable feat of winning a series of hat-trick medals for the country in a single edition of the Paralympic Games.

JOGINDER SINGH BEDI

The Hat-Trick Medal-Winning Maratha Sardar

"Success is not key to happiness. Happiness is key to success. If you will love what you are doing, you will be successful."

—Albert Schweitzer, German physicist

The Oxford dictionary defines happiness as a "feeling of pleasure or contentment". While the definition is certainly not incorrect, Albert Schweitzer's view on happiness is more in-depth. Joginder Singh Bedi, popularly known as Maratha Sardar, who won a hat-trick of medals in a single edition of the Paralympics, chased happiness throughout his life and, in the process, became a legendary Paralympian. The Maratha Sardar has left behind a legacy that has got the potential to inspire generations.

Murlikant Petkar won a gold medal in the 1972 Paralympic Games. The Indian contingent did not take part in the 1976 and 1980 Paralympic Games. When India participated again in the 1984 Games, it was in desperate need of the medal. Back then, every medal counted, for the decision-makers questioned the justification of sending teams for such events. One of the senior officers who worked with the sports ministry then said, "In those days, there was a feeling of negativity in the department.

Whenever any federation, player or coach would come with a proposal to take part in any international event, it was taken as if they were going out on the junket." In such an atmosphere, every medal or win counted, and it worked as justification to send the team for the next event. Moreover, it was also necessary to sustain the interest of a select few who supported the players then. In such a scenario, Joginder Singh Bedi grabbed three medals in the 1984 Stoke Mandeville Games.

The Maratha Sardar thus became the first Indian to win multiple medals in the single edition of the games. Though India has participated in every Paralympic Games after 1984, his record of winning three medals in the Paralympics has not been equalled till date. Even in the Tokyo 2020 Paralympics, where Indian para athletes made history in terms of the size of the contingent and the number of medals won, Joginder Singh Bedi's record of winning a hat-trick of medals remained unconquered. Avani Lekhara and Singhraj Adhana won two medals each, but none could touch the benchmark of three medals set 36 years ago.

The 1984 Paralympic Games had one more medal winner for the country other than Joginder Singh Bedi. Bhimrao Kesarkar won a silver medal in the javelin throw category. Bhimrao touched the distance of 34.55 metres. He competed in the men's 100-metre freestyle category too. However, there, he finished in the fifth position during the opening round. Before we go further into the inspiring story of Joginder Singh Bedi, an understanding of the historicity and significance of the 1984 Stoke Mandeville Paralympic Games will help us appreciate his achievements better.

The 1984 International Games for the disabled (or the 1984 Summer Paralympic Games) was historic in many respects.

There were two separate competitions within this event. The first one, organised in Stoke Mandeville in England, was for the wheelchair athletes with spinal cord injuries.

The second one, held at the Mitchell Athletic Complex and Hofstra University in Long Island, in the United States of America, was for the wheelchair and ambulatory athletes. This included amputees as well as cerebral-palsy-affected and blind and visually impaired athletes. In the chronology of the Paralympic Games, the 1984 Games is considered to be the seventh edition. The 1984 Games was also the last one where the host city of the Olympics and Paralympics were separate. Seoul hosted both the Games in 1988 and the trend has continued ever since.

The Soviet Union and some communist countries did not take part in the 1984 Games, claiming they lacked a disabled population. However, the USSR made its Paralympic debut four years later, during the 1988 Games, coinciding with the introduction of two crucial reforms, Perestroika (reconstruction) and Glasnost (openness), in the country. The 1984 Games saw participation from 44 countries, with Bahrain, China, East Germany, Faroe Islands, Jordon, Liechtenstein, Papua New Guinea, Thailand, Trinidad and Tobago and Venezuela making their Paralympic debut. India and Portugal also made their return after a 12-year absence. What was India like in 1984?

The year 1984 saw the assassination of Prime Minister Indira Gandhi, the unfortunate genocide of the Sikhs, and Rajiv Gandhi becoming the Prime Minister of the country. In the realm of sports, P.T. Usha narrowly missed the medal in the Los Angeles 1984 Olympics. Barring K.D. Jadhav, no Indian had won any individual medal in the Olympics. India, once a dominant force in world hockey, was on a downward curve in the same sport.

A year ago, the Indian cricket team had won the 1983 World Cup, which marked the ascendancy of the country in the sport. For the next two decades, Indian sport was primarily about cricket and cricketers, and there were rarely any noteworthy achievements in other sports. There were some stories of individual brilliance, but these were too far and few. Moreover, these achievements came despite the system and not because of it. There was hardly any awareness about the rights and facilities for the differently abled back then. Paralympic sport was at the bottom of the priority in the agenda of decision-makers. Ironically, the year which saw the mindless violence against the Sikh community also became witness to a Maratha Sardar rising to the occasion and grabbing three medals for the country in the Paralympics. The achievement did not create any buzz in the mainstream media. However, it was a silent reminder of the invaluable contribution of the Sikh community in the making of our great nation. The greatness of the Flying Sikh Milkha Singh has been deservedly celebrated and has become a part of the folklore now. It's high time we knew about the real-life story of Maratha Sardar Joginder Singh Bedi and acknowledge his invaluable contribution to the Paralympic Movement and Indian sports.

The story of Joginder Singh Bedi starts from Nagpur in Maharashtra, where he was born to Sardar Iqbal Singh and Surinder Kaur Bedi. He had two brothers and a sister. His is not a rags-to-riches story. But not every inspiring story needs to be a rags-to-riches story. Sardar Iqbal Singh was an army contractor. He used to supply essential commodities to the nearby army canteens and earn good money. He was an influential person in the area and well-respected in society. Sardar Iqbal Singh provided the best of facilities in terms of education and sports to his children. He always encouraged them to pursue their dreams with total dedication and hard work. It was perhaps this upbringing which imbibed the habit of chasing happiness in young Joginder.

Joginder Singh, one of Iqbal Singh's children, was disabled by birth. He had no forefinger in his left hand. Despite this, he was a physically active child and the beloved of the entire family. He always had a smile on his face and spread positivity all around. Right from the early days, he was loved and admired by family and friends. Joginder grew up in an environment where he learned to be confident of his abilities and did not take his disability as a liability. When he became an adult, he loved driving a scooter and then a car. Everyone used to talk about his passion for the wheel. But the thing which set him apart was his fondness for sports.

He played multiple sports and did well in most of them. As a cricketer, he was known for his powerful hitting, often scoring plenty of runs with one-handed strokes. He used the power in his right hand to dominate rival bowlers. In football, his skilful dodging of opponents captivated his friends. He also won medals in badminton. He played lawn tennis and was good in this sport as well. He loved participating in hammer throw and shot put. Supported and encouraged by his father, Joginder was able to follow his passion for sports. His versatility and success in various sports earned him the nickname "Tiger Jagga" among his college friends.

There is another significant aspect to Joginder's story. He was a very helpful person and used to go the extra mile to help others. His friends recount numerous instances where he assisted them and their relatives during times of need. He could not see anyone unhappy or in distress and did his best to help them out. His friends remember him as someone who had in-built leadership qualities. He would always take the lead in raising resources to help those in need.

While studying at GS College in Nagpur, Joginder founded an association for the disabled. After his classes, he dedicated himself to the association's work, which focused on providing essential support and assistance to individuals with disabilities in the region. The association was particularly active in the realm of sports, offering facilities such as a gymnasium and sports equipment to differently-abled people. From an early age, Joginder was a strong advocate for the transformative power of sports, believing that it could provide both physical and mental strength to those with disabilities and improve their lives. In this way, Joginder was far ahead of his time, especially during an era with limited awareness about the facilities and rights of the disabled.

In 1971, Joginder married Surinder in an arranged marriage. Surinder was a courageous woman who had been active in the National Cadet Corps (NCC) during her student days and had aspirations to join the Indian Army. However, after marriage, she chose to become a housewife and support her husband in all his endeavours. At that time, Joginder took on the responsibility of managing his father's business and the family finances were in good shape. The couple had one son and a daughter, and they provided their children with the best atmosphere and facilities possible. Despite his family commitments, what made Joginder the happiest was sports. When a friend introduced him to the Paralympics, Joginder saw an opportunity to elevate his association's focus on sports. He started aspiring to represent the country at the Paralympic Games and devoted all his energy to preparation. In those days, support and facilities for para sports were almost non-existent, and athletes had to manage everything on their own. His son, Pavneet Joginder Singh, recalls, "Despite many constraints, such was the commitment of my father to win a medal for the country in the Paralympics that his friends named him Maratha Sardar." Joginder set his sights on the 1984 Paralympic Games. He practiced from early morning until late evening and hardly deviated from his routine. At night, he dreamt of standing on the podium with the *Tiranga* (Tricolour) flying high. In addition to his rigorous training, he had to secure resources for travel and complete the necessary paper work for his participation. Finally, Joginder joined the contingent and set off to compete in the games.

Surinder accompanied Joginder as a team nurse for the Stoke Mandeville and New York 1984 Games. With a certificate in acupuncture, she provided crucial support to the Indian contingent throughout the event. Later, she shared her memories of the tour with their son, which remains the only available source of information about India's participation in that event. After a 12-year hiatus, India competed in the games once again, and the "Maratha Sardar" rose to the occasion. He won a silver medal in shot put L6 category. His throw of 10.06 metres made him the second Indian, after Murlikant Petkar, to win a medal for the country in the Paralympic Games.

Joginder did not stop there. His second medal came in the men's javelin-throw L6 category, where he won a bronze medal with a throw of 34.18 metres. In this same event, another Indian, Bhimrao Kesarkar, won a silver medal for the country. Joginder's third medal was in the discus throw L6 event, with a throw of 28.16 metres. Athletes from other countries wondered as to how Joginder and Kesarkar could win medals for their country despite having so many limitations in terms of facilities, encouragement and support.

Pavneet recalled, "I was just three years old at the time, so I don't remember much. However, my mother later shared many stories about the tour, and I still remember most of them. She spoke about the challenges in preparation and training, the atmosphere during the games, the performance of the Indian contingent and the reception they received upon returning home with the medals. My father was not satisfied with just one silver and two bronze medals; he aimed for a gold medal. Nevertheless, my grandfather was very proud of his son's achievements and the honour he brought to the country. My grandfather even travelled to Kamptee in Nagpur with his friends and my father's friends to welcome him home."

He added, "There wasn't much media coverage then, but some regional papers did report the news. Our experience with awards and accolades has been mixed. The Maharashtra government honoured my father with two Chhatrapati Awards, including one for lifetime achievement, and he also received the Arjuna Award. However, there were also many unfulfilled promises. Numerous people and institutions made promises that were never kept."

There was another aspect to Joginder's success in the games. The need to devote all his energy, resources, and effort to winning a medal had a significant impact on his business. As a result, the family had to go through tough financial times as the business began to falter.

Joginder had inherited his father's business as an army contractor supplying perishable commodities, but he suffered substantial losses. He explored other ventures as well, but faced setbacks in those too. Pavneet says, "My father lived his life with pride. He faced financial difficulties and many unfulfilled promises with a smile. He believed that awards and rewards should come naturally, not be demanded. He never asked for help for himself; he always sought help for others." However, financial constraints began to affect the entire family. When the family's finances were stable, Joginder encouraged his children to participate in sports and provided them with excellent facilities. His son excelled in table tennis and cricket, and one of his daughters also showed great potential. Unfortunately, as financial pressures increased, they had to give up sports and focus on earning a livelihood.

Joginder was a deeply religious person and a devoted believer in God. He visited the gurudwara every day and never missed his prayers. On 18 November 2011, he tragically passed away following an unfortunate accident. His son recalls, "Like every day, my father woke up early, had his breakfast, and went to visit his mother, who lived nearby. On that day, he arrived as usual but could not see her because she was bathing. My father returned home and went back later to meet her. Unfortunately, he met with an accident on the way. He was taken to the military hospital at Kamptee, where he passed away."

Joginder's mother could not cope with this loss and suffered a paralytic stroke six months later, leaving her bedridden for four years. She passed away on 13 January 2015. Pavneet still regrets for not being with his father at the time of his passing. He says, "I was in Delhi on business. More than just a father, he was my closest friend. He never refused anything and was a constant source of inspiration and motivation. He always looked at the positive side of life and made time for anyone who came to our home seeking help. He treated everyone, including the domestic help, as part of the family and even helped him build his house."

Joginder was always ready to help anyone who came to him in need. However, in the later stages of his life, when he required support from others, he was a loner and had to fend for himself. At that time, a career as a professional sportsperson was not financially rewarding, and there was limited support for para sports. Despite these challenges, Joginder devoted his active days to sports and to bringing laurels for his country.

Pavneet says, "My father must be smiling from heaven, seeing how well our para sportspersons are performing for the country now. The support, facilities, encouragement and exposure they receive today are truly amazing. He was a firm believer in the transformative power of sports, and this is evident now more than ever."

Pavneet, having heard many stories from his mother about the struggles his father faced to participate in and excel at the Paralympics, appreciates this change deeply. He shares, "My mother used to tell me about the numerous challenges my father faced while preparing for and competing in the games. There was not much support from the system back then. He made it to the games with the financial support of his friends. He trained largely on his own, without a coach. My mother accompanied him to the Paralympics and took care of the entire contingent during the event. Despite the limitations, my father performed exceptionally well."

Joginder did so well in the games, but his achievements were largely ignored by the media. There were many unkept promises, and he faced significant financial difficulties. And yet, all these did not make him bitter. He remained inquisitive and a keen student of life and sports until his last breath.

The greatest tribute to Joginder will arise from the next generation of athletes, who optimise the available resources and opportunities to excel for their country. His legacy should continue to inspire the future generations. Pavneet says, "I want to preserve his legacy. His true legacy lies in his pursuit of happiness rather than mere success. He always preached to 'love what you do, and success will follow'. Despite numerous challenges, he remained positive throughout and moved ahead in life." With a choked voice, he continues, "I don't have enough funds to preserve the places and belongings associated with his achievements. I want to preserve his childhood memories so that they continue inspiring the youth of our country. I've received support from various quarters. Sachin Tendulkar, one of the greatest cricketers of all time and a wonderful human being, generously contributed Rs 15 lakh. While there's much to be done, financial limitations are hindering my efforts."

More than Pavneet and his family, it is the responsibility of the citizens of this great country, who were close to Joginder until his last breath and who have reasons to be proud of him, to help preserve the legacy of the "Maratha Sardar".

In cricketing parlance, Murlikant Petkar, Joginder Singh Bedi and Bhimrao Kesarkar batted under challenging conditions— when the sky was overcast, the shining ball was doing enough, and the wicket was difficult. From there, the onus fell on another formidable and battle-hardened Devendra Jhajharia to carry the innings forward.

DEVENDRA JHAJHARIA

A Human Embodiment of Resilience and Willpower

"A champion is one who is remembered.
A legend is one who is never forgotten."

—Matshona Dhliwayo

This quote from Canada-based philosopher, entrepreneur, and author Matshona Dhliwayo aptly sums up Indian sporting legend, Devendra Jhajharia.

Rajasthan, known for its warriors in Indian history, particularly celebrates them for their fighting spirit rather than solely for their victories or defeats. Devendra Jhajharia, a sporting icon from Rajasthan, will be immortalised for similar attributes.

Years from now, when the annals of Indian Paralympic sports are chronicled, Devendra's legacy will echo through ages for the way he fought like a warrior in his personal and professional life, rather than by what he achieved.

Murlikant Petkar, Joginder Singh Bedi, and Bhimrao Kesarkar stand as the unsung pioneers of Indian Paralympic sports. Quietly, they laid the solid foundation upon which the grand edifice of Indian Paralympic sports now stands. Murlikant

opened India's medal account at the Paralympic Games, and after a long 12-year wait, Maratha Sardar Bedi clinched a hat-trick of medals upon India's return to the games. Kesarkar also brought home a medal. While this triumvirate forged the initial pathways, a concerning silence enveloped the scene following their era.

After the 1984 Paralympic Games, India participated in every subsequent edition, but for four consecutive games, they returned without any medals. "We had to literally beg, borrow and steal to justify our participation in the games before the officials," one of the Paralympians who participated in the games said on the condition of anonymity. As we reflect on the aftermath of the Tokyo 2020 Paralympics, the question arises: Who will become the first Indian to join the illustrious list of global legends like Trust Zorn, Ragnhild Myklebust, Beatrice Hess and Jonas Jacobsson?

In 2004, on the eve of the Athens Paralympic Games, there were doubts about whether India could secure another Paralympic medal and whether a new Indian Paralympian could rise to follow the illustrious trio of Petkar, Bedi, and Kesarkar. At the Athens 2004 Paralympic Games, a new legend emerged: Devendra Jhajharia claimed a gold medal, solidifying his place in history.

Devendra, hailing from the Churu district of Rajasthan, began his legendary journey in Athens in 2004, marked by three significant milestones in his sporting career. However, akin to the valiant warriors of Rajasthan, his story is about what transpired before and between these milestones, underlining his "never-say-die" attitude in overcoming life's major hurdles.

His first major milestone was achieved at the Athens Paralympics in 2004, where he, at the age of 23, clinched the gold medal in the F46 javelin throw category, with a world record throw of 62.15 metres, surpassing the previous record of 59.77 metres. His second major milestone occurred at the Rio Paralympics in 2016, where he won another gold medal by touching a distance of 63.97 metres, breaking his own world record set in Athens in 2004. The third major milestone was at the Tokyo 2020 Paralympics, where he won his third medal, becoming the most decorated Indian Paralympian. His third attempt, covering a distance of 64.35 metres, earned him the silver medal.

Devendra was born on 10 June 1981, into a small farmer's family in Jhajhariyon Ki Dhani, a small hamlet in the Surajgarh *tehsil*, approximately 175 km from Jaipur, the capital of Rajasthan. He had a typical childhood, playing with other kids and engaging in sibling mischief. He would playfully strike other children with sticks and swiftly flee before they could respond. Climbing trees and capturing animals and birds were among his favourite pastimes. After catching these creatures, he would tie them up, but upon receiving a scolding for this, he would release them and burst into laughter.

Recounting one of his childhood mischiefs, his sister Kirodpati Devi shares, "Our house was under construction then. As we stepped outside, we spotted him perched on top of the half-built structure. While the rest of us panicked, he remained composed, as if nothing extraordinary had occurred. After a few minutes, he climbed down."

Unfortunately, a few months later, when attempting a similar feat, Devendra nearly lost his life. He recalls, "I must have been eight or nine years old then. While climbing a tree in my village, I accidentally touched a live electric cable. It's said that the cable was carrying a power of 10,000 volts. When I was brought down from the tree, the villagers thought I was dead. My left hand was all burnt."

His father, the late Ram Singh Jhajharia, stated in an interview with a news channel, "One of his hands got almost totally burnt. The current was so powerful that it flowed all across the tree and impacted his entire body. His legs also got damaged. When we took him to the hospital in Rajgarh, the local doctors could not believe how he was alive after such an electric shock. In one of his hands, bones had charred, and skin peeled off. It looked like a baboon's hand."

After primary treatment, the local doctors advised the family to take Devendra to a better hospital, preferably in Jaipur. Ram Singh recalled further: "He was rushed to a hospital in Jaipur, where a board of doctors, led by Dr Pandey, assembled to discuss his case. They decided to do a surgery and amputate one of his hands. After obtaining consent, the operation was performed. The doctors closely monitored him for two days and then called me to their chamber. They informed me that although my son had survived, they didn't think he would develop further, physically and mentally. I was quiet and somehow kept my composure till then. But suddenly I could not take all that anymore. I said, 'Look, earlier you were saying that he will not survive. Now that he has survived you are saying that he will not grow for the rest of his life. Please leave him to his fate and there is no point in being judgemental about his future'. Deep inside, I had a strong belief that if God takes something, he has his own way of giving it back in his own manner and style."

When a life-altering event like this occurs, it takes time to process and accept. There are challenges galore before one can stand up and start walking again. This had happened in one of the rural regions of the country. In such places, awareness is limited, and people often rely on preconceived notions.

Devendra reflects on those days, saying, "When I recall those days, I think I didn't suffer a lot, thanks to my parents. It was they who had to go through demotivating and discouraging words at every step. As we are from a rural area, whoever we bumped into would look at me with pity and say, *'Iski zindagee to barbaad ho gayee* (his life is ruined)'. You can imagine the plight of the parents who have to listen to such comments day in and day out about their child. However, my parents absorbed all such outside heat themselves and protected me from its impact."

Devendra's sister, Kirodpati Devi, recalls her initial reaction, saying, "When he was undergoing treatment at a hospital in Jaipur, we were told that he had only lost his three fingers. However, when I first saw him without one of his hands, it deeply affected me, and I couldn't bear the pain. What will he do for the rest of his life? How will he earn his livelihood? Who will marry him? Though he has survived, I questioned the purpose of it all. Many such thoughts overwhelmed me and I eventually fainted and collapsed." Yet, once the family accepted this harsh reality, they displayed unwavering determination and resilience, pushing Devendra to fight hard and succeed.

As Devendra began to heal physically, he developed a mental block. "When I returned home after six months in the hospital, I realised everything around me had changed. People started treating me in an entirely different manner. The children I used to play with just six months ago now ridiculed me and shooed me away," Devendra recalls. It was at this point that his mother, Jeevan Devi, stepped in. She urged him to go outside and interact with the other children.

"Many other mothers would have asked their sons in a similar condition to become a doctor or engineer, but my mother directed me towards sports. I had confined myself to the house, telling her that other kids would taunt me and that I would not play with them. But she was the one who forcibly sent me to the playground again," Devendra says. Although it was not easy for him at first, he grew physically and mentally tougher, shedding his fears.

Devendra says, "Being back among the kids made me more determined. I consistently tried not to appear weaker than others. And the best way to do so was to compete against them and win. Sport is the only medium where this is possible. Through this approach, I developed a serious and personal relationship with sports. It became my way of demonstrating to the world that I am not weaker than anyone else in any respect."

As for his choice for javelin, Devendra explained, "In Rajasthan, while growing up, children hear stories of warriors and heroes from the region; we get to know about their spears and swords. Maharana Pratap Singh, one of the tallest warriors from the region, has a huge influence on many of us. We've heard stories and anecdotes from his life and battles in our early days. One of the stories was that he used to go to the battlefield laden with 208-kg weight. His spear weighed 81 kg and, his armour, 72 kg. He carried two swords, one with which he fought his own battles and the other which he offered to his enemies when they were unarmed. When you hear such stories as a kid, they get into your subconscious mind. This might be one of the reasons why javelin started attracting me from the moment weaker I saw it."

He adds, "I liked javelin because this was a sport I could

do it with one arm." Above all, this reflects the strength of Devendra's character. Whenever I have talked to any competitive javelin thrower at international level, they always emphasise the important role of the 'non-throwing' hand in javelin. Devendra didn't have this option and accepted it as a fait accompli. The mantra of his life is, "Don't dwell on what you don't have, and make the most of what you do have."

The village where Devendra grew up wasn't big on sport. His school had some basic track and field facilities, including javelin. Devendra began closely observing fellow students practising javelin in school. "The first javelin that I owned, I made it myself from a bamboo stick," he recalls. At the age of 14, competing against regular athletes with his homemade javelin, Devendra became the district champion. "Looking back, I consider this the turning point in my life. It was as if I had won an Olympic gold medal. I was able to convince myself that I am not weak and could compete with the best. Once you can convince yourself, it becomes easier to take on your opponents," he says.

Initially, people refused to accept him and ridiculed his participation. But after that, he let his javelin do most of the talking. "Whenever I went for competitions, people looked at me and thought I had come to compete because of someone's recommendation. But when they saw me actually performing with the javelin in my hand, they would apologise and accept me as the real champion. This has happened so many times in my life," he shares.

Another major breakthrough in his life came when Ripudaman Singh, popularly known as RD, saw him throw javelin for the first time in a para athletic competition in 1997. Coach RD was impressed by Devendra's talent and encouraged him to work hard. Undeterred by outside reactions, RD and Devendra, the *guru* and the *shishya*, began hunting together in pairs. One memorable story from their partnership involves an open, inter-university meet at the Lakshmibai National University of Physical Education in Gwalior, where Devendra participated among able-bodied athletes. Other coaches, support staff and athletes were surprised to see him there.

"*Kyon RD Sir, poore Rajasthan mein aapko koi do hath waala athlete nahin mila* (RD Sir, could you not find a single able-bodied athlete in entire Rajasthan that you brought a disabled athlete for the competition?)," they asked the coach in Devendra's presence. RD was shocked to hear this, but he kept quiet. Devendra's dominant performance left them in awe, and they had to admit their misjudgement. They started looking at him with admiration and awe. The stage was set for him to take another leap in life.

"I vividly remember my first experience of travelling to a foreign country. I was going to England to compete in the British Open Athletics Championships, and I got the gold medal, breaking all records. Some stakeholders were so impressed with my performance that they offered me lucrative deals to settle there and represent them in future events. However, I made it clear that I could never imagine representing any flag other than our *Tiranga*," he says. This journey abroad also opened his eyes to the vast expanse of the global sporting landscape and its potential.

Reflecting on his participation in the Busan 2002 Asian Games, Devendra says, "There were more than 2000 athletes competing in 17 sports. The scale and scope of the para sports stunned me." During those games, he had the honour of wearing an Indian jersey for the first time. "I received the jersey in the evening and tried it on at least five times before going to sleep. My father, who accompanied me on that tour, asked why I kept wearing the same jersey repeatedly. He thought it didn't fit properly. I explained that it was my dream to wear the Indian jersey, and I wanted to feel the joy and pride it brought over and over again," he says.

Soon, Devendra became a symbol of pride and inspiration for all those who aspired to don the Indian jersey. His first international medal came at the age of 21, when he claimed gold at the Far-East and South Pacific Games for the Disabled in Korea in 2002.

The countdown for his first Paralympic Games began. The country was waiting for another medal in the event after the 1984 Games. "As I was holding the Indian flag and leading the contingent in the Athens 2004 Games, I started feeling the added responsibility of giving my best for my country. I could feel the positive energy and sense that something big was going to happen," Devendra says. Winning the gold medal in his event made him the second Indian, following Petkar, to secure a gold medal in the Paralympics. The man from the desert state of Rajasthan ended India's over two-decade-long medal drought in the event. "When you are competing with 200 nations and win a gold and you see your national flag on the top and your national anthem being played in the background, nothing in life can match the feeling you have then. Nothing before and nothing after can beat that till I am alive," Devendra says.

However, Devendra's remarkable achievements went largely unnoticed by the mainstream media, reflecting the challenges and limited sporting ecosystem of the time. In this context, two facts shared by his father, the late Ram Singh Jhajharia, are relevant.

During an interview with *IBN7*, Ram Singh Jhajharia recounted their efforts to secure financial assistance for Devendra's training and participation in major events. "We approached everyone we could. Devendra and I had a meeting with Yunus Khan, a minister in the Rajasthan cabinet. He listened to our request with patience and mentioned that he would have been able to help if we had approached him sooner. 'After all, Devendra is competing in a major event,' he said. While Yunus Khan was speaking, Devendra confidently interjected, 'Don't worry; just get ready to give us a warm welcome when I return.' Yunus Khan responded that it might not be possible since the results would likely be announced by then. Unfazed, Devendra insisted that he wasn't just going there to compete; he would return with a medal, quite possibly a gold one. True to his word, Devendra returned with the gold medal, and Minister Yunus Khan honoured his commitment by organising a reception for him."

In the same interview, the late Ram Singh remarked, "Although Devendra won a gold medal for the country in an event of this scale, the mainstream media either completely ignored it or provided very poor coverage. Unlike today, information flow was not as accessible back then. I only learnt about his achievements while I was in Jaipur. It was the pre-internet age, and someone showed me a story on the *BBC* website. It pointed out that an athlete from a middle-class rural background had won a gold medal for the country in the Paralympics, but the mainstream media in the country had largely overlooked the news. Among the regional press, only Gopal Sharma's *Mana Times* provided detailed coverage."

From Athens 2004 to Tokyo 2020, there has been a sea change. Prime Minister Narendra Modi has set the tone by consistently engaging with the athletes before, during and after major events. More importantly, para athletes are now treated on a par with able-bodied athletes. This shift has prompted the mainstream media to provide more extensive coverage to their participation and achievements. Instead of foreign news agencies lecturing India on these matters, the country has been setting a global template, despite facing challenges on multiple fronts. The regional press and digital media have also compelled mainstream media to adopt a different perspective.

Devendra was honoured with the Arjuna Award for his gold medal-winning performance at the Athens 2004 Paralympics. However, just when it seemed like he would dominate major events, another challenge emerged in his life: a 12-year wait before he could compete again in his event at the Paralympics (the javelin throw event he competed in was not included in the Beijing 2008 and London 2012 Paralympics). During this period, he continued to excel in major competitions. In 2013, at the IPC Athletics World Championship in Lyon, France, he won a gold medal in F64 javelin throw. This was followed with a silver medal in the 2014 Asian Para Games at Incheon, South Korea. In 2015, at the IPC Athletics World Championships in Doha, he finished in second place with a throw of 59.06 metres, just behind China's Guo Chunliang.

Devendra says, "After winning gold in 2004, I had to wait for another 12 years for my next medal. It felt like waiting for the Kumbh Mela."

Twelve years is a long duration in competitive sports. While many athletes reach Devendra's level, only a few maintain their dominance for over a decade. Unfortunately, just as he was reaching the pinnacle of his career, Devendra missed two consecutive Paralympic Games. During this long gap, he was advised at times to quit sports and focus on other interests. "Yes, there were moments when my friends and acquaintances had such discussions. It was getting more and more difficult for me with every passing year, but I was determined not to give up. I had the total support of my family, and without their assistance, it would have been difficult for me to continue," says Devendra.

In 2007, Devendra married Manju, an accomplished Kabaddi player who represented her college at the national level. She made the selfless decision to sacrifice her own sports career to support Devendra and take care of the family. The couple is now blessed with a daughter, Kia, and a son, Kavyan. The family played a pivotal role in ensuring that Devendra's passion and determination continued to burn brightly, keeping him fully prepared for the moment when his next opportunity would arise. In many ways, they were a solid and constant support throughout his journey, guiding him from one milestone to the next.

"I kept myself in the loop by participating in the Asian and World Games. In 2013, while I was at the World Championship and broke the record, I learnt that my event would be included in the next Paralympic Games. After that, I left my hometown, my family, and relocated to Gandhinagar. It was painful to be away from my family, but I had to make this sacrifice to achieve something greater for my country. I used to practise throughout the day and evening, and after my practice sessions, I would call my family members individually and talk to them. During training, I often used to miss my daughter. Like every father, I was concerned about her studies and health. The best part was that despite all these challenges, I did not let my focus waver," Devendra says.

Finally, the moment for which Devendra had practised so hard for years and sacrificed so many things arrived. On 13 September 2016 in Rio de Janeiro, which was around 3 a.m. on 14 September in India, he was preparing for his third attempt in the javelin throw final. "My event was in the evening. I had told my media friends that not only would I win a medal but also break the record once again. They were amazed at my confidence, but it came straight from my heart," he recalled.

At that time, Devendra was leading the field and seemed certain to secure a medal. However, he knew that merely winning was not enough. The prolonged wait and intense pain had been an intrinsic part of his journey, but he was determined to achieve the ultimate goal. He got ready for his final throw. The javelin soared over 62 metres and ultimately reached 63.97 metres! He had started the evening as an underdog against world champion Guo Chuliang, but upon seeing the score on the screen, he broke into a dance. Two gold medals and two world records, separated by 12 long years! Dreams—they do come true!

After his Rio dream came true, another debate started surrounding him. Now that he had proven himself, was it the right time for him to retire from professional sports? In October 2018, Devendra was grappling with a persistent shoulder injury. In an interview with *PTI* from Jakarta, he said, "I will consider retirement after the Asian Para Games. I will discuss it with my coaches, friends and family. The thought has come to mind because I have been dealing with the shoulder injury for the past year and a half. My shoulder has a tear, and I have not been able to recover from it fully."

Then came the challenge of the COVID-19 pandemic, impacting his preparations for the games. Moreover, the Tokyo 2020 Paralympic Games got postponed for a year. For his ageing body plagued with injuries, every year was crucial. But then, from Athens 2004 to Tokyo 2020, facilities for athletes significantly improved. There has been a substantial change in the sporting landscape of the country, enabling him to continue and aspire for one more medal.

In 2020, he lost his father, Ram Singh Jhajharia, who was diagnosed with cancer. Devendra got to know about it while training at the Sports Authority of India centre in Ahmedabad. He returned home to be with his father, who, even in his final moments, wished for his son to win another Paralympic medal for the country. Devendra acknowledges his father's steadfast support, saying, "I would not have been here without my father. Even when he was unwell, he pushed me hard to train well and win a medal for the country. In the Tokyo 2020 Paralympic Games, he wanted me to win a medal for the country."

Devendra, who began his Paralympic journey during the Athens 2004 Paralympics, joined the largest-ever Indian contingent at the Tokyo 2020 Paralympics. His gold medal had ended the country's medal drought then, and now, he was part of a contingent poised to make history. The contingent he represented this time won many more medals than all the medals in all previous Paralympics combined.

Individually, Devendra won a silver medal in the men's javelin throw in the F46 category. He began the event with two throws just over the 60-metre mark, but his third throw, reaching 64.35 metres, reignited hopes for a medal. His fourth and fifth throws were fouls, and his final throw was 61.23 metres. Although the colour of his medal was not gold this time, the silver he won carried more weight than gold as it served as a fitting tribute to his father, Ram Singh. Years ago, when top doctors had nearly given up hope on Devendra, his father implored them not to be judgmental. In his heart, Ram Singh knew that if God had taken something from him, He would also give him something in His own way. Ram Singh must be looking down from heaven, proud to see his son become the most decorated Indian Paralympian.

In 2022, Devendra Jhajharia made history by becoming the first para athlete to receive the Padma Bhushan. Back in 2004, during the Athens Paralympics, another Indian, Rajinder Singh Rahelu, also found a place in the medals column. As we move forward, we will go through the life journey and heroic actions of our next real-life hero—Rajinder Singh Rahelu.

RAJINDER SINGH RAHELU

Challenging the Impossible

"Focus on your strengths, not your weaknesses. Focus on your character, not your reputation. Focus on your blessings, not your misfortunes."

—Roy T. Bennett in his book, *The Light in the Heart*

Rajinder Singh Rahelu. Who is he?

He's someone who has always focused on his strengths and paid little attention to his weaknesses. He's an example of the heights one can attain in life by focusing on character-building and not caring about one's reputation. He's someone who has counted his blessings without cribbing about his misfortunes.

Napoleon Bonaparte famously said, "The word *impossible* is not in my dictionary." In a similar vein, Rajinder Singh Rahelu, an Indian Paralympian-turned-coach, humbly tells his trainees, "I have deleted the word *weakness* from my dictionary." As his life epitomises these words in letter and spirit, his wards nod in full agreement.

Whenever I've mentioned Rajinder Singh Rahelu's name in personal and professional conversations, the first response from the audience has always been "who's he?"

As I learnt more about him and his life story, he emerged as a resilient character who literally rose from the ashes to attain the level of success he enjoys today. In fact, when I first heard his name in 2012, I knew nothing about him. At that time, I was heading the sports team of a leading news channel.

While our crew was in Jalandhar to interview India's star off-spinner, Harbhajan Singh, we encountered a slight hiccup. Upon arrival, Harbhajan Singh informed us that he wouldn't be available for the interview at the initially scheduled time. However, he offered us the option of conducting the interview later in the evening or early the following morning. Our plan was to do an extensive interview session with the country's most successful off-spinner at that time, during which we aimed to capture visuals of his early morning routine and practice sessions.

After finalising the interview schedule, we had our breakfast and checked into our hotel. Later that day, our local stringer proposed an intriguing idea, suggesting, "Sir, since you have the entire day free, why not visit a sports academy for the disabled in the nearby village?" With no other commitments on our agenda, we readily agreed and immediately headed to Gowahar village.

The academy was located on a modest plot of land, equipped with only basic amenities and lacking state-of-the-art infrastructure. Initially, the look and feel of the academy disappointed us, but our inquisitiveness took us further. As we learnt more about the academy, we discovered that the lack of world-class facilities was more than compensated by the remarkable stories of resilience embodied by those who managed the academy.

Within its first three years, the academy had produced 30 disabled players who won over 50 medals in national and international level competitions. These athletes received training in powerlifting, archery, and athletics. According to the minds behind the academy, it served two major purposes: First, it motivated the disabled to take up sports, and thus gave a new sense of purpose and meaning to their lives. Secondly, it inspired the able-bodied youth from the nearby villages to take up sports. Witnessing the dedication and determination of the disabled athletes encourages them to pursue sports and abandon bad habits in their lives.

Parvinder Singh, one of the founders of the academy, greeted us from his wheelchair. Prior to a tragic accident in 2002 resulting in a spinal cord injury, he was an active sportsperson himself. "After my accident, I spent two years bedridden. Piara Singh and Rajinder Singh Rahelu inspired me to take up sports. Though disabled now, I have won many medals for the country," he shared.

Parvinder made history as the first athlete with a spinal cord injury from the country to win a medal in the International Wheelchair and Amputee Sports Federation Games 2009, held in Bengaluru. He generously donated 700 square yards of his own land to start the academy. "What made you do all this?" I asked him. "The idea was to encourage youngsters and the disabled to take up sports for health benefits and to excel in their chosen sport. We have been able to make a small effort in terms of catering to the needs of the nearby villages. We don't have hostel facilities and so we have to be dependent on rented accommodation," said Parvinder.

As our conversation continued, Piara Singh, another founding member and director of the academy, joined us. A former weightlifting coach who had trained numerous athletes for Olympics and other international events, Piara assisted Parvinder in the academy's day-to-day administration.

After meeting Parvinder and Piara, I couldn't help but ask, "Who is Rajinder Singh Rahelu you mentioned earlier? Is he around?" They were surprised by my question. Parvinder said, "Sir, Rajinder Singh Rahelu is a Paralympic medallist and an Arjuna awardee. He is the coach of the academy but is currently away from the country for an important international commitment."

Parvinder's response impacted me deeply. *Here I am, introducing myself as the sports editor of a leading news channel, yet I have not even heard of Rajinder Singh Rahelu. Worse still, I have not bothered to do my basic homework before coming here*, I lamented inwardly. I tried to look up his name online and his profile stated "Bronze medal, men's powerlifting 56 kg, Athens 2004".

As I was going through a few online articles detailing his achievements and journey, my phone suddenly rang. It was my managing editor, inquiring about the status of the Harbhajan Singh interview. After updating him, I attempted to share the inspiring story of the disabled sports academy and Rajinder Singh Rahelu. However, before I could finish my sentence, he interrupted, asking, "Rajinder Singh Rahelu? Who is that?"

In his typical manner, the managing editor reminded me that our news channel prioritises stories that attract attention, not such "dry" narratives. But, at the same time, he wanted me to keep my spirits high as he was expecting headlines from the Harbhajan Singh interview.

He said, "Relax today and focus totally on Harbhajan Singh's interview. Ensure it makes headlines. I'll talk to the assignment desk. Just send visuals of disabled athletes practising in the academy. It'll be a good wrap-up masala for some of our bulletins." The managing editor then hung up.

Harbhajan Singh's interview happened the next day. My managing editor got the headlines that he expected. However, the story of Rajinder Singh Rahelu and the disabled sports academy didn't make it to the channel. To my astonishment, a few months later, I saw my managing editor felicitating Rajinder Singh Rahelu on stage at the Hero Awards, sponsored by the channel.

The journey of Rajinder Singh Rahelu commenced in Mehsampur village, nestled in Punjab's Jalandhar district. Born on 22 July 1973, he was the youngest among five siblings. He had two brothers and two sisters. Hailing from a poor Dalit family, Rajinder's father, Rattan Singh, earned his livelihood as a bandmaster, performing at weddings and other festivities. His mother, Meera Singh, worked as a maid in households to ensure her children got proper meals.

Meera Singh recounted that when Rajinder, affectionately called Sodhi, was eight years old, she noticed he had a high fever one afternoon while bathing him. Shortly after, he lost the ability to walk as his legs stopped functioning. The entire family became anxious. They rushed 20 km away from their home to seek medical help. Rajinder was diagnosed with polio. Over the next few years, his parents took him to every possible doctor for his treatment. Hoping against hope, they wanted to see their son walking again. They travelled extensively across nearby districts such as Patiala, Moga, Amritsar, and Ludhiana, exploring every treatment option suggested by relatives and friends despite facing severe financial constraints. Often, they would leave home early in the morning and return late at night. On the way, they would drink water from the tube wells so that they didn't feel hungry and have the need to buy food. When they saw all their efforts failing, they decided to accept the reality. The mother spent many sleepless nights pondering what her son's future would hold.

Meanwhile, Rajinder completed his education till class eighth in the village school. After this, he had to take admission to another school which was three kilometres from his village. His parents had to take him to school on the bicycle, drop him there, return, and then again go pick him up after he finished his classes. For a family that had to work daily to earn a livelihood, this was a very difficult task. The plight of Rajinder and his parents moved his teacher, Jasvir Kaur, at his school at Jajankalan. She raised resources to gift Rajinder a tricycle and encouraged him to use it while coming to school. This proved to be the game-changer in his life and added wings to his desires. Rajinder started using the tricycle to go to school every day. When his confidence increased, he started travelling as far as Ludhiana, Phagwara and Jalandhar. Psychologically, it gave him the confidence to travel on his own and plan his life accordingly. He was not dependent on anyone and this feeling liberated him.

Physically, it strengthened his hands and his upper body. Rajinder says, "Life has not been kind to me. I was not only disabled but was also from a family which struggled to make both ends meet. My father played in a wedding band to support our seven-member family. For me, life got tougher when I started going to school a fair distance away from my home. But then, this tricycle came at the right time, giving fresh hope to me. It made me independent. It liberated me."

After completing his higher secondary education, Rajinder had to discontinue his studies. However, this did not stop him from aspiring to do something meaningful and substantive in his life. And, it's here when a suggestion from his friend, Surender Singh Rana, proved to be crucial and timely. Surender was a power-lifter and had inspired Rajinder to take up the sport. Rajinder said, "One day, my friend Surender Singh, a power-lifter, who was based in Sweden, suggested me to take up the sport. He made me lift 70 kilograms. Once he saw me lifting 70 kg, he was convinced that with a little effort and training, I could be a state-level champion. I don't know what he saw in me and what gave him this confidence. I agreed and there was no looking back from there." After six months of training, he started lifting more than 100 kg. Rajinder got his first medal in 1997 in the Punjab Open Meet. In 1998, he won a medal in the national powerlifting championship in Hyderabad. This got him into a different league. He then bagged a gold medal at the 2002 Asian Beach Press Championship in New Delhi. After this, he set his eyes on the Athens 2004 Paralympics.

Rajinder won the bronze medal in the Athens 2004 Paralympics. He competed in the 56 kg category and this was India's first-ever medal in powerlifting in the Paralympics. In the final standings, he stood at number four after lifting the total weight of 157.5 kg. However, his position was upgraded to third, when Youssef Younes Cheikh of Syria, the initial bronze medal winner, tested positive for drugs and was disqualified. China's Wang Jian won the gold with a lift of 185 kg while A. Ahmed of Egypt grabbed the silver with 180 kg.

Rajinder's life started changing for the better after the 2004 Paralympics. In 2006, he was honoured with the Arjuna Award by the Government of India. He won a silver medal in the 2007 International Wheelchair and Amputee Sports

Federation (IWAS) World Games held in Taipei. Success cannot always be a straight line. In a professional athlete's career, highs are followed by lows. It's during the lows that they require the support of the system the most. After his purple patch period from 2004 to 2006, Rajinder could not convert his performance into medals for the next two Paralympics.

In the Beijing 2008 Paralympics, he was amongst the two para athletes who were part of the Indian contingent. After lifting a weight of 170 kg in his category, he finished fifth amongst 13 contenders in the finals. He was behind Polish Mariusz Tomczyk. The Paralympic medal winner of the Athens 2004 Games had to face the bureaucratic red tape to make it for the London 2012 Paralympic Games. He could finally make it only after his friends provided him with financial support. Rajinder was the lone representative from Punjab for the London Games. But he had to suffer from the serious anomaly in the Punjab government's policy for the sport of powerlifting. Ironically, on one hand, he was made powerlifting coach at Para Sports Academy in Jalandhar in 2010 on the basis of his 2004 medal. On the other hand, the state government refused to recognise the sports. Because of this, he was not given any financial assistance to participate in the games. He was also not granted official leave to be there. Amidst all these things, Rajinder failed in all his three attempts to lift 175 kg in London 2012 Paralympics. Many thought that his career was over.

But he didn't let the results of the 2008 and 2012 Summer Paralympics weigh him down, and he made a strong comeback in the Glasgow 2014 Commonwealth Games. He was granted leave for the Commonwealth Games only after the Central government intervened through a letter to the concerned departments. The letter directed the government departments across the country to grant leave to the athletes representing the country in the games. Only a few months back, the Punjab government had denied him leave to participate in the preparatory camp ahead of the Commonwealth Games. In the games, Rajinder lifted 185 kg and got a silver medal. After the success in the CWG, Rajinder gradually started preparing for the second innings of his life.

In 2019, the Sports Authority of India appointed Rajinder as the coach at the National Institute at Patiala. During COVID-19, coach Rajinder was at the forefront in terms of working with para athletes to keep them battle-ready for the upcoming Tokyo 2020 Paralympic Games. Rajinder was based out of the western zone headquarters of the Sports Authority of India in Gandhinagar. He stuck to his routine even during the unusual times of COVID-19. He used to start his morning with the conditioning, stretching and strengthening exercises and then move on to visualisation. He then interacted with the athletes over the phone, guiding and counselling them, as they tried to remain in shape. "We used to ask the trainees to post videos of their workouts on WhatsApp and thus keep them motivated," he says. From his playing days to the coaching years now, Rajinder's life has been a story of dedication and passion. Dr Manjit Singh, Director, Physical Education at Ramgarhia College in Phagwara, throws light on an important aspect of Rajinder's personality. He says, "He would come to our college every day on his tricycle and practise. As his tricycle could not go everywhere, he would move around walking on his hands. I feel it's this grit which has taken him so far. This inspired other sportspersons in the college as well."

Rajinder Singh Rahelu—who is he? While he may not have a widely recognised profile online, his contributions to the country are significant, even though he didn't receive the fame and attention he deserved. At the Athens 2004 Paralympics, where Rajinder earned a bronze medal, Devendra Jhajharia rose to prominence by winning the gold medal for the country. Rajinder's achievement, however significant, was somewhat overshadowed by the glitter of Devendra's gold. Unfortunately, Rajinder returned empty-handed from the Beijing 2008 and London 2012 Paralympics, partly due to a system failure when he needed the support the most. While new heroes are emerging on the Indian Paralympic scene, some have already surpassed Rajinder in terms of accomplishments. Yet, evaluating certain individuals necessitates an understanding of their background and the challenges they've overcome. Rajinder, born into a poor Dalit family, faced adversity from childhood with limited resources at his disposal. Still, he did not let all these obstacles come in the way of his success; he dared to dream and went all out to achieve them. Instead of succumbing to bitterness, he channelled his efforts positively and now mentors aspiring athletes, helping to shape their careers.

"Weakness jaise shabd mere dictionary mein nahin hain" (Words like weakness do not exist in my dictionary), says Rajinder. He has deleted the word "weakness" from his dictionary, and this spirit could be further seen when he says, "I could never have the food a powerlifter needed because of my economic condition. I used to travel 25 km to the neighbouring Phagwara district at least twice a week for training on the hand-powered tricycle. Perhaps this made me strong physically and toughened me mentally."

The real-life heroes who left their footprints in the Paralympic journey of India till the times of Rajinder Singh Rahelu were all from the western and northern India. In the coming two chapters, the protagonists of our stories—Girisha Hosanagara Nagarajegowda and Mariyappan Thangavelu—are from beyond the Vindhya Range.

GIRISHA HOSANAGARA NAGARAJEGOWDA

Defining the Moment

*"When a defining moment comes along,
you can do one of two things.
Define the moment, or let the moment define you."*

—Roy McAvoy

One of the most influential persons in my life was my grandmother, whom I affectionately called *Maa*. In her stories, there was one key point she would always emphasise on. "*Beta*, one of the most powerful actions you'll ever take in your life is when you make a decision," she would say.

There are moments in our lives, or in the journey of the institutions we represent, which we often refer to as defining moments. A defining moment is the point in our lives when we are urged to make a pivotal decision or when we experience something that fundamentally changes us. Truly defining moments prompt us to ask the question "why"; they challenge us to behave differently and they confront our set beliefs and norms.

As Roy McAvoy in the famous movie *Tin Cup* said, "When

a defining moment comes along, you can do one of two things. Define the moment, or let the moment define you."

When such moments come, the road ahead is bumpy and our commitment to the purpose is tested. Some individuals and institutions see these bumps on the road of life as obstacles, while some others see them as opportunities. Sheryl Sandberg, former chief operating officer of Facebook, in her book titled, *Option B*, which she has co-authored with Adam Grant, has written about one of her defining moments—the death of her husband on vacation. Her book is a roadmap on how to effectively handle your defining moments, face the adversity, build resilience and find joy. Most Paralympians are sportspersons who have dealt with such moments of their lives bravely.

This chapter is about the defining moment in the life of an individual named Girisha Hosanagara Nagarajegowda, also known as Girish N. Gowda, and an institution named Paralympic Movement of India. More importantly, it's about how an individual and an institution defined the moment.

Before we go through the individual journey of Girisha Hosanagara Nagarajegowda, we need to briefly know where India's Paralympic Movement stood after the first decade of the new century. This was the time when India's sporting system was desperately looking for an answer to the most fundamental question—how will a country as great and large as India start performing to its potential in sports.

India has been sending its contingent to every Paralympic Games since 1984, but there were inconsistencies in the journey. There were some games when heroes emerged out of nowhere and grabbed a few medals and the country was able to register its presence in the medals tally. This was followed by a "medal drought" in subsequent games. This also meant that the seeds of the Paralympic Movement in the country were taking a longer time than expected to germinate.

On the one hand, it reflected the low level of awareness regarding the inclusion of the differently-abled individuals in sports and other professions, as well as their broader role in nation-building. On the other hand, this was indicative of broader issues within Indian sports, which struggled to address fundamental questions such as why a nation of millions consistently underperforms in sports.

It was challenges like these that make the stories of real-life sports heroes even more compelling and absorbing. The colour of the medals that emerged out of such situations may have been gold, silver or bronze, but the sheer value of their stories in terms of inspiration and motivation was priceless.

Why do we describe the journey of India's Paralympic Movement from the 1984 to the 2012 Paralympics as inconsistent?

At the 1984 Paralympic Games, India sent five para athletes and won four medals: two silver and two bronze. At the Seoul 1988 Games, only two Indian athletes were part of the contingent, and India did not win any medal, thus failing to make the medals tally. In the Barcelona 1992 Games, nine Indian para athletes took part, but none of them finished on the podium. Similarly, at the Atlanta 1996 Games, India was represented by nine male athletes and no female athletes. Yet again, the team did not win any medal. In the Sydney 2000 Games, only four male athletes represented the country and India could not get any medal. In the Athens 2004 Paralympic Games, a 12-member Indian contingent participated. It comprised 11 male and one female members. There were two winners, Devendra Jhajharia and Rajinder Singh Rahelu. In the Beijing 2008 Paralympics, the strength of the Indian contingent fell to five athletes with no female representation. The contingent came back without any medal. In the London 2012 Paralympics, a 10-member Indian contingent competed in four sporting disciplines. It again had no female representation.

Girisha Hosanagara Nagarajegowda was the only medal winner for India at the London Paralympics. Following his achievement, Girisha remarked, "Athletes from other countries often asked me, 'Yours is such a large country with a huge population, and yet the size of your contingent is so small.' I had no answer." Indeed, the country's Paralympic journey could not have taken a decisive step forward until it addressed this most pertinent question.

In those days, we, as sports journalists, frequently faced another crucial question: Why does India, a large country with a diverse population, consistently rank at the bottom in major multi-sporting events? Even smaller countries have outperformed us in the Olympics and other significant competitions.

By 2012, it was almost two decades since India broke free from the licence-quota-permit raj, leading to the rise of a huge aspirational class, one that was bigger than the total population of some of the developed countries put together. The rising aspirational class had their friends and relatives working in and settled overseas and doing well in their chosen fields.

Members belonging to this segment of the Indian population would now visit developed countries of the world more often for their personal and professional work. They saw that there was immense talent in India, but they did not get the right environment and opportunities to excel. As the rising middle class got exposed to the best facilities overseas, they strongly felt that if the people of India got the same facilities, they could compete with the best in the world. This was also the time when satellite television and then the internet brought the rest of the world and their advanced practices closer to more and more Indian homes. Sports have got huge soft power. But unfortunately, the ruling dispensation and the bureaucracy were unwilling to acknowledge the changing reality.

They still saw sports with the prism of the socialist and pre-licence-quota-permit raj era when it was looked upon as a luxury. So, rather than finding right answers to the fundamental questions concerning Indian sports, they preferred to turn their heads away. Instead of using the soft power of sports, at least in public, they preferred to maintain a safe distance from it. As the sports editor of a leading news channel, I would like to list a few specific instances to establish the same.

First, N. Chandrababu Naidu, the then Chief Minister of Andhra Pradesh, sought to establish and launch the inaugural Formula One (F1) circuit in Hyderabad. He was seen as the new-age leader who had assiduously cultivated Hyderabad into a hi-tech city. The proposed F1 circuit would have helped him to further build on this image. The work for the proposed F1 circuit in Hyderabad could not even be started. Naidu lost the Assembly elections. Importantly, a big section of political commentators and the media felt that one of the reasons for him losing the elections was that he ignored the rural areas and the farmers and instead focused on Hyderabad and elitist projects like the F1 circuit. The reality is that there could not be any connection between the two. Secondly, the first F1 track in the country, Buddh International Circuit, came up at

Greater Noida in Uttar Pradesh. BSP leader and the then Chief Minister of Uttar Pradesh, Mayawati, played a crucial role in the making of the state-of-the-art circuit. But then again, she did not come to Greater Noida to inaugurate the circuit. Thirdly, this mindset was further visible during the Delhi 2010 Commonwealth Games. The games gathered headlines for all the wrong reasons. There was a brighter side to the games as well, in terms of promoting the multi-sporting culture in the country and initiating the piecemeal process of training and exposure for the athletes. Unfortunately, when the cases of corruption started coming in, it was the same mindset which prevented the leadership from coming forward, setting the house in order and to take the onus for a smooth conduct of the games.

Cricket provided a changing India with its first taste of being a strong power in sports. After the World Cup victory in 1983, the epicentre of world cricket gradually shifted from the Lords in London to the Wankhede Stadium in Mumbai. Another important game changer was India winning the inaugural T20 World Cup in South Africa and the birth of the Indian Premier League (IPL). A few years after its birth, the IPL became a leading sports property in the world. After the emergence of cricketing heroes from smaller towns and non-privileged backgrounds (led by the great Mahendra Singh Dhoni himself), the perception of cricket and sports being the domain of a privileged few and a luxury was further decimated. Most of India's sporting heroes came from lesser privileged and humble backgrounds, and sports was increasingly seen as a change agent and one of the crucial vehicles for the deprived to bring about transformative changes in their lives. After the huge success of cricket in India, the rising, aspirational middle class now wanted cricket plus. This explains the desperation behind the fundamental question being asked repeatedly, "Why is India not able to do well in sports?"

The Prime Minister Narendra Modi–led government should be credited for trying to find an honest answer to this question and to start working in that direction. On the one hand, it has boldly aligned with sports and sportspersons, leaving behind the old socialist mindset of sports being a luxury; on the other hand, it has tried to find long-term solutions for India's emergence as a dominant sporting power. Prime Minister Modi's government should be credited for utilising the soft power of sports towards the goal of nation building. In fact, Modi has set up a new template, in terms of using sports as a soft power to send out strong social messages. There are, broadly, five fundamental areas in which an effort is being made to lay the solid path for the country's emergence as a major sports power.

The first is the "Fit India Programme", which emphasises the importance of fitness amongst the youth of the country. The second is the "Khelo India Programme", which works with the objective of broad-basing talent at the grassroots level in a structured manner. The third, "Target Olympic Podium Scheme (TOPS) Programme", has the objective of nurturing identified talent and providing them with the best facilities in terms of training and exposure.

Then, there are frequent engagement programmes spearheaded by the Government of India that involve athletes participating in the run-up to and other major events. The Prime Minister has consistently interacted with both abled and differently-abled sportspersons before and after these events.

This has sent a message down the line that sportspersons, not bureaucracy or associations, are the real VIPs in the sports arena. The focus is on creating an environment and infrastructure conducive to achieving higher sports goals.

The fifth area of interest is the "Para athletes on a par with Able-bodied Athletes" programme. Its overarching goal is to use sports as a catalyst for a more inclusive society, treating para athletes on a par with able-bodied athletes in terms of engagement and preparation.

Prime Minister Modi's engagement with athletes, even in cases where they have failed to feature amongst the medal winners, has also sent in the message that the nation's sporting journey is a constant process. Defeats, or occasional bad days, cannot be deterrents in the forward march. This has again brought about a major change in terms of the mindset in the sports governance of our country.

The journey of India's Paralympic sport has greatly benefited from this and it has gone a long way in providing the right answer to the question which Girisha asked after his medal win in the London 2012 Games. The size of the Indian contingent has increased from 10 members in the London Games to 19 members in the Rio 2016 Games to 54 members in the Tokyo 2020 Games. The situation emerging after the London 2012 Games was thus the defining moment for the Indian Paralympic Movement. After the London Games, Sheryl Sandberg's concepts in *Option B* found expression in building a supportive environment for Indian sportspersons, and the initial results have been encouraging.

Now let's see what the defining moment in the life of Girisha Hosanagara Nagarajegowda was. Girisha was born on 26 January 1988, when India was celebrating its 36th Republic Day. The name "Girisha", which means the lord of mountains, represents his own identity, one which he built all by himself, brick-by-brick, and after successfully crossing multiple barriers in his life. "Hosanagara", in his name, represents the village in Karnataka where he hails from and reminds us of the ecosystem where his journey started. "Nagarajegowda" in his name represents his father, who was a by-product of the ecosystem. Like other fathers in a similar situation, he too had a number of questions to ask and several challenges to face when his child was born with deformity.

Girisha was born to Nagarajegowda and Jayamma, a couple from Hosanagara in the Konanur hobli of Arkalgud taluka in the Hassan district of Karnataka. From birth, Girisha had a deformity in his left leg. His father, confronted with this disability, thought, "*Why should a struggling family like ours keep a son with such a deformity? How would we manage the responsibility of caring for a disabled child? What benefit would a deformed child bring to improving the family's livelihood? Why has God done this to us?*"

In stark contrast, his mother Jayamma could not imagine parting with her child. Her approach to life was different; rather than cursing her fate or questioning God, she focused on finding solutions in a calm and composed manner. Her positive outlook had a profound influence on the family and significantly shaped Girisha's own outlook as he grew up.

"Girisha never felt that he had any form of deformity. It was only when others pointed out an issue with his legs that he realised he was different from the rest. His mother, Jayamma, was confident right from the beginning that Girisha would be like any other child in the village, if not better," says Harish, one of his relatives.

Right from his childhood, Girisha loved playing sports. When he was a kid, his mother would remember him tying ropes in the pillars of the house and jumping over them. He would compete with his brothers in the game. Never one to sit on his past performance, he would gradually increase the height of the rope and try to surpass it every time.

"As I grew up, I began practising by tying ropes between trees. I always tried to increase the level and better my performance. I won my first medal in the seventh grade, and that medal remains the closest to my heart till today," says Girisha. A quick learner, Girisha believed in learning from his mistakes and moving ahead in life. He was also good in his studies. His teachers recall him as a disciplined child who completed every task with full sincerity and dedication.

Girisha completed his primary education from a government school in the village. After this, he did his SLCC from the Government High School at Bannur Santhemala. He completed his pre-university education at the junior college at Shringala in the Kodagu district. Girisha got his Bachelor of Arts (BA) from the ANV first grade college at Gorur. When he was doing his BA, Girisha also took training in computers. While he was focused on studies, he did not allow it to distract him from his love for sports. Though he worked hard in sports, he did not receive much encouragement and support from others.

Girisha says, "Unfortunately, I did not receive any support in my younger days. People used to discourage me by saying I would not be able to achieve anything in sports as I am a disabled. My friends participated in the district and *taluka* level competitions. I always accompanied them. I used to carry their clothes, sporting gears and equipment, so that I could be closer to sports and sportspersons. Though I hardly got any chance, I used to closely observe the way other sportspersons used to train and perform. When I saw my friends performing in athletics, I always felt that I could do better than them. I used to eagerly wait for the day when my chance would come."

When one wants something desperately in life, one cannot be denied of it for long. Girisha made the most of it when his chance came. He won prizes at the state-level sports meet in Dharwad, while competing with able-bodied athletes. "I started preparing for the university level. But just when my event was to begin, the sports director of Mysore University informed me that I could not participate, as I am disabled. They thought it would be risky if they gave me the go-ahead to compete. This was very disappointing for me and I was in tears. But my friends fought very hard for me and it's because of them that I could get the permission to participate. Most of the people who saw me there were impressed with my performance," shares Girisha.

He won a bronze medal in the Mysore University sports meet. After that, he won a gold medal in the national high jump championship. His first moment of glory at the international level came when he won a bronze medal at the junior world championship sports meet for the disabled in Ireland in 2006. Unfortunately, just as his career in competitive sports was about to take off, he had to quit.

"I had no support. I was the eldest child and had the responsibility of looking after my family, which was struggling financially. Competitive sports don't come cheap and one requires more than a decent investment to be there. From food and training to clothes and equipment, everything is expensive. I realised that it will not be possible to bear the cost of all these and so I decided to quit competitive sports in 2009," Girisha says. He was out of competitive sports for two years. "During this period, I was working with ING Vysya Bank (now known as Kotak Mahindra Bank) as a contract labourer. But when my boss saw my passion for sports, he motivated me and asked me to pursue my passion. He strongly felt that I was an inspiration for many in society and should go back and concentrate on sports without wasting much time there. Another person who supported me immensely during this period was my friend and my coach Satyanarayana. He was confident about my success in sports. The Paralympic committee was also keen that I should return. It was because of all of them that I could make a comeback in sports," says Girisha.

He was also supported by a Bengaluru-based NGO, Samarthanam Trust for the Disabled. After he made his comeback in sports, his true potential started emerging to the fore. Girisha won two back-to-back gold medals in the Kuwait 2012 Para Athletics Championship and in the 2012 Malaysia Para Athletics Championship.

Girisha's next major assignment was the London 2012 Paralympic Games. When he was leaving for the games, he had promised his parents that he would return with a medal. Girisha had trained hard for his event and was confident of bettering the previous record of 1.80 metres. The gold medal winner in the Beijing 2008 Games had cleared the distance and Girisha had a strong feeling that he would cross this mark. Many times during the practice session, he had touched this mark. "While we were preparing in the Basildon sporting village, London Olympics 2012 was going on. I saw Sushil Kumar winning a silver medal for the country. In the Beijing 2008 Olympics, he had won bronze medal. After receiving the medal, he had the country's flag in his hand. This gave me goosebumps. I was confident of giving my best when my chance would come. But at the same time, I was also nervous. I started doing yoga and mental exercises to keep myself calm and focused. By the time the countdown for my event had started, I was feeling mentally tougher and I was not allowing the fear of losing to overpower me. I was in the best mental and physical frame of mind and confident of giving my best," he says. Finally, the time came for which he had prepared for months.

Girisha found himself amidst a massive crowd of about 80,000 spectators. Even in his wildest dreams, he had never imagined performing before such a large audience on the grandest sporting stage. The entire crowd was cheering on the athletes to give their best, creating an electric atmosphere. Girisha started with clearing a height of 1.60 metres in his first attempt. He then sailed over 1.65 metres and 1.68 metres in the next two attempts. However, he stumbled when the bar was raised to 1.71 metres. Though he cleared this mark in his second attempt and went past 1.74 metres after this, he had to be content with a silver medal. Iliesa Delana of Fiji won the gold medal as he cleared the target on his first attempt itself. Both Girisha and Delana tried to cover 1.77 metres but failed. In the final standing, Iliesa Delana won the gold medal, Girisha won the silver medal and Lukasz Maciej Mamczarz of Poland won the bronze medal.

This defining moment of his career is still etched in his memory. Girisha says, "I read my name on the screen. I also heard my name being announced. Soon, I was there on the podium with the two other medal winners. My coach had brought one flag, but soon I could count at least thirty to forty of them on the stands. I realised how passionately the Indians present in the stadium celebrated the medal win."

The child who was seen as a burden when he was born eventually lifted the burden of a million expectations. When the defining moment of his career came, he ensured that the Indian contingent would not have to return without a medal for one more time.

Immediately after the win, Girisha called his parents over the phone to inform them about his victory. It was almost midnight in India. After hearing about his success, the family was in tears. The boy about whom the father had so many questions when he was born with a deformity was now the pride of his parents, his village, and his country. As the feeling of victory started sinking in, Girisha had no bitterness for those who had discouraged him or refused to support him in his journey. Rather, he was grateful to all those who had been part of his incredible journey. From his boss in the bank where he worked when he was out of the sports to his coach Satyanarayana, he credited everyone for his achievement in his first press conference after the medal win. He specifically mentioned the role played by Sahana Kumari, an Indian athlete, for her help and support. When Girisha was training at the Sports Authority of India centre in Bengaluru before the London Games, Sahana Kumari was also training there. Both of them were under the supervision of the Russian coach Evgeny Nikitin. Girisha said at the press conference, "The training at the SAI centre helped me a lot, and Sahana had a big role to play in this. Last night also, she called me up to give me some tips."

What particularly impressed the journalists at the press conference were the issues Girisha raised. These concerns were not about seeking personal support but rather addressed broader problems affecting Indian sports. His appeal was an honest request for finding relevant solutions to these pressing issues.

Girisha said, "It's a pity that, in India, every sportsperson gets help, but as far as para athletes are concerned, only the government takes care of us. Unfortunately, we are not taken seriously, but our hard work is no less than any Olympic medallist. I hope that my medal will bring a significant change in India, and that para athletes will also get their due recognition. I dedicate this medal to the disabled community in India. I hope this will inspire them to become sportspersons." In this very press conference, Girisha rued the fact that, despite being such a big and diverse country, the Indian Paralympic contingent had only ten members. He said, "In London, the athletes and support staff from other countries often asked us why, despite our country being so big and with such a big population base, there are only ten members in the contingent. This is shameful. I hope we will have a bigger contingent in Rio in 2016."

A cricket buff, Girisha idolised Tendulkar from an early age. "I grew up watching him playing. He's like God for all cricket fans and I am one of them. He is such an icon and yet so humble. I want to meet him, but I don't know when this is going to happen," he said, while talking to Indian journalists. His dream came true within a few days after landing in the country when Girisha and Tendulkar talked over the phone. On his Facebook page, Tendulkar wrote, "It was wonderful speaking to Girisha yesterday. He is an inspiration to all of us. I wish him all the best for the coming years." Girisha said, "Tendulkar called me after the victory. I was very happy when he said I have become an inspiration for many people." Tendulkar was echoing the sentiments of the thousands of people across the country who wanted to see India as a strong "cricket plus" sporting nation.

After his felicitation functions in Delhi and Bengaluru, Girisha visited his village where he was given a hero's welcome. People of the village celebrated his victory as their own. Many of them talked about his strong determination to reach there despite so many constraints in his life. His success also inspired them to come out of their preconceived notions and treat the disabled as the differently abled and make them equal partners in growth and development.

Nagarajegowda, Girisha's father, who got emotional, said, "I never expected that my son could do this. When he was a kid, the doctors told me that he needed surgery to correct the disability, but I got scared and refused. It was mainly because I did not have the required money to bear the cost of his operation. But now I know, I made a huge mistake. And look at him now, he has made all of us proud with his achievements." He could not hold his tears when he said, "I couldn't support him as we were repaying the loan of rupees three and a half lakhs which we have taken for building our house and for our daughters' marriage. There were many days when we had to go to bed on an empty stomach. I cannot forget that phase in my life."

While it will be easier for many of us to blame Girisha's father for looking upon him as a burden when he was born disabled, the entire situation needs to be seen in a proper perspective. Girisha was born on India's Republic Day. But the nation can call itself a true republic only when it is able to lift lakhs of people under similar situations as Girisha's father out of the poverty so that they don't have to struggle for the basic needs. When the larger population of the country will be economically and socially secure, there will be many more Girishas waiting to excel in their respective fields. As Girisha says, "Being physically challenged is not my misfortune. Rather,

I feel gifted. If I had not been like this, I would not have been a Paralympian in the first place."

Girisha has many firsts to his credit. He was the first one from South India to win a medal in the Paralympic Games. He was the first Paralympian to get a major endorsement from the nutrition company Herbalife International. Girisha also became the brand ambassador of the election commission of Karnataka in 2017 and 2019.

From the era when the achievements of Indian Paralympians were largely ignored by the mainstream media, we now find ourselves in a transforming period where these athletes are beginning to endorse brands. This shift reflects a changing India. In the next chapter, we will revisit the journey of another real-life hero from South India, Mariyappan Thangavelu, on whose life a biopic is being made by the famous filmmaker Aishwarya Rajinikanth.

MARIYAPPAN THANGAVELU

The Commoner Who Dared to Take a Chance

"Emperor, king, general, duke, he whispered to himself. These are just labels. Climb up the family tree of any of them high enough and you will find a commoner who dared to take a chance."

—Ken Liu in his book, *The Grace of Kings*

The timeless tales of rags-to-riches and the themes of struggle and redemption are as old as civilisation itself. As human beings, we have progressed with the times because it's in our DNA to convert past tragedies into today's advantage. Our brains are inherently drawn to narratives of resilience and success; that's why many of the most commercially successful movies start with the saga of pain and struggle and culminate in a happy ending.

Similarly, impactful leaders among us often weave stories of adversity to forge a strong connection with their audience. In business boardrooms, the most compelling pitches often revolve around stories of struggle, sacrifice, dashed dreams and newfound aspirations. Nature's finest creations are often products of struggle; fruits and vegetables cultivated in harsh soils develop greater resilience and character. Mariyappan Thangavelu's journey is one such inspiring story.

The Rio 2016 Paralympic Games was a precursor to Team India's historic performance in the Tokyo 2020 Paralympic Games. India, with a 19-member strong contingent in Rio, nearly doubled its representation from the previous edition. Fast forward to Tokyo 2020 Paralympics, the Indian contingent swelled to 54 athletes. Officials from the Paralympic Committee of India are now eyeing an even larger squad of around 100 athletes for the Paris 2024 Paralympic Games.

The significance of Rio 2016 Paralympics lies not just in the increased participation but also in India's medal haul. India won 4 medals, including 2 gold, at the Rio Paralympics. Prior to that, India had amassed only 8 medals from 1968 to 2012. The figure reached the historic high of 19 medals in the Tokyo 2020 Games. Among the standout performers in Rio 2016 were Devendra Jhajharia and Mariyappan Thangavelu, both gold medallists in 2016 who repeated their success in 2020. One of these winners, Mariyappan Thangavelu, has a compelling rags-to-riches story and that is the focus of this chapter.

Prime Minister Narendra Modi took a personal initiative in engaging with India's athletes who participated in the Rio 2016 Paralympics, a trend that continued through the Tokyo 2020 Games. This effort also marked the beginning of increased mainstream media coverage for Indian Paralympic medallists. The winners of the Rio Paralympic Games were invited to appear on popular television shows, and plans were made for a biopic centred on one of its heroes, Mariyappan Thangavelu.

Mariyappan Thangavelu was born on 28 June 1995 in Periavadagampatti village in Salem district of Tamil Nadu. His early life is akin to many classic Indian movie scripts of the 1960s and '70s. He was one of six siblings, which included five brothers and a sister. When Mariyappan was a child, his father abandoned the family, leaving his mother Saroja to raise the family single-handedly.

As a single mother, Saroja had to face a lot of societal stigma, with people even reluctant to rent her house. She had to struggle from morning to evening to provide for her family, thus taking on various menial jobs. Mariyappan has memories of his mother carrying bricks as a labourer on construction sites. Despite being utterly exhausted after a long day's work, she would return home to complete household chores and cook meals so that her children never slept on empty stomachs.

When Mariyappan was just five years old, tragedy struck one morning as he walked to school. He was hit by a drunk bus driver. His leg below the knee was crushed and it had to be stunted. This incident dealt another severe blow to the financially struggling family. To afford her son's treatment, Saroja had to take a loan of Rs 3 lakh at a very high interest rate. Amidst all this, Mariyappan was the only silver lining for the struggling family. Against all odds, he managed to complete his schooling.

From a young age, Mariyappan loved playing sports, especially volleyball. His dedication caught the eye of his physical education teacher, who suggested he try high jump. Mariyappan heeded the advice and devoted himself to excelling in the sport. When he was 14, he participated in a major high jump competition for the first time, competing against able-bodied athletes. He impressed everyone with his strong performance and started getting consistent support from classmates and friends.

Meanwhile, Mariyappan completed his BBA from the AVA College of Arts and Science. This was also the time when he got in touch with 'Do or Die Club', which motivated him to dream big and live with a purpose. However, his sporting career got a major boost when Satyanarayana, a coach based in Bengaluru, recognised his talent.

Satyanarayana first noticed Mariyappan's talent at the Indian National Para Athletics Championships. Impressed by his performance, Satyanarayana invited him to Bengaluru in 2015 for further training. Under Satyanarayana's direct supervision, Mariyappan honed his skills at the Sports Academy of India for Differently Abled, receiving a monthly stipend of Rs 10,000. Mariyappan reflects, "After Satyanarayana sir saw me at the national level, he convinced my family and arranged training for me in Bengaluru for two years. He became a friend and guide, closely monitoring my progress, sharing valuable tips and always motivating me to aim higher and give my best." He further adds, "My deformed right toe is what gives me leverage in my jumps. I treat my right toe as my God."

What inspired Mariyappan to view the core of his disability as divine? Learning about this will shed light on Satyanarayana's teaching methods. Satyanarayana, who helped Mariyappan realise the immense latent possibilities in his "God", had coined the term to further motivate him. As Mariyappan discovered purpose and direction, other aspects of life began to fall in place. After a long struggle of 17 years, Mariyappan's family finally won their legal battle against the bus driver responsible for his injuries. They received compensation of Rs 2 lakh. His mother used half of this amount for legal expenses, while the rest was set aside for Mariyappan's future.

After months of intense training, Mariyappan began making strides in the field of professional sports. In March 2016, he soared to new heights by clearing 1.76 metres in the men's T42 high jump event at IPC Grand Prix in Tunisia, surpassing the 1.60 metres qualification standard for the Rio 2016 Paralympics. Then, on 9 September 2016, in Rio, he won a gold medal in the T42 category with a remarkable jump of 1.89 metres. In the same event, USA's Sam Grewe and India's Varun Singh Bhati won silver and bronze medals, respectively, with jumps of 1.86 metres. With this win, Mariyappan joined the ranks of Murlikant and Devendra as the third Indian to claim a gold medal in the Paralympic Games. Despite this historic feat, Mariyappan was rather calm at the podium after his victory. He simply raised his arm, waved and casually walked away as though the victory was inevitable after months of diligent work and training.

Few Indian leaders in post-Independence India, aside from Narendra Modi, truly understand and appreciate the effort required to rise from humble beginnings and overcome adverse circumstances. Prime Minister Modi, in his tweet, said, "India is elated. Congratulations to Mariyappan Thangavelu on winning gold and Varun Singh Bhati for winning bronze #paralympics."

A clear indicator of shifting attitudes, Mariyappan and the other medal winners of the Rio 2016 Paralympics were awarded prize money equivalent to that given to the Olympic medallists. J. Jayalalithaa, the Chief Minister of Tamil Nadu at that time, hailed Mariyappan's achievement, stating, "By leaping over a height of 1.89 metres, you have leapt into history and have done both the nation and state of Tamil Nadu proud. Your achievements overcoming several obstacles and hurdles will inspire more and more children and youth to overcome adversities and to participate and strive for greater achievements." The Tamil Nadu government announced a prize purse of Rs 2 crore in recognition of his remarkable achievement.

Mariyappan and the other medal winners were invited to some of the most popular Indian television shows, including *The Kapil Sharma Show*. They also attended programmes and events organised by academic institutions and management schools. Mainstream newspapers and dailies featured full-page stories tracing Mariyappan's journey from the beginning.

By that time, Indian cricketers had established a tradition of endorsing and standing alongside the journeys of India's Paralympic medal winners. An NGO backed by former India cricket captain Vijay Merchant funded Murlikant Petkar's participation in international events. Sachin Tendulkar, in his congratulatory message, praised Girisha Hosanagara Nagarajegowda's journey as inspiring for many.

On 3 October 2016, several personalities, including Tendulkar, felicitated four Indian Rio Paralympic winners, namely, Devendra Jhajharia, Mariyappan Thangavelu, Deepa Malik and Varun Singh Bhati with a cash prize of Rs 15 lakh each. More importantly, Tendulkar announced that a similar amount would be given to all Paralympians who had won medals for the country prior to the Rio 2016 Paralympics as well. In a conversation with Yours Truly, Pavneet Joginder Singh, the son of the late Paralympic medal winner Joginder Singh Bedi, thanked Tendulkar for this gesture. A nation truly becomes great not only by celebrating the present but also by honouring its past legacy.

The gold medal victory at the Rio Paralympics, along with subsequent awards and accolades, marked a turning point in Mariyappan's life and that of his family. "The first thing I did after winning the medal was to call my mother and inform her. Her voice choked up, and I could sense the tears in her eyes. She has sacrificed so much for me and our family," he says. Not one to miss a working day, Saroja was getting ready to go for work on the day of Mariyappan's event at Rio. Her other children had to literally force her to stay at home and watch the event on television.

Though the entire locality erupted with joy, her response was measured. Soaked in emotion, she could barely speak about her son's phenomenal success. Saroja says, "We were so happy watching him win gold on television. He's such a quiet and affectionate boy, the lifeline of our family. All of us love him so much."

Mariyappan wisely utilised a portion of his prize money to purchase a paddy field for his mother so that she could have a stable source of income. He also invested in building a house to provide his family with greater comfort. A few years earlier, when Saroja experienced chest pain from years of lifting heavy bricks and other materials as a daily wage labourer, Mariyappan borrowed money from one of his friends and gave it to her so that she could switch to selling vegetables for a livelihood.

In 2017, Mariyappan was honoured with the Padma Shri Award, India's fourth highest national civilian honour. He was India's flag bearer during the opening ceremony of the 2018 Asian Para Games in Indonesia. In 2020, he was bestowed with the Rajiv Gandhi Khel Ratna Award, the highest sporting honour in the country. However, Mariyappan faced a setback in 2017 when he suffered from an ankle injury, which required time to recover. This injury partially impacted his preparation for the Tokyo 2020 Games. But as the countdown for the games started, he regained his form. In an interview to a news channel prior to the games, Mariyappan said, "My performance at the selection trial, achieving 1.86 metres, was one of my best since the Rio 2016 performance. Although I had an injury in 2017 that took time to heal, I have been striving to regain my old rhythm. Now, I feel I've got that rhythm and am fully prepared for the games."

Mariyappan was designated as the flag bearer for India at the opening ceremony of the Tokyo 2020 Paralympics. However, just as the games were set to commence, we received a press statement from Gurucharan Singh, India's Chef De Mission, which read,

> We have received information from the Tokyo Paralympic Games COVID control room that six of our teammates have been in close contact with a COVID-19 positive person while travelling to Tokyo in a flight. Out of the six, two of them are Mariyappan and Vinod Kumar and both of them have been found to be in close contact. Regretfully, Mariyappan will not be able to take part in the march past today. Tek Chand will be the new flag bearer.

There was an apprehension that Mariyappan might not be fully fit for his event. Fortunately, both for him and the country, he made a complete recovery by the time his event started at the Tokyo Games.

Mariyappan settled for a silver medal after achieving a jump of 1.86 metres at the Tokyo Paralympics. He aimed for a height of 1.88 metres to secure the yellow metal but fell short. Sam Grewe from the USA claimed the gold. During the virtual press conference after the medal ceremony, Mariyappan expressed his disappointment, saying "I had hoped for gold, but the ground conditions at the Tokyo National Stadium posed lots of problems for me. Heavy rain during the competition made it difficult. I was wearing socks on the impaired leg, which got wet. This affected my stability during take-off. This disrupted my focus." He added, "I was confident of clearing 1.90 metres under better conditions because I started really well. The biggest difference was the weather; In Rio, it was very much like India's climate, but Tokyo's sudden rain disrupted my plans and execution." Looking ahead, Mariyappan stated, "My focus now is to win gold at the Paris 2024 Games."

After the event, Mariyappan's coach, Satyanarayana, said, "Under ideal weather conditions, clearing 1.88 metres would not have been a problem for him. Last month only, he jumped 1.98 metres at the Sports Authority of India, Bengaluru. He was also a bit upset that he could not be the flag bearer in the opening ceremony, which played on his mind." Irrespective of the change in the colour of the medal, Prime Minister Narendra Modi backed him as strongly as ever. In his tweet, the Prime Minister said, "Soaring higher and higher! Mariyappan Thangavelu is synonymous with consistence and excellence. Congratulations to him for winning the silver medal. India is proud of his feat." Responding to this, the champion athlete said, "PM Sir called me after the event and congratulated me in Tamil. I am happy that he is encouraging us like this." As he gears up for Paris 2024 and beyond, there are important life lessons which could be learnt from his journey till the Tokyo Games.

First, work hard. If you work with passion, you can turn any weakness into your strength. Mariyappan never let his stunted leg become a disability. Instead, he considered it his

God and a lucky charm, which propelled him to give the best of jumps in his career. Secondly, be positive always. Mariyappan approached every challenge with optimism and never gave up on his dreams despite so many obstacles. He excelled in sports and completed his studies as well. Mariyappan is now fully geared for a new career, anticipating the time when he will transition from professional sports. On 3 November 2021, Tamil Nadu Chief Minister M. K. Stalin appointed Mariyappan as a Deputy Manager in Marketing at Tamil Nadu Newsprint and Papers Limited. At that time, Mariyappan, a graduate in business administration, was working as senior coach at SAI, Bengaluru.

Thirdly, despite his success, Mariyappan has always been down to earth and remained connected to his roots. In one of his interviews, he says, "Though I have won medals, I feel bad when my best friends treat me as a VVIP." He has always been conscious of his responsibilities for his family and the society. To promote the culture of sports in his village, he aspires to run a school there. It's thus befitting that the first biopic on any Indian Paralympic medal winner is being made based on his life, encapsulating his wonderful journey and the life lessons one can take from his life. His is a rags-to-riches story which continues and holds us from the beginning to the end.

Girisha and Mariyappan, the two real-life heroes from South India, have one thing in common. Both of them were inspired and mentored by another real-life hero, Satyanarayana. He played a major role in shaping the careers of the two champion athletes and continues working with other aspiring athletes. In one of the popular television shows, the camaraderie between the *guru* and *shishya* (the teacher and the disciple) was in full display when Mariyappan was silent and let Satyanarayana do most of the talking. At one point, Satyanarayana intervenes to say, "Don't be fooled by his demeanour. No shy person can become a sportsperson." He then turns towards Mariyappan and asks him, "Are you shy or naughty?" To this Mariyappan replies, "*Saadhu*! Blameless and innocent." Those present there burst into laughter.

Satyanarayana himself has seen poverty from close quarters and understands the psyche of the athletes who rise from below. At one point of time in his life, he used to sell flowers for his livelihood. An international-level athlete himself, he had represented the country multiple times in international competitions. He says, "My vision is to have many more Girishas and Mariyappans. There is no dearth of talent in our country. We need to ensure that we provide basic amenities and facilities to sportspersons at the grassroots level and anything is possible after that." Another fascinating aspect of his coaching is his ability to make the best out of any situation. As he says, "For the able-bodied or differently-abled athlete, the most important part is to choose which events to participate in and which equipment to use. One must have read a lot about the marathon blade runner. Those blades cost a lot and cannot be afforded by many athletes in our country. So, athletes should choose wisely, depending on the available facilities." Another hallmark of his coaching is his ability to gauge the strength and weakness of his athletes. He says, "For Mariyappan, his right toe is very important as it helps him in his jumps. We have to look after it carefully so that it does not get dirty and infected."

Satyanarayana remains connected with the para athletes across the country. It's this constant connect with the grassroots level, which makes one aware of the direction in which the wind is blowing. As the Tokyo Paralympics was approaching near and Satyanarayana was training with his athletes in Bengaluru's Sree Kanteerava Stadium, he had said, "I can say with confidence that we will come back with all medals— from gold and silver to bronze—from the upcoming Summer Paralympics at Tokyo in 2020. Don't want to speculate on the exact numbers but it will definitely surprise most of you." He was bang on when the results came.

In the next chapter, the protagonist of our story is Varun Singh Bhati. Like Girisha and Mariyappan, Varun was mentored by Satyanarayana. But unlike both of them, he's from North India, closer to the capital of the country, Delhi. Also, unlike both of them, Varun Singh Bhati's story is not a rags-to-riches story.

8

VARUN SINGH BHATI

For Whom the Process Never Ends

"In the long run, we shape our lives, and we shape ourselves. The process never ends until we die. And the choices we make are ultimately our own responsibility."

—Eleanor Roosevelt

Eleanor Roosevelt, an American political figure, diplomat and activist, was the First Lady of the United States of America during the long tenure of President Franklin D. Roosevelt. Her thought provoking quotes have been a source of inspiration for generations. In one of her notable quotes, she expresses, "The purpose of life is to live it, to taste experience to the utmost, to reach out eagerly and without fear for newer and richer experience."

In another well-known quote, she says, "Remember always that you have not only the right to be an individual; you have an obligation to be one. You cannot make any useful contribution in life unless you do this."

These quotes are not hard to understand. When we closely observe successful people around us, we find that they embody these principles, either partially or fully. Personally, I found the echoes of these beautiful quotes in the life and approach of Varun Singh Bhati. When we dissect his journey

further, we discover that he is an athlete for whom the process never ends.

Life and sports have many things in common. In many ways, sports are often considered a genuine mirror of life. Contrary to popular belief, individuals in both sports and life don't solely pursue victories or defeats. More than the milestones, they prioritise the journey. Beyond mere wins or losses, they emphasise on the crucial moments leading up to them.

This is precisely why sports psychologists all around the world emphasise more on the process than the results. Given this context, there is much to learn from those who integrate sports into their approach to living. This is why our sportspersons, particularly para athletes, serve as our inspirations. Varun Singh Bhati, a real-life hero and the primary focus of this chapter, embodies this sentiment.

Varun Singh Bhati was born on 13 February 1995 in Greater Noida, Uttar Pradesh. He was diagnosed with Poliomyelitis when he was just six months old. Tragically, he was given a wrong medicine by the doctor, which led to a permanent handicap in one of his legs. While many of us would have resigned ourselves to this adversity as a permanent burden or a curse, such was not the case for Varun and his courageous family. They refused to take this obstacle as a deterrent and opted to move ahead in life. His family was clear from the beginning that the disability would not stop their child from living life to the fullest.

Varun developed a passion for sports and spent hours in basketball courts, refining his skills. His father, Hem Chand Bhati, is the village *sarpanch*, while his mother is a homemaker. They have always backed and encouraged their son to excel in sports.

Varun started doing well in basketball and represented his state for four consecutive years. However, in 2010, a teacher at St Joseph's School, Greater Noida, suggested he transition from basketball to high jump. And thus began his Paralympic journey. Reflecting on this transition, Varun explains, "Over my four years of basketball, my vertical abilities significantly improved. I had the basic reflexes necessary for high jump. Although I was very passionate about basketball, I started realising that I wouldn't be able to compete at national level despite rigorous training. It was then that my physical education teacher, Manish Tripathi, introduced me to high jump."

Varun recalls his first major high jump competition where he secured second place. "In 2012, I won a gold medal in high jump at Varanasi, and that is how my journey in high jump started," he adds.

In 2012, he made his first major headlines for achieving the "A" qualification standard for the London 2012 Paralympics, with a leap of 1.60 metres. However, due to limited slots available to India, he failed to qualify for the 2012 Games.

Why do coaches and psychologists in professional sports always stress the importance of systems and processes? One gains firsthand insight into this when conversing with Paralympian Varun. In 2014, Varun experienced both personal setbacks and triumphs. Varun recounts, "My participation in the China Open marked my debut in international competition, and winning the gold medal there boosted my confidence for the upcoming Para Asian Games in Incheon, Korea, later that year. But, more than the gold medal, I was happy for getting my classification done. In Paralympics, classification is paramount. Unfortunately, my performance in the 2014 Para Asian Games was disappointing, to say the least. I stood fifth in the event and it was my first defeat in high jump, a sport in which I had never been defeated before. I remember sitting in the stands, overwhelmed with emotion and contemplating quitting professional sports. But something inside me prevented me from making such a decision. This defeat proved to be one of the most important and motivating ones in my life. It inspired me to work harder and to train better. As a result of this, in the following games, I started achieving better results."

Varun is a quick learner, both in sports and in life. From quite early in his career, he had the knack of extracting invaluable lessons from both his victories and defeats. As the Rio 2016 Paralympics was approaching nearer, Varun participated in the IPC Athletics Asia Oceania Championships. There, he set an Asian record with a jump of 1.82 metres. Reflecting on this achievement, Varun remarks, "This was my biggest confidence booster in 2016. After standing fifth in the World Athletics Championship in Doha and returning to India on 22 October 2016, I changed my approach and trained differently for four months. For the first time in my career, I started strength training and focused on my biometrics. These two elements are fundamental for any athlete. Over the next four months, from November 2016 to February 2017, I dedicated myself to rigorous training, prioritising on these two key areas. Although I didn't see immediate results, the trials for the upcoming Asia Oceania Championships, held in Gandhinagar, Gujarat, proved disheartening as I managed only 1.70 metres. For a moment, I felt that my intense training over the past four months had been in vain. But I refused to give up. Instead, I meticulously analysed the mistakes I made during the trials and ensured they were not repeated in the Asia Oceania Championships in Dubai. I was on the topmost in the ranking and it was a great morale booster for me in the Paralympic year."

Shortly thereafter, Varun was in Rio along with the Indian contingent to participate in the 2016 Paralympic Games.

"Since 2012, competing at the Olympic stadium had been my dream. It's where the best of the best compete, making it the ultimate stage for any sportsperson, whether in the Olympics or Paralympics. We dedicate our entire lives to excel there. Among all my experiences, the Rio 2016 Paralympics holds a special place in my heart. Not because I won a medal, but because of the calmness I felt throughout. There were no worries, no tension, and even my heartbeat remained steady. Normally, in such high-stakes competitions, nerves can disrupt focus, but that wasn't the case for me. The Rio 2016 was a perfect competition for me. From the start till the end, it went as per the flow I wanted it to be. It went as per the plan I had mapped mentally. You won't believe this, the memories of that competition and the stadium are etched in my senses. I can still recall the distinct smell of the place and the precise locations where my coaches and mentors were seated. The moment on the podium was pure magic, indescribable in words. It remains the purest feeling I've ever experienced," shared Varun.

The day when he stood on the podium with the medal around his neck is etched in his memories for life, frame by frame. Varun won the bronze medal in this event with a jump of 1.86 metres. In the same competition, India's Mariyappan Thangavelu got the gold medal with a jump of 1.89 metres. Varun's success continued beyond the Rio Paralympics.

In the 2017 Para Athletics World Championships, Varun won a bronze medal with a jump of 1.7 metres, earning him a place on the podium. His close friend Sharad Kumar also won a silver medal in the same event. More than the medal, his performance showcased his focused approach and inherent belief in the system and the process.

Teekam Bhati, Varun's uncle, revealed in an interview with a popular English daily, "He was nervous because he had injured his leg during practice before the competition. Also, much of his time was spent in felicitations, which made him bad about missing practice. He felt that his preparations weren't at the same level as they had been before Rio. But we all were confident that he will do well, and he did. Varun is a special child."

There is another important aspect of Varun's life and that of his friends. It tells us about the refreshing change in the mindset of professional Indian sportspersons.

Earlier, sportspersons were content with one or two major performances throughout their careers and were satisfied with basking in the glory of those achievements for the remainder of their lives. Their primary objective was to get a stable job based on these performances. That era saw sports just as a means to attain a decent livelihood, preferably through a government employment. However, a shift occurred when sportspersons began aiming for exceptional performances in a select few events, striving to etch their names in history.

Today, what is most heartening is that athletes like Varun no longer settle for one or two marquee performances. Instead of viewing these achievements as final destinations, they consider them major milestones in their journey, extracting key lessons and pushing forward towards the next milestone.

In 2018, Varun won a silver medal in the Asian Para Games with a jump of 1.82 metres, following his gold win at the China

Open Athletics Championship earlier that year. This marked a solid three-year streak of medal-winning performances. It was no surprise that he was nominated for the Arjuna Award, India's second-highest sports accolade. On 29 August 2018, he was conferred with the Arjuna Award.

Initially hopeful for the Khel Ratna Award, India's highest sporting honour, Varun's coach Satyanarayana advised him that receiving the Arjuna Award first would be beneficial for his career. "Vijay Goel Sir had mentioned that Paralympic medallists would be considered for the Khel Ratna, so I had my hopes up for that award. However, I am content with the Arjuna Award because once you get the Khel Ratna, you become ineligible for the Arjuna Award. My coach reassured me that I am still young and have ample time to vie for the Khel Ratna in the future. So, I am genuinely delighted to get the Arjuna Award. It's immensely gratifying to witness my achievements being acknowledged and praised by the government," he says.

Varun was equally delighted to learn that one of his seniors and a revered figure in Indian sports, Devendra Jhajharia, had been nominated for the Khel Ratna award. He says, "Devendra *bhaiyya* is the first para athletes to be recommended for the Khel Ratna, and he totally deserves it. With two gold medals in the Paralympics and twice breaking the world record, this decision will undoubtedly uplift the morale of other para athletes."

Varun also expressed his joy regarding the increased media attention on Paralympic medal winners in contemporary India. He remarks, "I believe nearly half of those familiar with the Paralympics today were unaware of it before Rio. Since Rio, the media has been supportive, which was not the case earlier.

This is definitely taking forward the Paralympic Movement in India."

Varun could not meet the expectations at the Tokyo 2020 Paralympic Games. In the T42/T63 category, the gold medal was won by the USA's Sam Greave, while India's Mariyappan Thangavelu and Sharad Kumar clinched the silver and bronze medals, respectively. Varun finished seventh out of nine competitors. However, rather than being bogged down by this outcome, he had begun preparing for the future. For, he's a firm believer of the process, which he perceives as continuing throughout life.

As Varun's journey continues, he emerges as a source of inspiration, encouraging youth to develop mental fortitude, persevere through setbacks, and glean valuable lessons from failures to chart their futures. His refreshing perspective becomes evident in a speech delivered to students at his alma mater, St Joseph's School, after being honoured with the Arjuna Award. He said, "I don't intend to deliver an inspirational speech today, as I believe each one of you will reach great heights anyway. Instead, I urge you to make a commitment—to embrace a sport. It does not have to be a career option, but take it up for the betterment of your health and fitness. It could be any game—badminton, basketball, or athletics. Pick one and excel in it. I'll be looking forward to seeing more Arjuna Awardees from St. Joseph's." Here, we see a contemporary youth icon engaging with the youth of new India, advocating for holistic development through participation in sports.

What is Varun's advice for the youth of the country? First, he emphasises the importance of having a clear goal to achieve something significant in life. Without a clear goal, taking the first step becomes challenging, as every journey starts with that initial step. Clarity regarding the goal provides focus, preventing distractions from derailing progress.

Varun shares, "I stood fifth in the Para Asian Games and Para Athletics Championships, but I was steadfast in my commitment to high jump. So, throughout, I dedicated myself to finding ways to improve and excel in my chosen pursuit."

Secondly, Varun advocates for learning from mistakes and consistently striving for improvement, ensuring those mistakes are not repeated. According to him, learning from mistakes and avoiding their repetition is the only path to achieving excellence in one's chosen field.

Thirdly, he encourages individuals to believe in their abilities and minimise negativity. "I love being positive always in my life, so I surround myself with positive influences. I avoid negative individuals because positivity is crucial for staying in the right mindset and remaining focused," he explains.

Lastly, Varun emphasises the significance of embracing defeats and setbacks alongside successes. He believes that experiencing failure enhances the value of success, stating, "If you don't lose, the taste of success will not be the same."

Varun has been fine-tuning his skills under the guidance of Satyanarayana, who has also mentored Girisha and Mariyappan. One noteworthy aspect of Satyanarayana's protégés is that, despite competing in the same events at major competitions, they are great friends outside the field of competition. They support each other and celebrate each other's successes. In today's professional sports, where photo finishes and intense rivalries are common both on and off the field, this camaraderie among three leading para athletes, trained by the same coach, is remarkable. It serves as a valuable lesson for athletes across various disciplines and for the youth of our country. While we are surrounded by cut-throat competition, it's equally important to recognise the value of learning and growing together.

Moving forward in our journey through this book, our next real-life hero is the first Indian woman to win a medal in the Paralympic Games. She is the one and only Deepa Malik.

DEEPA MALIK

The Spirit in Motion

*"We have two lives, and the second begins
when we realise we only have one."*

—Confucius

Life, for most of us, unfolds in two distinct parts. There's Life 1.0, where we chase uncertainties and often compromise happiness in the pursuit of goals. We struggle to differentiate between temporary and genuine happiness. We tend to follow the path that society has consciously or subconsciously laid out for us, often without truly understanding ourselves. Then, something significant happens, and we come to realise that life is just one.

The second life begins here, which we call Life 2.0. Here, we grasp that happiness is found in the present, not in the past or future. We no longer feel the need to sacrifice our happiness just because we have not achieved what we had wished for. Instead, we start finding joy in the process and learn to appreciate the significance of small moments and activities. We learn to be grateful for everything we have, who we are and where we find ourselves. This is the inspiring story of a daring woman who has lived these two distinct lives and said "Yes" to every challenge that crossed her path. For Deepa Malik, it is cool to declare, "Being normal is not at all that cool!"

Deepa Malik's story is not just about the medals and trophies she has won; rather, it revolves around the barriers she conquered to accomplish what she did in her life. Much like many of us, she has lived through two distinct lives in a single lifetime. However, her transition from Life 1.0 to Life 2.0 is clearly demarcated by a mere seven days. As she recounts, "Before I underwent my next surgery, I was informed that I would be wheelchair-bound for the rest of my life. With just seven days remaining to celebrate my ability to walk, I transformed my home into a completely wheelchair-friendly space. I spent my free time in online chat rooms, connecting with the international community of individuals facing similar conditions, seeking solutions and hope. Even after my surgery, society viewed me as a lifeless body, but I had seen death, and that wasn't me. I still had a full life ahead of me."

Life 1.0 for Deepa was one of an army child who played various sports. She was a member of the Rajasthan state-level cricket team, played basketball, excelled in swimming, and even rode horses. She loved being on wheels and had a craze for bikes. However, those seven days changed her life forever. She accepted the new reality that she couldn't control the winds of fate and adjusted her sails to reach her destination. She began by tackling what was necessary, then moved on to accomplish what seemed possible, and ultimately achieved what appeared impossible. The incredible journey of Deepa Malik continues.

Deepa's journey towards becoming the person she is today commenced at the tender age of six when she was a spirited tomboy. A tumour was detected in her spinal cord, and although it was treated and contained early on, it was during this period that she learnt her first lesson of how to live life in the face of adversity. Her recovery took three years, during which she realised what it means if life threatens to be a bully and starts snatching the things you love and value one by one.

Deepa had a deep love for outdoors, climbing trees, and sneaking off with a friend's bike to ride into the sunset. But suddenly she found herself confined to a room, separated from the vibrant world she once knew. Remembering those early days, she says, "When you master the art of gratitude, you'll learn to focus on life's positives. Even while on that bed, I decided I had to enrich my mind and prepare for the future, for I knew life awaited me on the other side." It's this attitude that helped her overcome the worst crisis in her life. The tomboy transformed into a beautiful young woman who fell in love with a bike, ultimately leading to her marriage to the bike's owner.

Bikram Singh Malik, a young army officer, owned a state-of-art Japanese bike. Deepa recalls, "Every day, I saw this boy going for a run. One day, he came with this incredibly attractive motorcycle. I wanted to ride it, so I approached him and asked for the keys. He asked whether I could manage it. I insisted to hand me the keys, and he gave them to me. I rode the motorcycle, performed a few stunts and then returned it to him. I told him that I would marry a guy who would not question me why I needed a motorcycle and who would buy me one." The very next day, Bikram Singh approached her father, Colonel B. K. Nagpal, and said, "I'll get your daughter a new motorcycle. Can I marry her?" Deepa and Bikram got married, marking the beginning of a life partnership destined to achieve even greater and more substantial successes.

The couple began building a wonderful life together. Their first daughter, Devika, came into their lives. But before Devika could even start walking, she met with an accident. She got hit by a biker when she was barely one. Deepa says, "There was internal bleeding in her brain, her ventricles got dilated and her left side was paralysed. We rushed her to the Pune Command Hospital, and it was the same ward and same bed as mine from all those years ago." She adds, "There were rumours that I passed on my disability to my daughter. That was when I got to know the stereotypical images of disability in society's eyes. As a child, I was sheltered, but now I felt the venom. My father would tell me 'God distributes his challenges wisely. You have been chosen for this one'."

Deepa and Bikram began helping the child relentlessly. Soon after, the couple welcomed the second child, Ambika, who brought a breath of fresh air in their lives. In 1999, Bikram was summoned for the Kargil War, and as he left, Deepa began facing difficulties in walking again.

While her husband was away on national duty, Deepa was living in pain. However, when the pain became unbearable, she was advised by the doctor to go to Delhi for a thorough check-up. Initially, the doctor hesitated to share the details with her when he saw her medical reports and insisted on speaking to her husband. However, Deepa, being the daughter of an army man, did not want to disturb her husband while he was on duty at the India-Pakistan border in Kargil. The doctor had no other option but to inform her about the problem and the recommended course of medication. She recalls, "The doctors gave me seven days to prepare myself before getting admitted for surgery. They informed me of the potential consequences; in most cases, such surgeries resulted in paralysis."

Deepa had to accept many harsh realities at one go. Even if she survived the surgery, she would not be able to walk again. This was difficult for a young woman who loved bikes and passionately participated in multiple sports. Instead of succumbing to the impending changes, she started to prepare herself for the new circumstances.

Deepa had seven days left. She used that time in a way that no one would have to face difficulties if she were no longer there. Deepa wrote her will, put all her jewellery in the locker, and made her house wheelchair-friendly. She then called her mother to inform her that she would be sending her daughters to her along with the keys. As she prepared for the operation, the doctors refused to proceed without the consent form signed either by her husband or her father. She informed her parents, who signed the consent letter. She handed a letter to her parents addressed to her husband, outlining how to raise their daughters in case she did not survive. When her parents showed concern about the situation she was forced to face in life, Deepa replied, "Yes, things are difficult, but one has to face them." Her father, who was from the defence background, was stunned by the bravery and approach of his daughter.

Deepa was now in the operation theatre. The doctor asked her if she wished to say or do something before the operation. She requested two things. She was aware that she would be walking on her legs for the last time in her life. So, she wanted to enter the operation theatre walking, rather than in a wheelchair. Secondly, she wanted to speak to her husband, who was fighting the Kargil War. She was taken to the radio satellite room, and the officers connected her to her husband. Deepa says, "I said, 'I will never be able to walk again after the surgery. Over. I will be paralysed below the chest. Over.' And he replied, 'I will carry you in my arms for the rest of my life. Over. Just don't die, and wait for me. Over.'"

There are moments in life when the most crucial thing is to help family members realise that they are together in everything. Deepa reflects on her mindset as she prepared for the surgery, saying, "The Kargil War brought daily casualties and fatalities. The entire hospital was turned into an ICU. I found myself undergoing surgery alongside people who had lost their arms, eyes, and limbs through no fault of their own, not due to illness, but in service to their country. I had no reasons to complain. My mind was trained to look at things like that."

Once the operation started, her body and mind went through a lot of pain. But this was when her maternal instinct took over, and she wanted to survive the ordeal for her children. She recounts, "I felt utterly drained emotionally and mentally. I was determined to live through this, as I had no idea what my husband's fate would be. The mother in me took precedence; I had to endure for the sake of my children. Despite the surgery, severe complications arose. My cerebrospinal fluid leaked, necessitating a third surgery. I slipped into a coma for 25 days, battling yet another major battle in life."

Dr V.K. Batish, who performed surgery on Deepa at the Research and Referral Hospital of the Armed Forces in Delhi, told a news magazine, "In my 25 years as a neurosurgeon, I have never come across someone quite like her. Deepa's recovery and subsequent achievements are truly amazing. She's the type of person who can impart valuable lessons to both medical professionals and society at large." With her husband's return from the war, Deepa started the second innings of her life. This marked the beginning of Life 2.0 for Deepa.

Deepa started her second innings armed with two lethal weapons in her arsenal: a positive attitude towards life and a sense of humour. She says, "I am always on my wheels! Why call me wheelchair-bound when I am wheelchair-liberated? The Ashok Chakra has a wheel. I tell everyone like me, you have your inspiration right here, under you!" After a brief hiatus, sports once again emerged as her "Ashok Chakra", the wheel to propel her life forward.

One morning, Deepa accompanied her daughter Ambika to the swimming pool. Like many children, Ambika was initially reluctant to go to the pool out of fear. Deepa asked if her daughter would take a dive if she joined her. When Ambika agreed, Deepa jumped into the swimming pool. She felt liberated and decided to pursue coaching in swimming. This marked her entry into the competitive para sports.

Deepa began researching about what disabled people like her were achieving globally. She explored various paths. Just as Deepa was gaining momentum in the second innings of her life, an unexpected twist occurred. Her husband Bikram was summoned for national duty following a terrorist attack on the Indian Parliament. As the wife of the squadron commander, Deepa started taking care of 30 families whose husbands were called for duty overnight.

Deepa, who was then in Ahmednagar, Maharashtra, opened a garden restaurant named "Dee's Place" on her farmhouse premises. With the assistance of domestic staff and some painters already engaged there, she brought her vision to life. Soon, Dee's Place became a popular restaurant and a favoured spot for young officers to hang out. Deepa says, "I began serving around 250 people in the restaurant daily and overseeing about 100 home deliveries. I also supported some of our employed youths in returning to school and completing their tenth-grade exams. When I became disabled, some women doubted how I would provide for my own family. Well, now I was feeding theirs." It was during this time and in this very restaurant that Deepa reignited her passion for bikes.

Deepa recounts, "One day, an army officer named Atul arrived on his new bike. I found myself momentarily lost in nostalgia, remembering the days when bikes were my biggest passion. Atul approached me and suggested that I could still ride the bike. At first, I gave him a piece of my mind and a reality check. 'Nothing below my chest level functions properly. My injury is at the T1 level, leaving me with no torso balance, limited sensation, compromised lung functioning, and no temperature control. My nerve endings are haphazardly cut, and I lack ladder or bowel control. Yet, here I am, running the restaurant. And now you are telling me I can ride a bike?'"

Atul then googled and showed Deepa how people like her could have a customised bike created, allowing her to rekindle her passion. This revelation provided Deepa with an opportunity to pursue her other passion. Throughout all these endeavours, she had the total backing of her husband. As she renewed her romance with the wheels, it eventually earned her a place in the Limca Book of World Records.

Deepa had dedicated herself to rigorous training, primarily focussing on swimming. One day, an individual noticed her swimming on television and recognised her talent. This person promptly informed sports authorities about an upcoming national tournament, and advocated for Deepa's inclusion. Deepa, thus, received an invitation to compete at the national competition. Despite being 36 years old at the time, she didn't hesitate to take the plunge. In her own words, "Why not? Opportunities knock on your door, and winners are those who have the courage to seize them. I did just that and earned many medals. In 2006, I went to Kuala Lumpur and even won a silver medal ."

Deepa continued her successful journey by winning a medal in the 2010 Para Asian Games and set her sights on the London 2012 Paralympics. Unfortunately, she couldn't qualify for the games due to the absence of a quota. But this setback only fuelled her resolve to make it to the Rio Paralympics in 2016. There, she won a silver medal in the women's shot put event, achieving a personal best throw of 4.61 metres. Fatema Nedham of Bahrain won the gold with a throw of 4.76 metres, while Dimitra Karokida of Greece bagged the bronze with a throw of 4.28 metres. That was Deepa's best effort in that season. She, thus, became the first Indian female medallist in the history of the Paralympic Games. After debuting in the 1968 Paralympic Games, it took India 48 long years to produce its first woman medal winner.

Deepa has participated in three Asian Para Games. She won a bronze in javelin throw during the 2010 Games in China and a silver medal in javelin throw during the 2014 Games in South Africa. In the Jakarta Games in 2018, she participated in two events—javelin throw and discus—winning bronze medals in both. She is the first Indian female para athlete to win medals at all three major tournaments: World Championships, Asian Para Games and Paralympics. In total, she has won 17 international medals and 58 national gold medals in various sports events. At the age of 42, she became the oldest recipient of the Arjuna Award in 2012.

Deepa holds several other firsts in her name. She is recognised as the first paraplegic woman in the world to drive a quad bike on the highest motorable roads of Leh and Ladakh. She says,

"I began my homework by contacting the army adventure cell since I was an army wife. But I soon found out that only serving army officers' wives were allowed to participate. I did not give up, even though I had to wait for three more years. I was present at the flag-off for the Desert Storm rally in Delhi in February 2009. During the entire event, I interacted with various teams and shared my desire to participate in a rally. I got mixed reactions; some thought I was crazy, while others admired my courage. Finally, I was accepted by the Pune Millennium team, who taught me navigation skills and prepared me for the rally's challenges."

Afterward, Deepa approached the Himalayan Motorsport Association and the Federation of Motor Sports Clubs of India (FMSCI) to accept her as a formal competitor. This endeavour was met with some hesitation, as it was the first time a disabled person had approached them. She says, "They took their time, but I'm happy that they appreciated my passion for motorsport. I held my breath until I saw a ray of hope when they agreed to accept me, although I had to complete all the required paperwork."

Obtaining the required documentation posed another challenge for her. The most difficult task was getting personal accident insurance under heavy-risk conditions. But when you desperately want to achieve something in life, you attract the right people who help you reach your goals. Deepa received proactive support from various stakeholders, including Maruti Suzuki and Rakesh Diwan, a three-time Raid-de-Himalaya winner. Finally, her dream came true, and her husband Bikram backed her throughout her rally journey, joining as her attendant.

Deepa reflects, "After a long struggle for permissions,

sponsorships, a rally vehicle, a professional team partner and procurement of snow clothing, I found myself in Shimla. At first, people were taken aback, and some even appeared shocked to see me there. They assumed I had come to cheer a friend. However, as time passed, they began to notice the name sticker on my car, the competitor's licence and an identity card on my back. They started taking me seriously after seeing all these visible markers. I was very happy to see the surprised expressions on everyone's faces. For me, it was a moment of achievement and contentment as I watched my dream turn into reality. I was able to prove to the world that disability is a state of mind rather than a condition of the body."

On 7 October 2011, the rally got flagged off in the morning. It was a nine-day, 1700-km drive in sub-zero temperatures. Deepa says, "Even at an altitude of 18,000 feet and with oxygen shortage, I managed to endure it. It was tiring, but the adrenalin rush was so high that I never felt tired. We held the third position in the adventure category until an accident took place."

Deepa was honoured with the True Grit Trophy for her exceptional courage. But, more than the trophy, what she holds most dear is the profound impact it had on the inclusivity of disabled individuals in motorsport. Deepa's efforts paved the way for people with disabilities to participate in such events. Throughout the nine-day journey, she crossed nine high-altitude passes and went through extreme conditions. This remarkable feat earned her a well-deserved place in the Limca Book of Records.

In fact, Deepa holds four records in the Limca Book of Records in the Adventure Category. These include swimming in the Yamuna river against the current for 1 km (2008), covering

58 km by riding a specialised bike in 2009, driving across nine high-altitude passes in Ladakh in just nine days along the world's highest motorable roads in 2011, and completing the longest pan-India drive (spanning 3,278 km from Chennai to Delhi) in 2013 by a paraplegic woman. What motivates her to undertake such adventures in life? She says, "Biking and sports have become powerful tools for shattering the stereotypical image associated with people in wheelchairs. To be heard, one must become an achiever. To discover your voice, you must do something extraordinary." It is this life mantra that inspired her to explore and conquer new things in life.

Deepa has set yet another record by doing a pan-India drive to promote para sports in the country. She has contributed immensely to improving sports policies for the physically challenged during her tenure as a member of the Working Group for the formulation of the 12th Five-Year Plan (2012–17). In 2020, she was elected as the President of the Paralympic Committee of India. She has been awarded an Honoris Causa Doctorate by ITM University in recognition of her outstanding contributions to the fields of sports and adventure sports in India. She was also awarded another Honoris Causa Doctorate by Raffles University, India, in recognition of her contributions to social work. She is the "Clean India" brand ambassador for the New Delhi Municipal Council and serves as an expert consultant for disability-inclusive accessible infrastructure for the Ministry of Housing and Urban Affairs' Smart Cities project. She is the founder of the Wheeling Happiness Foundation, which advocates for enhancing the emotional well-being of persons facing challenges and empowering women through outdoor sports, motor sports, and adventure activities. The foundation also offers training and sports equipment to para athletes and organises awareness and advocacy sessions on disability sports in various schools and colleges, in addition to empowering individuals from lower socioeconomic backgrounds.

Deepa, honoured with the Padma Shri in 2017, is the role model in her family. Addressing an event at the Rashtrapati Bhavan, she famously remarked, "There was a time when I was emotionally distressed and confused regarding what I could offer my daughters. Initially, societal stigma, taboos, and stereotypes surrounding my physical condition loomed large. However, I'm proud that my motherhood and womanhood became sources of strength, empowering me to recover and reclaim my life with a lot of passion. My determination paid off, and I was able to bring home the first-ever female Paralympic medal for my country in 2016."

Her elder daughter Devika says, "The whole family is proud of my mother. People read books to get inspired and achieve something in life. I look up to my mother. Everywhere we go, people are in awe of her. It is an adventure being her daughter."

I often wondered what made her undergo such an incredible transition from "Life 1.0" to "Life 2.0". I got to know her closely when we invited her for the DD Sports conclave. During her address, she shared insights into her transformation, stating, "The things I once took for granted before my disability now seemed like big hurdles. Even the same six-inch step that I never paid attention to before started restricting my accessibility. Earlier, I was crazy about fashionable and branded clothes and loved gossiping. However, disability brought clarity to my life. I started a restaurant, supported the education of a few children and worked on a mission mode to motivate people like myself through my activities. I learnt the importance of giving back to society and discovered the true sense of living."

DEEPA MALIK

She then invited four gentlemen to lift her from the wheelchair and place her on the stage. After this, she said, "Many of you might think that it's ordinary for four people to assist someone in my condition, but for me, it is like four handsome men carrying the palanquin of a queen. It all depends on how you look at life." For Deepa, it's not cool to be normal.

Deepa Malik's journey is a testament that no challenge is unconquerable. With determination, courage, and unwavering self-belief, anything becomes within reach. In the upcoming chapter, we will go through the story of another young Indian girl, Avani Lekhara, who continued to raise the bar.

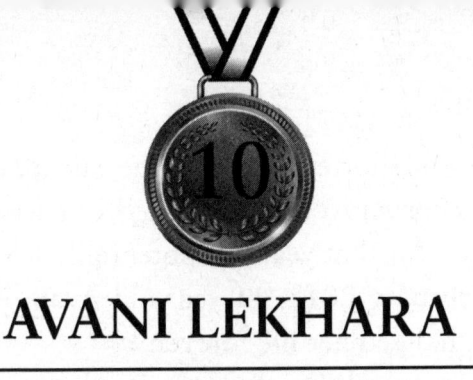

AVANI LEKHARA

A Win Against the Self

*"Life consists not in holding good cards
but in playing those you hold well."*

—Josh Billings

Josh Billings, the pen name of Henry Wheeler Shaw, was an American humourist whose plain-language philosophical quotes gained widespread popularity after the American Civil War. His quotes, featured in his newspaper pieces, books, and articles, are known for their straightforwardness and rustic charm. The aforementioned quote by Billings has deeply resonated with me since I first read it. It signifies that while you receive what is given to you, you have the power to choose how you use it.

In this chapter, we meet Avani Lekhara, our superstar. She met with a life-changing accident just when she was about to enter her teenage years. This incident could have left her in a state of helplessness, while her father, who was with her in the car at the time, could have carried a lifelong burden of guilt. It took time for both Avani and her father to overcome the aftermath of this unfortunate accident. However, once they did, their journey became not about holding good cards, but how well they played those cards.

February is the shortest month in the calendar, but for Avani Lekhara, the February of 2012 turned out to be the longest month, not only for that year but potentially for the rest of her life. On 20 February 2012, 11-year-old Avani met with a car accident that changed her life forever.

Born into a financially affluent family in Jaipur to Praveen Lekhara and Sheetal Lekhara, Avani was the apple of her family's eye. On that fateful day, she was supposed to stay at home when her parents were leaving on a road trip from Jaipur to Dholpur. At that time, Praveen was posted at Dholpur, Rajasthan, and Avani was studying at a school there. Despite her parents' desire for her to stay back in Jaipur at their ancestral home, she insisted on accompanying them because she wanted to participate in a dance competition at her school.

"I loved dancing, and chose to travel to Dholpur with my parents for the dance competition. My mother, father, brother and a cousin were with me in the car. I was sleeping in the back seat of the car and didn't actually see what happened. I just felt a sudden jolt while sleeping. I sensed the car had turtled and it kept on rolling before finally coming to a stop. I could see that we were surrounded by fields. The car had landed in the fields beside the road. I tried to get up and exit the car, but at that moment, some sand and mud entered my eyes, and I couldn't open them. I could neither feel my legs nor move them. I experienced a terrible back pain. I was taken to Jaipur's SMS Hospital, where they revealed that I would have to use a wheelchair for the rest of my life," Avani recollects with a heavy heart.

Avani was still a pre-teen when she faced one of the most challenging situations imaginable. After the accident, she spent three months at SMS Hospital in Jaipur, and then another four months at the Indian Spinal Injury Centre in Delhi. Over the next two and half years, her family took Avani to various treatment centres in Delhi, Mumbai, and Ahmedabad. Amidst these struggles, she withdrew into herself. In a way, she had to start her life from scratch. Learning to sit again became a monumental task for her. Seeing their vibrant daughter confined to such a desperate state was a harrowing experience for the Lekhara family. Avani's father, Praveen Lekhara, tearfully confessed, "I was hospitalised when I learnt of her spinal cord injury and paralysis below her waist. My heart broke, and I just wept. I pleaded with God, wishing the burden had fallen on me instead of my girl."

After the initial trauma and pain, the biggest challenge for the Lekhara family was to lift Avani from her distress and infuse her life with a new meaning and fresh objective. "To be honest, I thought this was just a long nightmare and that one day, I would regain my ability to walk and run. I was just 11 years old when it happened—too old to forget, and too young to understand the situation. Eventually, I accepted that my disability was permanent. I had to relearn everything in a different way, even how to sit properly, as my body had lost its sense of balance and I had to balance my upper body to sit again. It was as though I was born in a new body and had to learn to do everything, akin to a baby's journey. It was really tough. Physically I was a different human being now, and it had a direct impact on my emotional and psychological health also. I didn't want to go out or talk to anyone. I became very shy and very introverted. I never liked being looked at with pity. I didn't have any friends during those two years of homeschooling. My family and my house became my entire world," Avani shared in a candid conversation with *NDTV*.

In this backdrop, when Avani returned to school in 2014, she felt like stepping into a whole new world. She reminisces, "Going back to school after two years was a totally different experience. The faces were familiar, yet it felt like I needed to make a fresh start with everyone. Initially, I was taken aback by the loudness of everyone around me. But as I made new friends, I found myself opening up and gaining confidence."

The Lekhara family rejoiced at the progress she was making in her life. However, Avani's father recognised that besides academics Avani needed another outlet to vent out her innermost frustrations and disappointments. With her disability, Avani's options were limited. Sports emerged as a potential avenue for her, which could act as a catharsis for her. And this is where the story of one of India's most successful para athletes was about to start.

"After the accident, once everything settled, I found myself evaluating the options that remained. I was determined not to give up on life. Bedridden for nearly eight months and homeschooled for two years thereafter, I pondered my future. It was my father's suggestion that I engage in some sports. While he may not have the Paralympics in mind initially, he believed sports would benefit both my body and mind. Being physically weak, traditional athletic pursuits like discus, javelin, or shot put were out of reach for me. So, in a sense, I feel shooting found me, rather than the other way around," Avani shared during her interview with the news channel.

Was shooting an automatic choice? Avani responds with a giggle, "No, not at all. I actually tried my hands at archery, but it was very tough. It required a lot of physical strength, which I lacked due to the accident at the age of 11. Moreover, being an outdoor activity in the sweltering heat of Rajasthan, archery wasn't quite my cup of tea," Avani admits, acknowledging her weak areas.

Realising that she was accustomed to a certain level of comfort and that her body couldn't endure excessive strain, her father, Praveen Lekhara, sought an alternative. He introduced her to shooting, hoping it would help her channel her energy constructively and manage her frustrations. This decision finally clicked.

"When I first went to the shooting range, I was immediately relieved by the cool air and the absence of intense heat. It didn't seem too physically demanding at first glance. After observing other shooters for a while, I mustered the courage to ask one of them if I could borrow his rifle for a few minutes. To my surprise, not only did he agree, but he also took time to teach me how to properly hold a rifle. I still vividly recall my first shot—it hit the inner black spot, a perfect 10-pointer! In fact, my first 10 shots all hit the inner black circle, and I couldn't help but feel a rush of excitement. I knew then that shooting was a sport I could truly invest my time in," reminisces Avani about her first day at the shooting range.

Despite her initial excitement, Avani admits that she wasn't fully committed to her shooting endeavours in the beginning. She only visited the range once or twice a week. It was her father's encouragement that eventually motivated her to take the sport more seriously. However, there were challenges galore. Avani lacked the physical strength to hold a rifle. She also didn't have a rifle of her own. She lacked a wheelchair that would provide her with comfort and stability she needed while shooting. Most importantly, she faced the hurdle of finding a coach who could accommodate her needs and help sharpen her skills.

Talking about the challenges she faced while starting her shooting journey, Avani says, "To say that shooting came naturally to me or that I just picked up the rifle and started winning golds are totally far from reality. Initially, it was extremely challenging. I lacked the physical strength to lift a rifle for more than a few minutes, and here was a game that required holding the rifle for nearly 90 minutes. It was very tough. I was unfamiliar with how classification worked based on disability, unsure of which events to pursue, and oblivious to the impact even slightest adjustments to my wheelchair, such as the cushion I used, could have on my performance. There was no literature available on para shooting in the country, so we had to do a lot of research on our own. Initially, I didn't know how to customise a rifle according to my needs, and there wasn't a proper coach who would tailor their guidance to accommodate my disability. Those early days of shooting felt like being a hen lost in the farm, darting around aimlessly and trying anything and everything."

As the family tackled each hurdle one by one, Avani found solace and clarity through her love for reading. She was very intelligent and used to do well academically. It was around this time that she read Abhinav Bindra's autobiography, *A Shot at History: My Obsessive Journey to Olympic Gold*. Bindra, the first Indian to concurrently hold the world and Olympic titles for the men's 10-metre air rifle event, had achieved those feats at the 2008 Summer Olympics and the 2006 ISSF World Shooting Championships. He had also won 7 medals at the Commonwealth Games and 3 medals at the Asian Games. Bindra's book really influenced Avani's perspective, not just in terms of shooting but also in shaping her entire life. It made her realise that shooting would not only define her sporting career but also deeply impact her personal life.

"Shooting is more of a personal journey; it is a constant battle against your own mind. When I read Bindra's autobiography, I was really inspired by it. Some people might assume that an athlete's struggle is only in financial aspects, but like me, Bindra didn't have much of a financial crisis; rather, we both had to fight our inner demons," explains Avani about the impact the book had on her.

As Avani found her hero in Bindra and aspired to follow in his footsteps, her father began accompanying her frequently to the Jagatpura Shooting Range. In 2016, under the guidance of her coach Chandrasekhar, Avani focused on the 50-metre and 10-metre air rifle events. As she got comfortable shooting from a wheelchair and made necessary adjustments to accommodate her physical condition, she went from 50 to 200 shots in a session. Avani's dedication to training and her growing passion for shooting started to yield tangible results.

"Initially, I started with school competitions. I studied at Kendriya Vidyalaya No. 3, and participated in the regional tournaments of KV schools. I won a gold medal at the Kendriya Vidyalaya National Tournament. Competing against able-bodied shooters rather than para shooters was a significant morale booster for me. During these regional tournaments, I didn't have my own rifle because I wasn't entirely sure if shooting was the sport I wanted to pursue. The rifles, shooting kits, gloves, and ammunitions cost a lot of money. Despite my parents' support, I wanted to be sure before investing in the equipment. Representing the Rajasthan state, I won 3 gold medals in the nationals and was selected for international tournaments," Avani reminisces her initial success.

Avani secured the gold medal at the 2015 National Shooting Championship, representing the state of Rajasthan.

Nevertheless, in every athlete's journey, there comes a crucial moment when they transcend their threshold level and reach the take-off stage. For Avani, that moment arrived in 2017. It was the year when the sporting community began considering her a serious talent. During the Para Shooting World Cup at Al Ain in the UAE, she clinched a silver medal in the women's 10-m air rifle event in the SH1 category.

"My silver medal at Al Ain World Cup really boosted my confidence. All the shooters who had participated in the Rio 2016 Para Games were there. The gold medal was won by the shooter who had won the gold at Rio. So, winning silver by defeating other Paralympian shooters was truly exhilarating. It solidified my belief that I could achieve accolades at big tournaments," says Avani.

In the same year, she bagged a silver medal at the Dubai Paralympic Championships in the women's 10-m rifle event in the SH1 category. Just a few months later, she bagged a bronze medal in Bangkok at the 2017 WSPS World Cup.

The year 2018 was remarkable for Avani as she won 3 gold medals in three different events at the World Shooting Para Sports World Cup. She excelled in 10m rifles, Prone and 3 Position events.

Continuing her stellar performance, in 2019, at the 63rd National Shooting Championship in Bhopal, Avani grabbed 3 gold medals and a bronze in a single championship. Later that year, she won a silver medal at the 2019 WSPS World Cup held in Osijek, Croatia. Her back-to-back impressive performances led to her selection for the TOPS (Target Olympic Podium Scheme) by the Ministry of Youth Affairs and Sports in 2020, earning her a place to represent India at the Tokyo 2020 Paralympics.

When Avani's father had introduced her to shooting, his intention was to help her break free from her constraints, internalise her anger and embrace life with a fresh objective. However, as she immersed herself in the sport, achieving one milestone after another and setting new goals a new challenge emerged. How much physical pain could she endure in the process? How long and to what extent could she push her endurance? She found herself pushing her boundaries to the limit, causing concern for Praveen Lekhara and the entire family. Amidst all this, COVID-19, one of the worst pandemics in more than a century, hit the world, bringing with it a different set of challenges. So, more than her Olympic aspirations, medals and achievements, it was her resilience in facing the circumstances leading up to the event that deserves recognition and contemplation.

First, COVID-19 and the resulting lockdown disrupted her physiotherapy routine. Due to her spinal cord disability, Avani does not have any sensation in the body parts below her waist. This means she must exercise her legs every day. A dedicated physiotherapist usually visits her home in Jaipur every day to assist her with leg exercises and stretches. However, after March 2020, because of the lockdown, this became impossible. Despite being sponsored by the Go Sports Foundation, which would have allowed her to obtain a government-issued pass for her medical caregiver (the physiotherapist) to visit without hindrance, Avani chose not to do so. Her physiotherapist came from a distant part of the city, and she did not want to expose him to any risks during these uncertain times. So, she had to depend on her parents for her daily exercises during this period, and they did the best they could.

Secondly, the Olympic and Paralympic Games 2020, initially slated for 24 July-9 August 2020, were cancelled due to the pandemic. The lockdown had greatly impacted Avani's practice sessions and preparations for the event. Unable to practice at the shooting range, she was forced to train at her home, utilising spaces from halfway in the kitchen to half way in the master bedroom. However, distractions such as cooking noises in the kitchen or the television hindered her focus and concentration. Eventually, with the guidance from her coach, she devised a schedule for herself and stuck to it.

Thirdly, Avani had qualified for four events at the Tokyo 2020 Paralympics. While her inner champion drove her to push her limits, her body was not cooperating. She began experiencing severe back pain, which troubled her throughout the day. In March 2021, during the World Shooting Para Sport World Cup, the pain became so intense that she feared it might prevent her from participating in the Tokyo Paralympics. By May-June, the problem had worsened to the point where she had to stop shooting entirely and focus on physiotherapy. But even then, she remained steadfast in her goals.

Avani turned to mental exercises, visualising various scenarios in her mind. Mental mapping and training are crucial in modern sports; we've heard many stories of sports legends, from Sachin Tendulkar to Virat Kohli, who use mental visualisation to plan their performances ahead of important games. Avani, too, harnessed this unique ability to its fullest during her time away from shooting due to pain and physical limitations. Her father and family had genuine concerns that she was pushing herself too hard, which might lead to distress or a breakdown. But legends-in-waiting, like Avani, are made of different stuff and they do give hints of their brilliance when confronted with difficult situations. By this time, she had become a dedicated student of the sport, making notes and continuously exploring different strategies to navigate various situations.

"In the last two months leading up to the Tokyo Games, our base was the Dr Karni Singh Shooting Range in New Delhi, where we received exceptional care. It felt like a complete lockdown, cut off from the rest of the world, yet inside the shooting range, we created our own universe. Our coaches were training us very hard. They were leaving no stone unturned. They subjected us to hypothetical scenarios to gauge our performances under varied conditions. I had qualified for four events, so maintaining focus was tough, but it was also a time of self-discovery," remembers Avani about her days during the final preparation.

As the countdown for the Tokyo Paralympics began, Avani found herself among India's brightest medal hopes. Stepping onto the 'land of the rising sun' marked her debut at the Paralympic Games, necessitating her to confront personal mental struggles ahead of commencing her campaign on one of the world's grandest sporting stages. Before her, only one Indian woman, in the entire history of the games, had won a medal for the country. Deepa Malik, who was part of the Indian contingent in her capacity as the President of the Paralympic Committee of India, had won a silver medal in shot put at the Rio 2016 Paralympics.

"When we arrived in Tokyo for the Paralympic Games, I was very anxious. It was my first Paralympics, and there were definitely butterflies in my stomach. Despite the uncertainty leading up to the Games, we were thrilled that they were finally happening. I was just happy to be there. However, upon arrival, I quickly realised that I needed to meticulously plan my time, as

I was taking part in four events. After careful consideration, I came to the decision, along with my coach, to focus primarily on two events as my main priorities, using the other two events to test myself and gain valuable experience for the future. This was my last junior year. So, I gave ambitious targets for myself: set a world record, a Paralympic record, a junior world record and also win a gold medal. I just wanted to achieve it all. People close to me advised me not to think so much, but I felt compelled to test my boundaries. With many events cancelled due to the COVID-19 pandemic, this Paralympic Games marked the end of my junior career. I was determined to make the most of it," says Avani.

As Avani arrived at the Games Village, the enormity of the challenge loomed over her. *Would she succeed? Would she live up to the expectations? How would her loved ones and those who had shared her dream react if she fails?* These uncertainties plagued her thoughts. Looking back on her career, from the Nationals to the Para Shooting Championship in Al Ain in 2017, she had won numerous silver and bronze medals. However, when it truly mattered, gold medals had always eluded her. Would history repeat itself?

After some time, her personal coach, Suma Shirur, joined her at the Games Village. "What if I didn't win the medal?" Avani asked her coach. "Suma Madam told me that whether I win or lose, whether I get the medal or not, our relationship is not going to change. She would still be by my side and offer support whenever I need it in the future. All she asked was for me to give my best, to perform to the best of my abilities, so that I wouldn't have any regrets later on," Avani recalls. This reassurance, coming from someone who had experienced it all before, somehow helped ease her nerves.

"On the night before my event, I was a little nervous. It was going to be my biggest day up to that point. More than me, the expectations of those around me weighed heavily. Everyone kept saying, '*Avani ka medal to pakka hai, practice ke barabar bhi agar perform kar degi to bahut hai* (Avani's medal is a sure thing; if she performs even close to her practice, it will be great)." This was always there in the back of my mind. My coach advised me to trust the process I had been following. The outcome, whether a medal or not, lay beyond our control, and worrying over it served no purpose," says Avani.

It was 30 August 2021, the day scheduled for her favourite R2 (10 m rifle) event. Avani's journey in the competition didn't commence on the smoothest note. *Of all days, why is this happening with me today?* she wondered as she struggled through the qualification round. Despite a shaky start, she managed commendable scores of 104.9 and 104.8 in her third and fourth attempts, respectively. Her final attempt yielded a score was 104.1, culminating in a qualification round score of 621.7, placing her seventh among the eight finalists. In sports, we often talk of "peaking at the right time". In a discipline like shooting, particularly in the Paralympic arena, timing is everything. As she geared up for the finals, she had a feeling which raised breaths of fresh hope. She started the finals with a formidable momentum, consistently scoring above 10 points. Only two of her shots fell below the 10-point mark in the first stage of the competition, by the end of which she held the second position. Avani finished with a Paralympic record, winning the gold medal with a world-record-breaking score of 249.6 points.

Avani Lekhara made history as the first Indian woman to win a gold medal in the Paralympic Games. Prior to her remarkable achievement, only three Indians had got this distinction for the country: Murlikant Petkar in 1972, Devendra Jhajharia in 2004 and 2016, and Mariyappan Thangavelu in 2016.

This was a 19-year-old girl's debut Paralympic Games. "I can't describe this feeling. It's like being on top of the world. I was just saying that I have to take one shot at a time. Nothing else mattered—just one shot at a time and finishing it through. Beyond that, I tried not to think about the score or the medals tally," Avani says.

Before Avani, many athletes have scaled the Everest of success in various sports. As a sports journalist, I have had the privilege of watching some of these golden moments from ground zero. On other occasions, we have seen history being made on the big screen. The best part is about how, on most of the occasions, if not all, the winners talk and emphasise on the process that propelled them to reach there. It seems that many of them were focused more on the journey rather than the end result.

As India's Chief National Coach, J.P. Nautiyal, commented, "Avani has executed exactly what we practised in training and followed the process meticulously. She has definitely set an example for aspiring shooters in the country. I never tell my players to chase medals for the country; instead, I urge them to give their best in every shot, knowing it can lead to great results. Certainly, Avani has matured as an athlete now. She knows what's best and how to achieve it. She realises that reaching the top requires nothing but hard work, hard work and more hard work."

Abhinav Bindra, the hero who inspired Avani Lekhara to take up the sport despite the odds, tweeted, "Gold it is! Brilliant display by @AvaniLekhara to win India its Paralympic Gold

Medal in shooting. Immensely proud! Many congratulations on your shot at history!"

Days after winning the gold, on 3 September 2021, Avani scaled yet another summit. She etched her name in history as the first Indian woman to win two medals in the Paralympics and the second Indian, after Joginder Singh Bedi, to claim more than one medal in the same edition. Avani won the bronze medal in the women's 50 m 3 Position SH1 event.

During the finals, Avani initially stood fourth after the first three kneeling series with a score of 149.5. However, she surged ahead with a remarkable second three prone series, scoring 153.9 and climbing to the sixth position. Despite the pressure and looming threat of elimination, Avani displayed exceptional composure. She delivered two standing series with scores of 50.5 and 50.7, to be placed fourth before the single-shot elimination started.

Maintaining her optimism, she stayed in contention with scores of 10.3 and 10.2 in the single-shot rounds, securing fourth place just behind Ukraine's I. Shchetnik, trailing by a mere 0.3 points. . In the crucial elimination shot, Avani shot a commendable 10.5, while Shchetnik managed only 9.9. With this, Avani got the bronze medal, trailing behind Germany's Natasha Hiltrop's silver and China's Jhang Cuiping's gold. Avani's performance was particularly noteworthy considering she had begun competing in 50m 3P event only after winning the silver medal in the 10m air rifle event at the Al Ain World Cup in 2017.

"My bronze in 3 Position (3P) event is just as special to me as the gold medal, as it requires a lot of fitness. Each position—kneeling, prone and standing—requires different equipment, and adapting to them on a wheelchair took considerable effort and time. A table (the support platform) acts like my body. People use their knees for kneeling, so the table is like my knees during the match. Since the distance is 50 m, even the slightest body movement can significantly affect accuracy at the target end. So, we need to train a lot physically to endure a match lasting nearly two hours and forty five minutes. It requires a lot more physical and mental strength than the 10 m standing events," she says, explaining why the bronze medal holds equal significance to her as the gold.

With such great accomplishments in her debut Paralympics at just 19 years of age, accolades and honours were bound to follow. She was conferred with the Padma Shri and Major Dhyan Chand Khel Ratna awards.

This Indian shooter also won the Best Female Debut honour at the 2021 Paralympics Awards for her record-breaking gold medal performance at the Tokyo Games. The lives of champion athletes comprise two contrasting facets. On one side, there is the allure of name, fame and popularity; on the other, there is the solitude of grappling with the newfound identity and perception. On one side are the medals, the awards and accolades. On the other side is the urge to leave them behind and move on to scale a new summit.

While Avani's journey continues, her father, who introduced her to shooting as a means to channel her inner turmoil, looks back with a lot of satisfaction. For both daughter and father, it's been a lesson in realising that life isn't merely about the hand you're dealt with, but how skilfully you play your cards.

In the next chapter, we will go through the life story of Sumit Antil, often called India's Sergey Bubka—the legendary pole vaulter—earning him the moniker of "The Tiger".

SUMIT ANTIL

The Tiger

"To be a champion, compete;
to be a great champion, compete with the best;
but to be the greatest champion, compete with yourself."

—Matshona Dhliwayo

It is often challenging to find the right words to describe the subtle distinction between a champion, a great champion and the greatest champion. Matshona Dhliwayo, a Zimbabwean-born and Canada-based philosopher, entrepreneur and author, has beautifully summarised this. When looking for a perfect example of Dhliwayo's definition of the greatest champion, one name stands out: Sergey Bubka. Although many great champions have graced this world, Bubka is remembered for his consistent pattern of breaking his own records in nearly every major event he competed in. His journey exemplifies the making of the greatest champion. We saw a similar narrative in an Indian athlete during the Tokyo 2020 Paralympics. This athlete possesses elegance, strength, agility, and immense power. Known as "The Tiger" among his friends, he is Sumit Antil.

"Oh wow! ... Oh man! This boy is India's answer to Sergey Bubka," shouted one of my sports-crazy friends when he was

watching the historic performance of India's Sumit Antil at the Tokyo 2020 Paralympic Games.

"Sergey Bubka! Come on, he's an once-in-a-lifetime athlete. How can you compare someone with the Ukrainian legend?" countered one of the seasoned journalists watching the event alongside him. "Bubka from the undivided USSR broke the world record for men's pole vault 35 times during his career. To be likened to an athlete of Bubka's stature, one has to have a spectacular career. Sumit Antil has just started," he said.

After a brief pause, he added, "But what an incredible performance! I can't recall any Indian athlete dominating in such a manner at such a big stage. He has miles to go before he reaches there, but Sumit Antil has given us a glimpse of Sergey Bubka, and this speaks volumes about him."

The date, 30 August 2021, holds a special place in the history of Indian para sports. It was the day when Sumit Antil was on a record-breaking spree. On his way to winning the gold medal, he shattered his own records multiple times. But, before making his mark on this truly special day, Sumit had his share of personal battles all along.

Sumit Antil was born in Khera village in Sonepat district of Haryana. His father, Ram Kumar, was a Junior Warrant Officer in the Indian Air Force. He passed away after battling cancer when Sumit was just seven years old. His mother, Nirmala Devi, and his three elder sisters took great care of him, doing their utmost to ensure that Sumit never felt the absence of his father. He began to grow up like any other child in the area.

Like many youngsters from the region, Sumit fell in love with wrestling. Haryana, sandwiched between Delhi and the border state of Punjab, has produced numerous international players and Olympians, owing to its rich wrestling culture. Amidst this backdrop, sports, particularly wrestling, became Sumit's first love. When Sushil Kumar won the bronze medal in the Beijing 2008 Olympics, Sumit became more passionate about the sport. This is how one champion inspires many others to follow the sport seriously and aspire to become champions in the future.

Sumit began training with local *pehelwans* (wrestlers), and adopted their dietary habits and workout regimes to build a strong physique like them. In 2012, another popular Indian wrestler, Yogeshwar Dutt, became his role model. Yogeshwar, a freestyle wrestler, won the bronze medal in the 60 kg category at the London 2012 Summer Olympics—a moment witnessed by millions of Indians. Yogeshwar's journey to the podium, marked by decisive victories against all odds, is still etched in the memories of those who were witness to the event that day. This bout had a deep impact on 14-year-old Sumit, prompting him to fervently follow Yogeshwar and his wrestling style.

Even though Sumit had managed to strike a perfect balance between his studies and wrestling, an unfortunate accident on 5 January 2015 changed his life forever. In January, north India experiences extreme winter weather and dense fog. Sumit was 17 years old then and was returning home one evening. "I was riding pillion on my friend's motorcycle after returning from tuition," he recalls. "Suddenly, a tractor hit us from behind, causing our bike to slip on the road. The tractor driver failed to apply the brakes in time, and it ran over my left leg. Everything happened in a matter of seconds. People rushed to the accident site. When some of them helped me to the side and tried to make me stand, I realised that I couldn't even feel my leg. I was in terrible pain. As I cried out, they took me home in one of the vehicles," he added.

"Initially, my family assumed it was a simple bone fracture. But, the X-ray report disclosed that my bone had broken into small pieces and there was no chance that it could be reconstructed. There was gloom and silence in the entire house," Sumit recollects with tears in his eyes. As his father was a former Air Force employee, Sumit was admitted to the Air Force Hospital, where the doctors had no choice but to amputate his leg below the knee. Just as his life seemed to be taking flight, it was forced into an emergency landing.

Sumit's mother, Nirmala Devi, was totally heartbroken and fell into complete silence for days. "I still can't bear to recall those days. We had barely begun to cope with the loss of his father when my son lost his leg. In our society at that time, it seemed preferable for one to die rather than become disabled," said Nirmala Devi. "Just imagine a young, handsome, well-built boy, who wanted to excel in wrestling, suddenly losing his leg forever. He was in shock, feeling as though his entire life had come to an end. As a mother, I felt lost, unsure of how to help him through those initial days. But soon I realised that I couldn't stay like this. I made efforts to lift his spirits, continually motivating him. I showed him pictures of individuals with disabilities who had succeeded in their lives. I shared inspiring stories of those who had excelled against all odds. It wasn't easy for me; I had lost all hopes in my own life. Yet, as a mother, I couldn't think of giving up on my son, who had his whole life ahead of him," Nirmala Devi recounted.

"After the accident, the first thought that struck me, *how can I pursue my dream of becoming a wrestler now that I've lost my leg?* I couldn't even imagine my life without wrestling, and now I had to accept this as a fait accompli. I spent 53 days in the hospital, and throughout that period, my mother never left my side. She kept on motivating me. I can't even begin to explain the struggles she went through. She is a brave woman. She lost her husband when I was barely seven years old. I lost my leg when I was 17 years old, and I can't even fathom the mental turmoil she has gone through. She was all alone in this fight. It was a struggle to come to terms with the reality, made even harder by the insensitive comments from some friends and relatives, who saw my situation as hopeless. But amidst the darkness, my mother and I found solace in each other's company. Our bond grew stronger. She lifted me up when I felt low, and when she seemed on the verge of collapse, I reassured her, promising to start running again soon," says Sumit. Despite the gloom that surrounded them, the unique bond between the mother and the son was the only silver lining.

Nirmala Devi and her son Sumit embarked on a journey of progress, taking one step at a time. After 53 days, Sumit was shifted to the artificial limb centre in Pune, where he got a prosthetic leg. This enabled him to stand on his own feet again after undergoing rehabilitation. While Nirmala Devi was coping with this, she also had to take care of her three daughters, Kiran, Sushila and Renu. Life presents a multitude of obstacles, yet when crisis arises, the challenges often push us forward rather than holding us back. Perhaps, this happened with Nirmala Devi as well.

Meanwhile, Sumit began taking baby steps towards reclaiming an active life. "After getting the prosthetic limb, I visited the stadium. I yearned to resume wrestling. After all, it was my first love. However, due to the limited movement of my knees, I felt crippled. I realised that I will not be able to do wrestling again. It shattered me. I cried continuously," he says.

One of life's truths is that when it seems like everything is coming to an end, a new beginning is just around the corner. This new start must begin from within, and soon, you'll find people who become part of your renewed journey. Sumit experienced this firsthand. Supported by his mother, he took the initial leap, soon joined by his friend Mohit. Over time, Mohit became an integral part of Sumit's odyssey. Sumit reflects, "Mohit is my childhood friend. We were classmates, and when he learnt about my accident, he quit his job as a merchant navy officer to stand by my side. He pledged his support to help me pursue my dreams and passions. Mohit became my pillar, lifting me up when I faltered. During exhaustive practice sessions, he became both my physiotherapist and masseur. Not once did he feel ashamed that he was pressing my legs and hands. When I realised that I could go no further in wrestling, I turned to javelin throwing, a decision Mohit wholeheartedly supported. During training sessions, as I threw the javelin, he retrieved it again and again, never showing irritation. His smile spurred me on to refine my technique. Many others would have become irritated in his place, but he would urge me with a grin, "Throw it again, and this time, with perfect technique".

With the blessings of his mother and the support of friends like Mohit, Sumit started focusing on the positives in his life. Determined to cast aside negativity, he embraced a fresh perspective. What were these positives he began to recognise? First, he found solace in his rural upbringing, where sports were not just a pastime but a way of life deeply rooted in the culture. His village had produced many national and international sportspersons who could guide and mentor him. It was during this phase that he first heard about the world of para sports. Rajkumar, a fellow villager and once a notable para athlete, was now an accomplished coach.

Sumit had completed his senior secondary education and was studying in the prestigious Ramjas College of Delhi University. "Delhi's atmosphere was quite different. People around me here were more understanding and accepting. Moreover, I used to wear loose trousers and because of this, many did not even realise that I don't have one leg. As I moved to Delhi, the biggest challenge I faced was the arduous daily commute between Sonepat and Delhi on the state transport buses. It was very painful. Initially, I felt totally drained out. But I had no other option. This toughened me physically and mentally," says Sumit.

Secondly, during this period, Sumit came in contact with Virendra Dhankar, who happened to be one of his relatives. Virendra was a decorated athlete who had established himself in para sports. He had participated in the Rio 2016 Paralympics and had won many international medals, including a silver medal in shot put at the 2018 Para Asian Games.

"The moment I saw Sumit, I knew he had great potential. With his early training in wrestling, his upper body strength was remarkable. If he could choose a sport that could fully utilise all his abilities, he could do wonders," says Virendra. At that time, Virendra was training under Naval Singh, a Dronacharya Awardee coach known for his rigorous training methods and exceptional coaching skills. Virendra introduced Sumit to Naval Singh at Delhi's Jawaharlal Nehru Stadium, which proved to be a major turning point in Sumit's journey.

"When I first saw Sumit, I recognised his immense potential. He had a very innocent face but his eyes conveyed a strong determination. Standing tall at 6 feet 2 inches, he had a strong physique, particularly in his upper body. After our initial interactions, I straightaway knew that my role had to be two-fold: on the field, I had to train him in a new sport, and off the field, I had to make him emotionally stronger. But today when I look back, I take pride in Sumit's dedication as a student. He wholeheartedly embraced my coaching methods. Most importantly, he never shied away from hard work. When I asked him to practise something 20 times, he would do it 25 times, showcasing his unmatched drive for excellence. In this sense, he is exceptional," says coach Naval Singh.

When Sumit came for the trials, his coach gave him the options of discus throw, javelin and shot put. Ultimately, it was javelin that captured Sumit's interest. "When I first held a javelin, I assumed these sticks couldn't cost more than Rs 700– 800. But, I was shocked to learn that the one I held was worth around Rs 1.5 lakh. I initially thought that they were joking and poking fun at me. However, when I discovered the truth in their words, it came as a complete shock and disbelief to me. At first, javelin throwing looked simple—just throw the stick as far as possible. But as I got deeper into the sport, I discovered its complexity, technicality, and challenges. But by then, I was already immersed in the sport, and from that point on, there was no turning back," recalls Sumit.

When Sumit began his training, his throws initially reached an average distance of around 35 metres. His primary obstacle was his prosthetic leg. The artificial leg he used for both practice and everyday walking was a plastic model unsuitable for high-endurance training. Naval Singh explains, "A high-end prosthetic leg could cost us nearly Rs 4 to 5 lakh, but we had no means. It was then sports journalist Mahavir Rawat did a story on young Sumit, highlighting his dire need for a good prosthetic leg. Once the story got aired, a Germany-based company, Ottobock, came forward to help. They gave Sumit a specialised prosthetic leg tailored for javelin throwing, and he never looked back from there."

After addressing this fundamental problem, Sumit began to push himself to the limit, ensuring every step he took counted. His days started at the early hour of 3 a.m., followed by relentless hard work throughout. Initially, his body rebelled, but gradually it adapted to the pain. He embraced the adage "No gain without pain". Soon, his efforts bore fruit. With the combination of hard work, great practice ethics, focused coaching and suitable prosthetics, Sumit started honing his skills and picked up the required speed. He started making an impact at the international level. His confidence surged after reaching the fourth position at the Paris Handisport Grand Prix in 2018 and finishing fifth at the 2018 Asian Para Games at Jakarta. He won a silver medal at the World Athletics Championship in Dubai in 2019, followed by silver medals at the 2019 Paris Open Handisport and 2019 World Para Athletic Grand Prix. By the time Tokyo 2020 Games approached, Sumit had elevated his abilities to a level where a podium finish was inevitable; the only uncertainty was the colour of the medal.

In the lead-up to the Tokyo 2020 Games, Sumit had honed another trait: consistently surpassing his own records and setting new benchmarks. The stage was thus set for this specific trait to be showcased at its fullest during the Tokyo Games.

"When Sumit started his javelin career, Sandeep Chaudhary, another student of mine, dominated the category. I set a goal for Sumit to reach Sandeep's level. In almost every tournament where Sandeep got the gold medal, Sumit used to get the silver medal. As a coach, it was great to see both of my players doing so well. But deep inside, I had a strong belief that Sumit could achieve even more. I somehow felt that he wasn't fully tapping into his aggression during competition," recalls Naval Singh. He adds, "Together, we addressed this aspect of his personality. The results were astounding. In the 2019 Italy World Para Athletics Grand Prix, he shattered the world record in F64 category. This was followed by another record-breaking throw at the World Para Athletics Championships in Dubai later that year. As the Tokyo Paralympics drew closer, one question occupied my mind—*what heights could he reach there?*"

As Sumit was gearing up for the Tokyo 2020 Paralympics, the world was struck by the COVID-19 pandemic, impacting every facet of life including sports. Another aspect of life is that even in the biggest of the tragedies, there is a positive side to it. The lockdown imposed due to COVID-19 provided an opportunity for many to cherish quality time with their loved ones. Sumit chose to spend this period in his village with his mother. During this time, he became aware of his mother's declining health, a fact previously unknown to him. After a thorough medical examination, it was revealed that she was suffering from a heart-related condition, leading to breathlessness and frequent fatigue. Despite her health issues, she chose not to burden Sumit with her concerns, prioritising his preparation for Tokyo 2020 and his overall journey in sports.

Since his father's passing, Sumit's mother had been his pillar of strength. When he met with a devastating accident and it appeared to be the end of the road for him, she became his constant companion on the road to recovery. He couldn't bear to see her wither away like this. So, Sumit decided to spend more time with her. As he devoted himself to caring for his ailing mother, his rigorous practice sessions and preparations naturally took a backseat. Due to COVID-19 and fresh developments in his family, he practised in Sonepat while his coach Naval Singh was based in Delhi.

The COVID-19 phase was a tough time for athletes, especially those training without the direct support and guidance of their coaches. Sumit faced these challenges head-on. For instance, if the technique diverged in the wrong direction while practising, there was no coach available to detect this deviation early and initiate corrective measures. This also posed a risk of faulty technique becoming ingrained as a habit, thereby affecting the athlete's performance. Naval Singh observes, "I wouldn't say that Sumit's technique was faltering, but I sensed that something wasn't quite right with his throws." Unfortunately, things took a turn for the worse when Sumit suffered a back injury. Although he was in excellent physical condition, the back pain limited his ability to cover the distances he was capable of.

During the Tokyo Para Games qualification trials, Sumit was still recovering from the injury. Despite this, he managed a throw of around 62 metres, securing his qualification for Tokyo. But he trailed significantly behind Sandeep Chaudhary, who touched the distance of around 66 metres, setting an unofficial world record. Sandeep, who had stood fourth at the Rio 2016 Para Games, was determined to grab the gold in the Tokyo 2020 Games. During the build-up to the event, there was a healthy competition between Sandeep and Sumit, both standout protégés of the coach Naval Singh.

As the games drew near, Sumit started to pull ahead of Sandeep. Dealing with a back injury, Sumit opted to train alone, unwilling to leave his ailing mother under any circumstances. So, a compromise was worked out: Coach Naval Singh would travel twice a week to Sonepat, which is around 100 km from Delhi, to personally monitor Sumit's training sessions. On other days, Sumit would concentrate on weight training and core muscle-building exercises. This arrangement continued for two months, yielding encouraging results. Sumit was back to his peak fitness, with his throws matching the levels achieved prior to the injury.

As India's largest-ever Paralympic contingent geared up to depart for Tokyo, the nation celebrated the culmination of its most successful Olympics campaign to date. Neeraj Chopra emerged as India's greatest sporting hero after winning the country's first-ever gold in athletics with a monumental javelin throw of 87.58 metres, forever ingraining himself in the hearts of sports lovers across the country. Neeraj's achievement served as a catalyst, inspiring many young people to take up the sport. Perhaps, this was the chosen moment for Sumit to contribute to the fervour and popularity of athletics. "I had met Neeraj Chopra and trained with him in Europe for a few days. We were aware that he was an exceptional athlete, yet we never imagined he would eventually rise to become one of the greatest legends in Indian sports history. His triumph also made it clear to many of us that, for the majority of our countrymen, the only significant medal was the one earned at the Olympics or Paralympics. I realised that such a medal had the power to transform an athlete's life forever. I was thus determined to go out and give my best possible shot," says Sumit.

Unlike the Olympics, where India got its first athletics medal more than seven decades after gaining Independence, the country has seen commendable performances in the Paralympics in the past. In the 2004 Games, Devendra Jhajharia made history by winning a gold medal in javelin throw. In the London 2012 Games, Girish N. Gowda won a silver medal in high jump. This was followed by a record haul of 4 athletics medals in the Rio 2016 Games, including two golds, one silver and one bronze.

Certainly, India has had its share of remarkable moments in Paralympic athletics. However, 30 August 2021 surpassed all those previous milestones. This was the day scheduled for the F64 category javelin throw event at the Tokyo 2020 Games. Sandeep Chaudhary was the clear favourite to bring the gold medal, given his exceptional form and peak fitness. He also held the world record of 66.18 metres. "I was definitely restless the night before, but beyond a point, I stopped thinking on it. I spent time talking to my friends and family over the phone. My mother and coach wished me luck. I was confident about myself. Despite still recovering from an injury and not achieving a great qualification result, I was determined to give my best shot. During the warm-up, my body felt excellent. It seemed like all the hard work put in by both me and my coach had aligned perfectly when it mattered the most," says Sumit, remembering the night leading to the truly special day.

When the event's start list was announced, Sumit found himself as the first athlete to throw the javelin among the 10 contenders. Sandeep, on the other hand, was at number five in the line-up. Beginning first carries both advantages and disadvantages. On the one hand, it offers a fresh start, devoid of any pressure from the performance of the previous athlete. On the other hand, it means being unaware of the javelin's response to the conditions. But, what followed with Sumit gripping the javelin left many spellbound. What Sumit displayed there was one of the most commanding performances by an Indian athlete to date. He repeatedly shattered the world record in a stunning debut at the Games. In the span of six throws, the Haryana boy beat his own previous world record of 62.88 metres three times! His sequence of throws read as 66.95, 68.08, 65.27, 66.71, 68.55 and a foul. His first throw of 66.95 metres not only beat his previous best of 62.88 metres but also the previous world record. His second throw of 68.08 metres broke the world record for the second time in the day. While his third and fourth throws of 65.27 and 66.71 metres may seem comparatively modest in terms of his scoring sequence that day, on any other occasion, they might have also broken the world records in the F64 category.

Sumit's fifth attempt, reaching 68.55 metres, set up the world record for the third time that day, clearly surpassing his own world record five times on his way to securing the gold medal. Australia's Michal Burian won the silver with his best throw of 66.29 metres, while Sri Lanka's Dulan Kodithuwakku claimed the bronze medal with his best attempt of 65.61 metres. This was an Indian making history with authority on the grandest global sporting stage. While many in the sports fraternity were stunned with his performance, Sumit exhibited exemplary self-belief. In conversation with a few close friends after the event, he said that had he not been injured, he believed he would have crossed the 70- metre mark.

"It feels great. In every tournament, I aim to give my best and set new benchmark in para sports. I had hoped to cross the 70-metre mark, but it did not happen, and that's okay. I'm happy to have broken my record three times on my way to winning gold. During the qualification, till the last month, I was injured. But I worked very hard, and it eventually paid off. This being my first Paralympics, I was a bit nervous. All the competitors were great. I was hoping for 70-metre-plus throw, maybe even 75. It was not my best," Sumit shared with journalists immediately after his "Sergey Bubka moment".

Sumit's performance was one of the most commanding ever by an Indian athlete on the global stage, yet he remained unsatisfied. By channelling this discontent and hunger, he has the potential to elevate his performance with each high-level competition. And if he can maintain this consistency, the rising India may well see its own "*swadeshi* version" of Sergey Bubka, inspiring generations of athletes to strive for greatness in every significant outing.

As Sumit Antil's journey of becoming one of the greatest athletes of our times unfolds, our endeavour to document the progress of Indian Paralympic sports also continues. In the chapter ahead, we will talk about the "Pocket Rocket" Krishna Nagar.

KRISHNA NAGAR

Pocket Rocket

"Satsaiya ke dohre jyo naavik ke teer,
Dekhan mein chote lage ghaav kare ghambir."

—Bihari Lal Chaubey

The above *doha* or couplet, roughly translated into English, means, "Like the arrow of a sailor, it may appear small in size but causes severe injury." This couplet, by Bihari Lal Chaubey, who hailed from Govindpur near Gwalior and spent his boyhood in Orchhaa, Madhya Pradesh, fits perfectly with the life and achievements of Krishna Nagar, affectionately known among his friends as 'Pocket Rocket'. Just as the arrow in the couplet, he may look smaller in size, yet he has set his sights high and achieved big in life.

"I used to grow without really growing up," Krishna Nagar chuckles heartily. Hearing such words during his school days would have hurt the champion para badminton player from Jaipur. But he has come a long way since then. Krishna Nagar won the gold medal at the Tokyo 2020 Paralympics in the category of people with short stature. His life is now a living lesson on how to turn one's disability into super-ability.

On 12 January 1999, Sunil Nagar and Indra Nagar welcomed a baby boy into their family in Jaipur. They named him Krishna.

The Nagar family had a daughter earlier, so they felt blessed to now have a son in their arms, completing their family just like many others in the region. For the first two years, everything seemed normal with Krishna Nagar. Then, something caught their attention, and the script changed completely.

"He was as innocent and loving as any other baby of his age. There was nothing abnormal with his body, mind or behaviour that would raise any suspicion in us. It was only when he turned two years old that some elders of the family noticed Krishna wasn't growing as tall as other children. When others observed this abnormality in his height, we decided to seek some medical help," says his father, Sunil Nagar.

After many medical tests, scans and assessments, it was discovered that Krishna suffered from growth hormone deficiency in the pituitary gland, leading to dwarfism. This revelation came as a big shock to the Nagar family, as there was no history of dwarfism in their lineage. Sunil Nagar, though not very tall himself at 5 feet 5 inches, had dreams of joining the Indian Army. However, his height fell just below the average Indian height, making it a deterrent. Sunil had taken this in his stride and started working as a fitness trainer. However, he was completely heartbroken when doctors told him of his son Krishna's growth impairment.

"We were truly shocked! For a couple of days, we couldn't believe what the doctors were telling us. Throughout our lives, we had assumed that dwarfism occurred only if one of the parents was a dwarf. This diagnosis seemed to come out of nowhere, completely out of our control. We couldn't confide in anyone, worried about how people would react. Moreover, we were deeply concerned about our child's future, knowing how insensitive society can be towards people with disabilities," says Sunil.

As is often the case in such situations, the family gradually began to open up and share their struggles. They received advice on various treatment options and visited numerous hospitals and yoga centres. They consulted traditional doctors and explored different medications, including allopathy, homeopathy and Ayurveda. Unfortunately, none of these efforts yielded favourable results or had any significant impact. Some doctors recommended surgery, but the family learnt that the success rate of such surgeries was very low and that there were considerable risks of side effects. After careful consideration and consultations, the family took a firm decision. They opted against surgery and instead chose to accept their child as he was.

Sunil was an accomplished athlete who competed in a variety of sports, including taekwondo, judo, baseball, and softball. His background as a sportsperson and fitness trainer proved to be a blessing in this situation. Sunil introduced Krishna to sports at an early age, which ultimately turned out to be a game changer. "We stopped all medication and treatment for Krishna and accepted our fate. I believed that by involving him in sports, he could unlock his potential. We didn't know how tall he would grow, so, we didn't focus on training him for any specific sport initially. Our priority was to ensure he engaged in some physical activities regularly. His mother consistently encouraged him, unconcerned with others' opinions," Sunil says. "I also held onto the belief that his active involvement in sports might alleviate his dwarfism, envisioning a day when my son would lead a normal life," he adds, his eyes gleaming.

Those suffering from dwarfism often suffer from huge

mental stress during their developmental stages. Unlike their peers, they have to constantly confront societal perceptions, which affect their personality and emotional growth. One consequence is that many in their age group start avoiding them, leading to negative self-esteem and a gradual withdrawal from social interaction as they feel isolated and marginalised. While attempting to integrate into the community, they often experience discrimination, which profoundly affects their psychological and emotional well-being. They are bullied by others and this hurts them deep inside.

Krishna, who was shorter in height, often found himself compared to other kids in his circle and sometimes subjected to bullying. As parents, it's our duty to instil empathy in our children for those facing similar challenges. Despite facing hurtful experiences in his childhood, Krishna quickly bounced back and refused to allow negative thoughts consume him. Reflecting on those times, he remarks, "In some ways, I was just like any other kid, but in other ways, I stood out. Fortunately, I had some amazing friends who never let me feel different. Honestly, I never felt that there was something wrong with me. All my body parts were intact—I had a functioning brain, I studied, I played. I was simply one foot smaller than average, and that's it."

Following in his father's footsteps, Krishna began to excel in various sports as he progressed through life. Encouragement from his parents fuelled his passion further. Despite his stature, he proved himself to be a very good sprinter and an adept volleyball player, making his mark as a strong defender. His athleticism compensated for his height, and he often outshone his peers in school sports. However, as Krishna transitioned from childhood to adolescence, the taunts and comments from others began to weigh heavily on him.

Reflecting on this period, he recalled, "Classmates and people in general had various names for me, some of them quite hurtful. It made me feel depressed and frustrated. I didn't seek any special treatment; I simply wanted to be treated equally. So, I started avoiding public gatherings and unfamiliar faces. I had my set of friends with whom I used to feel comfortable and at ease. My family was my biggest comfort zone and it included my uncle and aunty, apart from my parents." Recognising the impact this had on Krishna, his father effectively utilised sports to pull him from the situation.

Krishna's father, being a sportsperson and accomplished physical trainer, devised various fitness techniques for his son. He dug a pit near their house, where Krishna honed his skills in high jump and long jump, leveraging his sprinting prowess to excel in the latter. The fact that Krishna was a very good sprinter helped in his long jump. While Krishna initially explored cricket with enthusiasm, his height posed challenges in gripping the bat and ball effectively, hindering his performance. Recognising that his height was a major hindrance in various sports, he made the transition to badminton, where he felt confident in his ability to compete with and surpass his opponents. Moreover, the skills acquired from previous athletic endeavours proved to be handy when he played badminton. His movement on the badminton court was quick, benefiting from his background as a proficient sprinter. His jump and stay in the air, referred to as 'hang time' in basketball, was also excellent. Thus, badminton became his sport of choice where he could truly shine!

"In my journey through various sports, badminton emerged my favourite. I began playing badminton around 2015-2016, when I was 16 years old. Although I had been developing my athletic abilities for quite some time, it was badminton that I felt I had a level playing field with other competitors. Back then, I wasn't even aware of para badminton or any separate category where I could compete based on my height. I was simply driven by my love for sports, and a desire to excel in badminton," recalls Krishna. Eager to refine his skills, he joined a local badminton training academy at Sawai Man Singh Stadium in Jaipur, where he immersed himself in learning the basic nuances alongside fellow athletes.

Krishna honed his skills in the game by competing against able-bodied people. Excelling at district-level tournaments, he began representing his school at the national level. It was during one of these tournaments that he heard about para badminton, and that there were categories tailored to players with various disabilities. In early 2018, Krishna competed in his first para national tournament and won a gold medal in the SH6 category, designated for people with abnormal height. It was here that he caught the attention of Gaurav Khanna.

Gaurav Khanna had dedicated himself to para badminton and gained a reputation as one of the top coaches in the field. "When I first saw him, I was really impressed with his raw physical abilities. He was very agile on the court, with lightning-fast reflexes. His ability to jump and hang in the air was exceptional. However, what he lacked was a professional setup and a structured training regimen typical of professional athletes. Obviously, it was not his fault; he was simply following the guidance he had received from his coaches," says Gaurav Khanna, remembering his first impression about Krishna Nagar.

"When able-bodied players compete in badminton, they perceive the court as standard. But, for SH6 players—those with short height—the court looks more like a tennis court. Also, what seems like a standard net to most of us appears much higher for them, akin to volleyball net. Since their height is short, everything appears taller and wider to them," Khanna explains the problems faced by SH6 players.

After years of coaching para badminton players, Khanna has developed his own customised practice sessions tailored to each player's category and competitive level, drawing on his extensive expertise and exposure in the field. Under the guidance of Khanna, Krishna's perspective on the game underwent a profound transformation. In addition to hours of intensive training, he adopted a thoroughly professional approach. It was during this training period with Khanna that Krishna had the opportunity to meet Pramod Bhagat, a distinguished veteran in para badminton, revered across nation like a deity by players.

"Pramod *bhaiya* is a legend," reflects Krishna. "I've never met a more humble and helpful person in my life. His face always radiates with a smile, and his presence exudes positivity. Not only for me, but if you ask any para badminton player in the circuit today, Pramod *bhaiya* is a family, a mentor, a coach, and a companion, all wrapped into one. On the court, he is my favourite player," he adds.

Under the mentorship of Khanna, Krishna's immense talent began yielding rapid results. Within just a year of entering the professional circuit, he qualified for the 2018 Para Asian Games, marking his debut in a major tournament. Despite losing in the semi-finals, he clinched a bronze medal in this prestigious event.

After the Para Asian Games, the announcement that badminton would debut in the upcoming Tokyo Paralympics sparked excitement among players worldwide. It was a monumental opportunity for the para badminton players to be part of the biggest sporting event on the planet and contend for

Paralympic medals. To qualify for the Tokyo 2020 Paralympics, one of the criteria was to rank within the top 6 in their respective categories. To meet this requirement, players had to actively compete in numerous tournaments.

Krishna had a prolific year in 2019, competing in all major tournaments and consistently finishing in the top four in his category. He clinched bronze in singles and silver in doubles, teaming up with Raja Magotra. As the countdown to the Tokyo Paralympics began, Krishna's world ranking rose to number 2, guaranteeing his participation in the games. However, Khanna was concerned about one thing: Krishna's tendency to falter in the semi-finals of major events, seemingly succumbing to pressure at crucial junctures. Khanna diligently addressed this mental hurdle in their training regimen leading up to the event. While Krishna and Khanna were putting in significant effort, the entire world came to a standstill due to the COVID-19 pandemic. Para badminton players were more anxious than athletes in other sports because their discipline was set to debut in the Paralympics. Furthermore, the looming possibility of the games being cancelled altogether due to the pandemic only added to their concerns.

"I won't say it was a tough time just for me. Like everyone else, I too spent a lot of time at home with my family. My elder sister and my younger brother were also there. It was actually nice at first, since we hadn't spent that much time together in ages. However, it soon became a repetitive cycle of eating, sleeping and passing time. For days, we found ourselves stuck in this routine. The badminton courts were closed for nearly six months, so besides basic stretching exercises, there wasn't much we could do at home," says Krishna, talking about the lockdown period in Jaipur.

When the lockdown eased for players representing their country at the international level, Krishna rushed to the nearby badminton court. He began with the basics that he has been practising for so many years.

"Seven of our players had qualified for the Paralympic Games. We stayed in touch regularly," says Khanna. "There were exercises one could do within the confines of one's home. It was crucial not to completely shut down for such a long period of time," he adds.

In January, the seven players reunited and began training together. However, the COVID-19 protocols made the situation tougher for them. Their residences were regularly sanitised, and they were advised to minimise contact outside their bubble. These players could not train with others and could only enter the court after thorough sanitisation. Finally, the countdown to their competitions started.

"Over the past six months, we poured all our efforts into our training regimen. We used to train in the morning, have lunch, rest for some time and get back to training. This was our daily schedule. Initially, we dedicated six hours a day to training, gradually increasing to nearly 10 hours daily as our departure date drew nearer. We ensured that we were exposed to various training conditions to excel in any scenario. We focused more on the mental approach required at various phases of the play. For me, it was more about increasing positivity. I had a mental barrier regarding the semi-finals, but I was determined to overcome it," says Krishna.

Badminton was one of the concluding events of the Tokyo Games. By the time the matches began, several gold medallists from our country, such as Sumit Antil, Manish Narwal and

Avani Lekhara, had already returned to India due to stringent COVID-19 protocols.

In Krishna's category, there were a total of six players, divided into two groups of three players each. Jack Shepherd from Great Britain held the top seed, while Krishna was second-seeded and placed in Group B. Krishna faced a tough battle in the league stage, winning his match against Malaysia's Didin Taresoh with scores of 22-20, 21-10. In his next match against Brazil's Vitor Tavares, he won with a margin of 21-17 and 21-14. Krishna was now in the semi-finals. His opponent was Krysten Coombs of Great Britain, who had defeated his top-seeded countryman, Jack Shepherd, in the league encounters.

"Personally, I feel that semi-finals of any tournament are tougher than the finals. Also, I had a bad history of losing in big semi-finals. But this time, I was determined. Actually, my semi-final match was scheduled on 4 September, but all the attention was on Pramod (Bhagat) *bhaiya*. He had his gold medal match, and people were talking about his match and his preparation. Even the media was more focused on him. This turned out to be a blessing in disguise for me. It helped me to stay calm and relaxed mentally," says Krishna, recalling the hours leading up to the famous semi-final match.

Krishna went for the match with all guns blazing. He thrashed his opponent in little over half an hour, with a margin of 21-10 and 21-11.

"What can I say? Anyone who saw that match was in awe of Krishna. Everything just fell into place. His movement, reflexes, jumps, smashes and game sense—everything was top class. I guess when people watched his game back home, they became his fans. He has a pacy game with impressive jumps and smashes, which look very good on TV. I remember on the same day Pramod won his gold and we were all emotional about his achievement. But everyone also knew that Krishna Nagar had reached the finals and he was a hot favourite," says Khanna.

The Tokyo Para Games concluded on 5 September 2021. By this time, the excitement surrounding para badminton had peaked. Pramod had won a gold medal, L. Y. Suhas claimed a silver and Manoj Sarkar grabbed a bronze. India had already won 18 medals by then, an unprecedented achievement. The entire country awaited the final match eagerly. Having overcome the demons of the semi-finals, Krishna was considered the favourite against Hong Kong's Chu Man-kai. Chu Man-kai had won the gold medal in the 2018 Asian Games, where Krishna had to remain content with a bronze medal.

Krishna won the first game 21-17. However, in the second game, he faltered and suffered defeat with a score of 21-16. Spectators watching the game were dismayed by his unforced errors. It appeared that Krishna became overconfident after his first-game victory, leading to overly aggressive play and a rush to conclude the match prematurely. But, in the third game, Krishna came back stronger and finished the match with a score of 21-17. This was India's fifth gold medal at the Tokyo Para Games. Among the seven para badminton players representing India, four proudly adorned medals around their necks.

"I just went blank. I didn't know what I did after that. I was just jumping on whomsoever I met. It was such a relief. It was such a big achievement," shares Krishna, reflecting on his victory. "Then there was the medal ceremony where the Indian flag ascended, and our National Anthem was played. I had tears in my eyes," he adds.

Krishna further revealed that Prime Minister Narendra Modi had personally called to express his admiration for his performance. "It was like a dream come true," said Krishna while talking to reporters after his famous victory.

Coincidentally, 5th September is celebrated in India as Teacher's Day. And on this auspicious day, Krishna paid his biggest tribute to his coach by winning the gold medal. Upon their return to India, Krishna and all medal winners received an astounding welcome. Subsequently, rewards and awards poured in. Krishna was bestowed with the Major Dhyan Chand Khel Ratna Award, the nation's highest sporting accolade.

As Krishna and his family were having the best of times, an unforeseen turn of events occurred. They were eagerly waiting for 13 November 2021, the day Krishna was set to receive the award. On 10 November, Krishna was in Jaipur finalising his travel arrangements to Delhi. He was supposed to be in Delhi by 11th November, along with other award recipients. Rehearsals for the award ceremony were scheduled for 12 November, with the ceremony itself set for 13 November.

As Krishna prepared to leave for Delhi on 10 November, his mother had prepared a meal for everyone. His father had also returned home early from work by 12.30 p.m. "My mother and father were supposed to accompany me to the award ceremony, and we were getting ready to leave for Delhi together," Krishna recalls. "They have been my pillars of strength right from my childhood. We enjoyed lunch together, reminiscing and laughing about old times. We packed our things and prepared for our Delhi departure. I had just finished bathing and was putting my towel in the sun to dry when I heard a loud thud from top of the house," he adds.

Krishna rushed down to find that his mom had fallen from the terrace to the first floor. "She was in real pain. We hurried her to the hospital, where the doctors admitted her to the ICU," recalls Krishna with tears in his eyes.

The doctors and family members informed Krishna late in the evening that his mother was showing signs of improvement. They urged him to proceed to Delhi to collect his Khel Ratna award, knowing it was what his mother would have wanted. Krishna, in a state of shock, reluctantly complied. With a heavy heart, he arrived in Delhi and took part in the rehearsal. However, later that evening, Krishna's mother, Indra Nagar, succumbed to her injuries and passed away. The family was devastated. On the one hand, Krishna was about to receive the greatest award of his life, while on the other, he had lost his strongest support system who had played a vital role in his achievement. The family didn't know how to break the news to Krishna. They turned to Pramod Bhagat, the only person they believed could handle the situation.

Pramod recalls, "At midnight, I got a call from Krishna's uncle informing me about his mother's death. I was shocked! They gave me the responsibility to break the news to Krishna, who is like a younger brother to me. My mind went numb. I understood that once I instructed him to leave the function and head home, he would know the reason. So, I approached him, wrapped my arm around his shoulders, and simply told him to leave for Jaipur. Neither of us exchanged more words. I had also called my parents for the award ceremony, but upon receiving the news, none of us were in the mood to celebrate. How could we?"

Before the awards were presented, a two-minute silence was observed at the Rashtrapati Bhavan to pay homage to Krishna's mother.

"She struggled hard for everything. On the surface, it was my father taking charge, but my mother was the true source of strength. She instilled in me all the virtues and taught me never to feel ashamed of myself. Only God knows how she managed to run the house during crunch financial situations. I had so many plans for her. However, everything seemed futile and devoid of meaning after her death," Krishna recounts, his voice choked with emotion.

It took Krishna quite a long time to overcome this personal loss. Yet, it was his mother's spirit that eventually motivated him to return to the badminton court. Now, he aspires to excel in the sport for her. He competed in the nationals and won 3 gold medals. "My height is small, but it was my mother's wish to see the flag of *Bharat Maa* soar high. I am determined to make her proud and bring more laurels to my motherland," asserts Krishna.

Krishna Nagar, although short in height, has sky-high determination.

Some players excel in their sport, while others are looked upon as mentors even during their active participation. Coming up next in this book is the story of Pramod Bhagat, a revered figure in para sports who has earned the respect of many as a senior statesman.

PRAMOD BHAGAT

The Silent Leader

*"Become the kind of person that people would follow,
even if you don't have the title of the leader.
Because if you do and enough people follow you,
then soon enough the title will come."*

—**Brian Tracy**, *Canadian-American motivational speaker
and author*

If one is seeking a living example for this popular quote by Brian Tracy, look no further than Pramod Bhagat. While he may not hold a formal leadership title per se, Pramod is a leader for many athletes, regardless of their abilities. To some, he is a friend, philosopher, mentor, and guide, all rolled into one. We caught a glimpse of his leadership prowess in the previous chapter and his pivotal role in Krishna Nagar's life during crucial moments. As we go through this chapter, we can visualise a full-fledged film of his leadership qualities unravelling before us.

Pramod Bhagat's life, according to his mother, Malti Devi, resembles many aspects of Lord Shri Krishna's life. Like many Indian women, Malti Devi holds a deep reverence for the deity, passionately recounting parallels between her son's life and that of Lord Krishna.

Pramod was born in a small village in Hajipur in the Vaishali district of Bihar, as the fourth of six children to Rama Bhagat and Malti Devi. Rama Bhagat, a small-scale farmer, lived in Bihar, one of India's least developed states, where life for many small farmers was a constant struggle to make ends meet. At the tender age of four, Pramod was struck with polio. The entire family felt hopeless and clueless, as if the daily struggles in their lives were not already enough! They were unsure of what to do and how to react.

"One morning, Pramod woke up with high fever. His entire body was trembling. It was a convulsion that we initially thought was due to an extremely high fever. But as his condition deteriorated, we took him to a doctor. It was only then we came to know that Pramod has been infected with the poliovirus, and that his life would not be like that of other children," remembers Pramod's mother Malti Devi.

The doctor strapped Pramod's hands and legs before sending him home. They advised his parents that while there was no cure for polio, proper treatment could aid in his recovery and limit the impact of the disease. Disheartened, the family returned home. Poverty can be one of life's greatest challenges, and when compounded by disability, it can lead to a lifetime of misery. As word spread about Pramod's disability and poor health in the family, Rama Bhagat's sister, Kusum Devi, arrived to offer assistance to her grieving brother. Kusum Devi was married to Kailash Bhagat and lived in Attabira in the Bargarh district of Odisha. Compared to others in the family, Kusum was slightly better off financially. Kailash Bhagat worked in rice mills, and was able to fulfil the basic needs of the family. Yet, the couple had a different problem in their life.

Kusum Devi and Kailash had been married for years without having a child, while her younger brother Rama had four children at that time, with Pramod being the youngest. Kusum Devi offered to take Pramod with her and care for him as her own child. At first, Pramod's mother was reluctant to part with her four-year-old child due to his polio condition. However, influenced by her husband's persistence and her concern for her child's well-being, she eventually agreed to send her child with Kusum Devi and Kailash. Both families realised the potential benefits of this arrangement, especially for Pramod. Kusum and Kailash raised Pramod as their own son, and he began to look at them as his parents, referring to them as "*Maa-Papa*"—the words were music to their ears. Despite his weak and thin left leg, Pramod did not fully grasp his disability until others began to remind him of it. From a young age, there was something special about Pramod. He was the centre of attraction wherever he went. Right from childhood, he never really bothered about what others said or felt about him. He was a bright kid and excelled in studies and extra-curricular activities. He displayed enthusiasm and passion in whatever he did. He had a cheerful disposition, which led to him having a wide circle of friends. However, what truly excited him the most was participating in sports activities.

"At my home, studies were always the priority. The prevailing mindset was that since my upbringing would be challenging due to my polio, I should prioritise studying and aim for a government job to secure a comfortable future. Therefore, before going to play with the neighbourhood kids, I had to always ensure my schoolwork was completed. Maybe it was an extra responsibility on my parents to shape my career, hence they were more focused on my education," says Pramod.

Pramod participated in various sports like cricket and *gillee-danda* (a popular game in rural India), both in his locality and school. But he was never considered a force in any of the sport, as his disability somehow affected his performance. When Pramod was 13 years old, he saw a badminton match for the first time at a district tournament and instantly fell in love with the sport. "Two players were involved in an intense match that held the audience spellbound. It was then that I realised badminton was the perfect sport for me, despite my disability. The game emphasised footwork and movement on the court. From that moment, I decided to focus all my energies into excelling in badminton," recalls Pramod.

"I had neither heard nor read about para sports in my life. When I picked up the badminton racquet for the first time, it was purely for enjoyment, not with the intention of pursuing it professionally. Yet, it was in badminton where I found myself on a par with everyone, and where my disability wasn't any hindrance," says Pramod, remembering his first badminton match.

However, badminton, an indoor game, requires a shuttle and racket to play with. At that time, indoor wooden courts were rare in the country. Pramod lived in Odisha's remote area of Attabira, where mud courts were the norm. "I requested Papa to buy me a badminton racket. I got a cheap one, but I was over the moon. Then, along with some of my friends, I cleaned a nearby field and marked lines on it with chalk powder to create a makeshift badminton court. Since we had rice mills around our area, we used to tie a rope on two sticks and hang rice sacks on it to give it a feel of the net. When you are a kid, these things hardly matter. But the flip side was that the shuttle would not last even one hour. The cheapest ones cost us Rs 10 each. Even if we all contributed to buy them, it was still an expensive game," says Pramod with a smile.

It was around this time that Pramod caught the eye of Shiba Prasad Das, an employee at the National Aluminium Company (NALCO). Shiba, popularly known as SP, was a local badminton coach who trained kids lacking resources. Impressed by Pramod's attitude towards the game and life in general, SP immediately took him under his wings. The child had an aura which made him distinct and special. "He definitely had a spark in him. He was a natural player on the court. His movements, anticipation and game sense were that of a champion. He was very committed and sincere from his early days. The best thing about him was that even after giving his 100% on the court, he would forget the results and reset with fresh vigour. There was always a smile on his face, even when things didn't go his way," says SP about his most famous student.

Pramod retains this trait to this day. No one has ever seen him lose his composure, whether during practice or in a match. It is as if the man keeps an ice-pack on his head. When asked about it, he credits his serene disposition to his hero and idol Sachin Tendulkar, widely regarded as one of the greatest cricketers the country has ever produced.

"I learnt this quality from Sachin Tendulkar. When we were growing up, there was no bigger sporting star in the country than Sachin. I vividly recall numerous instances where he found himself at the receiving end of poor or incorrect umpiring decisions. In an era where there was no DRS (Decision Review System), replays often exposed the errors made by the umpires. Yet, Sachin's response was always exemplary. Instead of reacting, he would simply glance upwards and gracefully make his way back to the dressing room He was aware that millions of children watched him, followed him and tried to mimic him. Sachin didn't want to let any child pick up any bad habits by observing him. Sachin's ability to maintain his composure in such tough or unfair situations sets him apart from his peers," explains Pramod about his favourite sporting idol.

Pramod first began playing on the mud courts, where his legs often got stuck, disrupting his concentration. He had to focus hard, afresh. Transitioning to cement courts posed new challenges due to the shape of his polio-affected leg, increasing the risk of slips and injuries. Yet, his passion remained steadfast, undeterred by setbacks. After dedicating himself to badminton, Pramod emerged victorious in the very first tournament that he took part in. This boosted his confidence. His prowess quickly gained recognition, both at school and district levels. As he delved further into the sport and ascended the ladder of success, it necessitated more practice hours and increased time spent on the badminton court. This meant early arrivals and late departures from the badminton court. This was not acceptable to his parents and they asked him to stop playing badminton.

"*Ye game hum logon ke liye nahin bana hai, chup chaap apndi padhai par dhyaan do aur ye bhoot apne dimag se utaar do* (this game isn't meant for people like us; focus quietly on your studies and rid your mind of this obsession)," his father would often admonish when Pramod returned home late. Eventually, the day arrived when Pramod was forbidden to play badminton. "There was a district tournament, and I was part of the school team. My papa denied permission, insisting sternly that I focus on my studies instead. My heart was broken and tears rolled down my eyes. I knew this time my father had really made up his mind," recalls Pramod. "I informed my teammates that I wouldn't be able to participate in the tournament and advised them to look for a replacement. When I returned home from school, my teammates had already gathered at my house, pleading desperately with my father to allow me to compete. My papa thought that I was the mastermind behind the entire drama. He smiled and reluctantly granted me permission. However, it was the other kids' heartfelt pleas that swayed him; he didn't want to break their hearts. He simply said, '*Iss baar chale jaao (Go this time)*'," says Pramod, his voice choking with emotion as he recounts the incident.

Pramod advanced to the finals of the tournament, an impressive feat for a ninth-grader competing against students much older than him. Though he lost in the finals, his agility and stamina garnered admiration from all, showcasing his determination despite his disability. Alongside the trophy, he received a prize money of Rs 2,000. "When I returned home with the trophy, Papa asked me if I had really won it! He wondered whether I played exceptionally well or if others simply performed worse," says Pramod with a hearty smile.

As time passed, Pramod discovered about para sports and para badminton. In 2005, he made the decision to pursue badminton professionally, dedicating his entire focus and efforts to the sport. However, the journey was not easy. After losing his father, Pramod had to take care of his family apart from focusing on his own game. Nonetheless, his mother, Kusum Devi, remained a pillar of support, encouraging him to prioritise his sport. When Pramod decided to pursue a professional career in the sport, international tournaments were scarce and very expensive to participate in. Additionally, awareness about para sports was limited. This lack of recognition was evident from the minimal discussion surrounding Devendra Jhajharia's gold medal win at the 2004 Athens Paralympics, both within the sports fraternity and in the media.

Pramod's challenge was far more difficult, as the sport of his choice, badminton, was not yet part of the Paralympics. Pramod began to dominate in national tournaments, but it wasn't until 2013 that he tasted success on the world stage. Alongside Manoj Sarkar, Pramod won the bronze medal in the 2013 Dortmund World Championships. The following year, he claimed another bronze medal at the Incheon Asian Games. His remarkable consistency in both national and international competitions set him apart.

As Pramod achieved these commendable successes at the international level, a noticeable shift began to unfold in the country's sporting ecosystem. What was particularly heartening was the inclusion of para sports in this transformation. With the stellar performances of athletes like Saina Nehwal and P.V. Sindhu in badminton at the highest levels, people across the country began to follow their footsteps. Many people with disabilities also took up badminton, and looked up to Pramod Bhagat as a hero. Pramod, in turn, lived up to these expectations. We can often see Pramod surrounded by young para badminton players who want to play like him and succeed like him. Pramod loves sharing insights and tips to help them refine their skills.

Despite belonging to the SL3 category, he willingly offers guidance to players irrespective of their disabilities. In a way, he has become a silent leader for many passionate followers of the sport. "During my first national tournament in 2013, everyone knew who Pramod Bhagat was. When I saw him, he was least worried about his match. Instead, he was busy talking to a player set to compete against him in the final match. That's the kind of person Pramod *bhaiya* is," says Sukant Kadam, an international para player who partners with Pramod in the doubles. In a cut-throat competition scenario of today's world, it's this rare quality that truly distinguishes Pramod from his peers.

"When I started playing, there was no one to guide me. I used to design my own shoes, go to the cobbler and have them stitched to fit my feet perfectly. I had no clue about pacing my game or what drills to focus on for my category. It was all trial and error. But I don't want new kids to go through the same hardships and waste precious time. That's why I'm determined to pass on as much knowledge as I can," says Pramod, the silent leader. Even today, if you attend any national tournament, you will find Pramod surrounded by large groups of young players. Those close to him affectionately call him *Daadi-ma*, meaning grandmother. They say he's like a grandmother, always ready with solutions for everyone's problems, be they professional or personal.

Meanwhile, the evolving ecosystem of the para sports across the globe also meant a new set of challenges for Pramod.

As para badminton gained global popularity, more tournaments and events were organised in various parts of the world. More tournaments also meant more practice sessions and a higher frequency of matches. As Pramod excelled in more tournaments, he found himself pushing harder to maintain his winning streak. This took a toll on his ankles, particularly his polio-affected leg, which began to weaken. Although the injury initially appeared in 2016, Pramod ignored it and continued to play, making his injury worse. "*Ye dard hi ham-dard hota hai khiladi ka*" (Pain is the only friend that an athlete has) was the catchline which Pramod would use in a quite filmy style, when reminded about the injury. Nonetheless, the injury eventually began to impact his performance and results. He didn't perform up to his reputation in both the World Championship and Asian Championship. Disappointed with his performances, he made a weird promise to himself.

Pramod says, "Dhoni had made a secret pact that if he won the 2011 World Cup, he'd shave his head. As a die-hard Dhoni fan, I vowed not to cut my hair until I won a big tournament. I didn't realise then that the next big tournament was the 2018 Asian Games at Jakarta. Over time, my hair grew long, and I had to tie a pony tail. My coach, unaware of my pledge, got angry and said that this was not football or tennis I was playing where I could flaunt my hairstyle. During that time, I met our Prime Minister Narendra Modi sir, and if you look closely at the pictures, you'll notice that I had long hair," says Pramod reflecting on the tough phase.

It wasn't until he won the gold medal at the 2018 Asian Games that Pramod finally cut his hair. By then, he had fully recovered from his injury. After this event, it was officially announced that badminton would debut in the Tokyo 2020 Paralympics, marking a historic moment for para badminton players. However, qualifying for the Paralympics required being in the top six in their respective categories. This meant playing more tournaments and winning crucial points leading up to the event.

In 2019, Pramod had a whirlwind of activity, as he competed in over 20 tournaments, both major and smaller ones. As he was juggling between singles, doubles, and mixed doubles, the load and wear and tear of the body was thrice when compared to the usual times. He won in nearly every tournament that he participated, and was the top-ranked player in the world. He was in a fine form in terms of fitness and raring to go. But then COVID-19 brought the world to a standstill.

"Now, when I look back, those days stand out as some of the finest moments I've spent with my family. For nearly 15 years, I was seldom there with them. They had learned to live without me, while I had built my own family within the badminton community. But this forced lockdown period brought us back together. My younger siblings had grown up, and my mother, advancing in age, became a comforting presence. I ate a lot of *aaloo ki bhujiyaa* and *bhindi ki bhujiyaa* which were my childhood favourites. In hindsight, I believe that period brought a sense of calmness in me. In a way, it prepared me to excel in the upcoming biggest event in my life," muses Pramod philosophically.

However, tragedy struck during the second wave of COVID-19 when Pramod's mother succumbed to the merciless virus. Looking back, Pramod feels that God wanted him to spend some quality time with her during the lockdown.

When some restrictions were relaxed for sportspersons, Pramod began going to the nearest badminton court and immediately got back his rhythm. Nearly three months before the games, the entire para badminton team made their base in Lucknow. During the camp, the Tokyo-bound players trained together under the watchful eyes of Chief Coach Gaurav Khanna. With seven badminton players in training, the chief coach had set a target of 5 medals, including 3 golds.

Going into the Paralympics, Pramod wasn't worried about his form. But he knew that participating in two different events would be taxing for his body. The match schedule was such that Pramod had to play two matches in a single day. In the singles event, Pramod was placed in group A along with India's Manoj Sarkar. He won both the matches in group stages and reached the semi-finals. In mixed doubles, Pramod Bhagat and Palak Kohli lost one of their group matches but still reached the semi-finals. After losing in the semi-finals, the pair played in the bronze medal match, which lasted almost an hour. Pramod was also scheduled to play in the singles final on the same day.

The moment had arrived. In the finals, Pramod was to face Daniel Bethell of Great Britain. For quite some time, these two players had been the best in the world, frequently competing against each other in important tournaments and being familiar with each other's game. "Daniel and I have played against each other so many times that we know each other's game very well. And when I saw the draw, I knew that we would be facing each other in the final. So even when I was playing against other opponents, I would be thinking about my strategy against Daniel. I was mentally prepared for the final match," says Pramod.

In the first game, both players exercised caution, opting for a safe strategy. It was a matter of who blinked first. Pramod held his nerve at crucial points and won the first game 21-14. But it was the second game that shocked everyone. No one could comprehend what happened between the two games. It seemed like Pramod had completely lost his touch. In no time, Daniel took a commanding 12-4 lead. It looked like it was a matter of time that he would run away with the game. Daniel wanted to push the match into a third game, knowing that Pramod, who had already played a mixed double match earlier, might be at a disadvantage.

"I didn't know what happened. Maybe I had already started thinking about victory. By the time I could regain my focus, he had taken a lead of 8 points over me. But I had made comebacks from far worse situations in my career. I was determined not to give him easy points. Gaurav Khanna Sir was keeping me motivated. He kept on saying, 'You can do it, just hang in there'," says Pramod about the final match. The strategy worked. As Pramod started to win points, Daniel lost his composure and started making unwitting errors. In a remarkable display of composure and determination, Pramod won the second game 21-17. The moment he won, he leaped onto Khanna. "I knew it was an emotional moment, but I had never imagined that Pramod would jump on me. That's not his usual way of celebrating. But I guess the moment was so intense that even Pramod couldn't control his emotions," says Khanna.

The entire group was elated. The triumph of the silent leader meant victory for each one of them. Celebrations and felicitations followed. But there was one meeting after his famous victory that will forever remain etched in his memory. "I always wanted to meet Sachin Tendulkar, but I wanted this meeting to happen only when I achieve something big. After this famous victory, when I met Sachin, he held my medal and said 'You have got something that I cannot even dream about'. I was so happy. It was such an emotional moment for me. The man I had admired and dreamt of meeting all through my life was saying this. It was so satisfying," says Pramod, recalling the day he met Sachin Tendulkar.

This was not just a fan boy meeting for Pramod Bhagat. This was a meeting of two legends. Both of them have traversed long paths in their careers. Sachin might not have been the captain of the team for a greater part in the later stages of his career, but every captain of the team considered him the leader and sought his advice. Likewise, Pramod Bhagat is the undeclared leader of the para badminton fraternity. One can always see *Daadi ma* talking to youngsters and teaching them the tricks of the game.

Name, fame, money and leadership—Pramod Bhagat dedicates everything to his parents, Kusum Devi and Kailash Bhagat. He believes that, akin to the boundless love Yashoda and Nanda showered upon Lord Krishna, he too was raised by Kusum Devi and Kailash Bhagat. "Forget the medals; I dedicate my entire life to them," he asserts. His mother, Malati Devi, sees shades of Lord Krishna in him.

As we move ahead in our journey in this book, we go through the life and achievements of yet another extraordinary athlete and champion—the emerging shooting star, Manish Narwal.

MANISH NARWAL

The Rising Shooting Star

"Yeh Dil Maange More" (This Heart Desires More)

—Pepsi slogan (1998)

This popular slogan, first released as a tagline for the beverage brand Pepsi in 1998, had already taken the nation by storm. It took a new meaning a year later when the martyred braveheart "Shershah" Captain Vikram Batra adopted these lines as his war cry during the 1999 Kargil War. The iconic slogan is the brainchild of Anuja Chauhan and was the adaptation of the "Ask for More" commercial for Pepsi. The adaptation became more popular than the original, as the latter was asking for more of a drink, while the former was more about wanting more from life.

The slogan reverberated once again on 7 September 2021, when Manish Narwal, the rising shooting star, declared, "I want to win at least five Paralympic medals for my country; *yeh dil maange more.*" This came after the 19-year-old had just smashed the Paralympic record to win a gold medal in his debut outing in the Tokyo 2020 Paralympics. This chapter tells the story of Manish Narwal's *"yeh dil maange more"*.

At just eight years old, Manish Narwal excelled as a runner, followed by football at the age of 10 and wrestling at 12. Finally,

at the age of 15, Manish found his true passion in shooting. His life serves as a powerful lesson about how nothing can come in your path if you passionately love sports.

From birth, Manish faced the challenges of a congenital disorder, which resulted in underdeveloped functionality in his right hand. Congenital anomalies, also known as birth defects, include structural or functional defects that occur during intrauterine life. Manish's parents learnt about this condition only months after his birth. They felt heartbroken. However, Manish's disability did not come in the way of his pursuit of excellence in sports.

"The entire family was delighted. The birth of the first child, a son, in our Haryanvi society is a matter of great pride and happiness. But months after his birth, his mother noticed that though Manish looked very normal, movement in his right hand was very limited. After a number of tests and clinical inspections, it was found that Manish suffered from a rare disability. His right hand was not fully functional due to dysfunction in the nerves. There was nothing we could do. The entire mood in our home was dampened after getting this news. No one knew how to deal with the situation. We tried all possible systems of medicines—allopathic, homeopathic, and others, but they were ineffective. Finally, we had to accept the situation and reconcile to the fact that the disease is incurable," says Dilbagh Singh Narwal, father of Manish Narwal.

When did Manish realise that he was different from others? Manish was then in his seventh standard. The kids around him started pointing towards his weak right hand. While some of them were curious, others began making fun of him. One day, Manish returned home crying from school. It was another day of listening to comments from classmates about his weaker right hand. He could not bear it anymore. He wanted to get his hand cured at any cost.

So, Manish's father took him to their family doctor and got all the tests done again. After going through the reports, the doctor said, "We are ready for the surgery, but there is a risk involved. Either your hand will regain all its strength or it will lose all mobility forever. Also, when we operate on the nerves, there are chances of some more organs being affected after the surgery."

Now, the ball was in the court of the Narwals. They had to decide whether they were ready for the risk or happy with what they had. Most importantly, Manish realised the seriousness of the surgery and hugged his parents for all their struggle and support. The entire exercise had one important implication: Manish came to terms with the harsh reality and decided to move on from there.

The house of Narwal family was situated near a playground where people used to come and exercise. This ground became a favourite spot for youngsters who trained there in hopes of joining the army. Manish was a big sports lover, and particularly enjoyed outdoor activities.

"Initially, I used to run alongside the young army aspirants and participate in physical exercises. I started liking it, and my parents were delighted to see my dedication," recalls Manish. They knew that if I will be physically strong, the impact of my weak hand will be lesser in my life. Despite being the youngest among them, Manish devoted nearly three hours every morning to various physical exercises.

Apart from running regularly, Manish also played football. Since his legs were normal, he could keep up with other kids in the game. He admired Lionel Messi and tried to emulate the dribbling and juggling skills of the Argentinian legend. Manish's father, Dilbagh Singh, was a respected wrestler at the regional level. Wrestling is the most popular sport in the state of Haryana. Manish, too, tried his hands at wrestling but, somehow, things did not click for him.

During this journey of exploring various sports such as running, football, badminton, and wrestling, Dilbagh Singh was captivated by Manish's passion and saw a future for him in the field of sports. Around this time, someone advised Dilbagh Singh to consider introducing Manish to para shooting, particularly the pistol discipline. Since shooting with just one hand was feasible, para shooting emerged as a promising option for Manish to excel in para sports.

The father and son shared a unique bond, built on absolute trust. When Dilbagh told his son, "*kal se tum shooting karogay aur ab isee khel mein poora focus lagaana hai* (from tomorrow, you shall start shooting and dedicate your full focus on this game)," it became a command that Manish wholeheartedly embraced. Dilbagh was highly protective of Manish, not even allowing him to ride his bike to the shooting range. Instead, a relative would pick Manish from his house and drop him back after the practice.

"I still remember the date. It was 15 January 2016 when I stepped into a shooting range for the first time. Prior to that, I had only seen outdoor shooting ranges that were 50 metres in length. So, I went in with the perception of a huge outdoor area where we would be taught shooting. But, to my surprise, it turned out to be a small indoor shooting range with minimal light. The only light was focussed on the shooter and the target," reminisces Manish.

But the lack of light wasn't his only issue. For 15 years, Manish had lived as a free spirit, playing physically demanding outdoor sports. All of a sudden, he found himself confined to a narrow 15-metre room with no equipment to practice with. So, did Manish adapt to shooting effortlessly, like a fish to water? No, absolutely not.

"I felt trapped. There were nearly 20 young shooters, but the range had only three pistols, which were reserved for the seniors. There were no dummy pistols available for practice at that time. We were given bricks to train with. The coach instructed us on how to stand and how to set our eyes on the target. Instead of using a dummy pistol, we each held a brick and were told to treat it as a pistol. For the first few days, I practised for about two to three hours daily. I used to pick up a brick, take aim at the target, and then put the brick down. It was only after five days that the seniors allowed me to hold a pistol and taught me how to aim properly. I continued this routine for 15 days," recounts Manish.

However, there was another interesting aspect to this journey. The more Manish was pushed towards shooting, the more he found himself drawn to other games. He often left shooting classes early to spend the rest of the evening playing football with his friends. This diversion from shooting initially fell short of his father's expectations for his progress.

"One day, Rakesh Sir, the head coach of the shooting academy, approached me to assess my progress and asked me to shoot at a target card. My shots were scattered all over the place. It was the first time my month-old shooting practice was put to test, and I failed miserably, in front of a large gathering. I felt terrible," shares Manish. This incident weighed heavily on Manish, and more than for himself, he felt disappointed for his father, who had supported him against all odds. Determined to improve, Manish decided to give his all in the practice sessions.

He reminisces, "After 10 days, the coach once again asked me to shoot at a target card. This time, my shots showed a good grouping. He then made me fire at another card, and again I performed well. He repeated the exercise, and that day, I hit the mark consistently. I am sure the coach saw something in me that day, which made him trust me. I, too, started to believe in myself. A month later, there was an internal tournament at the academy, where the top eight shooters were to compete. I don't know what was going through my coach's mind, but he urged me to participate. Surprisingly, I defeated the shooters who had trained for years and stood second in the tournament."

This proved to be a turning point in Manish's career. He was now convinced of his potential in the sport. He realised that if he could defeat seasoned shooters without giving his hundred percent, then the sky would be the limit for him, especially if he devoted his mind, body, and soul to the sport.

But then, there was one technical problem: all the shooters in the academy were right-handed, and so the three pistols available were designed for right-hand shooters. Manish, on the other hand, was left-handed, and there was no separate pistol available for him. For the next seven to eight months, he had to practice with pistols that were not tailored to his needs. Despite this challenge, his results in the competitions were very encouraging. By now, Dilbagh Singh was convinced that his son could be a champion in a sport. However, shooting is an expensive game. The costs of ammunition, target cards, coaching fees, range fees, and tournament fees among others make the sport prohibitive for many. Shooting, thus, is largely considered an elitist sport.

MANISH NARWAL

Dilbagh Singh was a skilled wrestler and kabaddi player. However, due to heart ailments and lack of family support, he could not pursue his dream of becoming a famous sportsman. He, however, understood what it takes to be a champion. Money was always scarce. Manish was the eldest in the family, with a younger brother and sister whose education needed to be taken care of. Additionally, Dilbagh Singh had to take care of his ageing parents. His business was also struggling, and mere survival was becoming difficult. Despite these obstacles, Dilbagh knew that it was a now-or-never moment for Manish. Somehow, Dilbagh Singh managed to buy a left-handed pistol for Manish, which cost him Rs 1,30,000, a significant sum for the family.

"I asked my mother where father got so much money from, but she remained silent on the matter. Later, I came to know that he had borrowed it from some friends and lenders at a very high rate of interest. Today, there are schemes like Target Olympics Podium Scheme (TOPS) and Khelo India, but at that time, there was no support from anyone," shares Manish. However, this episode inspired Manish to leave no stone unturned and carve a niche for himself in the sport. With the pistol came results too.

Manish rose to prominence when he won a gold medal at the 2017 World Shooting Para Sport World Cup. It was his debut on the international stage, where he grabbed gold in Men's P1 10m Air Pistol SH1 category. The following year, he bagged a silver medal at the 2018 World Shooting Para Sport World Cup, held at Al Ain, achieving a score of 234.6. The gold medal in this event was won by Chinese shooter Xiaolong Lou. Later in 2018, at the Asian Games, Manish added another gold medal to his name in Men's 10m Air Pistol SH1 category and a silver medal in the P1–Mixed 50m Free Pistol SH1 event.

Notably, he also broke the previous junior world record during the championship, thus securing his spot in the Indian Team for the Tokyo 2020 Paralympics.

In 2019, Manish continued his winning streak by securing a gold medal in the P1, P4, and P6 team events, along with a silver medal in the individual P1 category at the World Cup in Croatia. After this, he bagged two bronze medals at the 2019 World Para Shooting Championship in Sydney, in the Men's 10m Air Pistol SH1 and Mixed 50m Pistol SH1 events. He achieved all these feats while he was still a teenager.

In 2020, Manish's remarkable achievements were recognised by the Government of India, and he was honoured with the prestigious Arjuna Award. However, just things seemed to be progressing smoothly, there was yet another change in the script.

In 2020, Manish returned from the World Championships with three bronze medals, yet he appeared a mere shadow of his former self. He was unwell throughout the tournament but refrained from taking any medication. With the Tokyo Paralympic Games approaching, he dreaded the possibility of inadvertently consuming a drug as part of medication that could lead to a violation of anti-doping regulations. Manish had maintained a clean record in this regard all his life and was determined not to jeopardise his chances of participating in the Tokyo Games.

His father grew increasingly worried about his declining health. Instead of taking any allopathic medicines, Manish turned to homemade soups and *desi* treatments. After three months, his weight plummeted from 68 kg to 58 kg. This prompted his father and him to seek the advice of a specialist doctor before things got out of hand. The doctor's diagnosis was alarming! "You can only play if you're alive. You have Tuberculosis (TB). You need six months of medication to fully recover," the doctor said after examining Manish.

The news shook the entire Narwal family. With the Tokyo Games looming, they feared that the Paralympic dream they had nurtured and for which Manish had worked so hard might soon be shattered. Throughout the treatment, Manish lost an additional 6 kg, bringing his weight down to 52 kg. Reflecting on this ordeal, Manish recalls, "I remember that harrowing period. It was a struggle to even lift a leg, forget walking or running. I had lost 16 kg and looked like a skeleton. I was prepared for the worst. Yet, with care, support, and medication, I recovered from TB."

However, overcoming TB did not mark the end of Manish's ordeal. He was infected with the deadly COVID-19 virus. Fortunately, he experienced only mild symptoms. However, the virus subsequently struck Dilbagh Singh, whose condition deteriorated day by day. He had to be admitted to the intensive care unit for nearly a week before he showed signs of recovery. After a month of care and medication, Manish's father finally returned home. Just as things seemed to be getting back on track, Manish's maternal grandmother (*naani*) got infected with COVID-19, with her oxygen level continuously dipping. Despite the family's utmost care and efforts to get the best medication, she succumbed to the virus. Facing one disease after another, the family found themselves grappling with significant financial constraints. When so much was happening around the family, Manish's focus on shooting took a backseat. He had given up hope of excelling in the Tokyo Games due to inadequate preparation.

By then, the games got postponed, breaking the hearts of hundreds of athletes who had meticulously planned their preparations around the year 2020. However, for Manish, it came as a relief. It provided him with the much-needed breather and time to mentally recover from a challenging period and start fresh preparations for the games. Even though he had 14 world records to his name, the journey felt like starting from scratch. Beginning training wasn't easy, as most stadiums or shooting ranges remained closed due to strict protocols. Thanks to the consistent perseverance of the chief shooting coach, Jai Prakash Nautiyal, camps were organised with the support of the Sports Authority of India.

Eventually, Manish arrived in Tokyo with hope. Although he had qualified for two events—50m pistol and 10m pistol events—it was the latter where he believed he stood the best chance. Manish had dominated this category on the world stage in the years leading up to the Paralympics.

The competition had started on a positive note for the Indian shooting contingent, with Avani Lekhara setting the tempo. All eyes were now on Manish. As the 10m air pistol event began, expectations were high in the air. Manish emerged as the top performer in the qualification stage and the hype around his medal started getting louder. But what followed was both shocking and unbelievable for many. Manish sums it all when he says, "I just allowed the pressure to overpower me. I started doubting my abilities, with numerous voices echoing in my head, and I struggled to control my breathing. It being my first Paralympic Games, there was a lot of pressure. I started losing confidence in my practice and technique, and ultimately, I just faltered. I got eliminated at the seventh position. Throughout my month-long training, my lowest score still exceeded the score that won the gold medal by three points. I couldn't even match my lowest practice scores. I just lost it."

Although Manish did not reach the top three, his friend and training partner, Singhraj Adhana, secured a bronze medal. Manish was happy for Singhraj as India didn't return empty-handed. However, he was utterly disappointed with himself for missing out on the opportunity.

"Everyone around me was trying to console me. Even some IPC officials who had witnessed my journey in shooting for years came to offer advice, urging me to let go of the disappointment. But deep inside, I was broken. Years of hard work, averaging nearly 12 hours of daily training, seemed futile. I was hurting inside but tears refused to fall. As it started raining outside, I decided to be alone. I walked outside in the rain. One volunteer even offered me an umbrella, but I declined. It was only when I ventured out in the rain that tears began to flow. I cried uncontrollably. After 10 minutes, I returned to the team bus. I was drenched in rain, but I didn't change anything. I remained silent and uninterested in conversation with anyone. Quietly, I made my way back to the hotel," Manish recalls, reflecting on the moment.

For the next two days, Manish was like a body without a soul. He didn't speak to anyone and found no solace in words of comfort from coaches or teammates. Lost in thought for hours in the bathroom, he believed everything was over. Later, it was the words of the legendary Devendra Jhajharia that eventually stirred him from this despair.

"I was sitting on the floor when Devendra *bhai sahab* passed by me. He knew that I was a talented shooter. He said to me, '*Bhai, tere paas to ek aur mauka hai, humare paas to ek hi event hai. Isliye jo ho gaya usse bhool jaao, aur aane waale event par dhyaan lagao. Main to apne event ke liye 12 saal baitha raha, tera agla event to 2 din baad mein hai'* (Brother, you have one more opportunity, I have only one event. So, forget whatever has happened and focus on the coming event. I had to wait for my event for 12 long years, your event is only two days from now)'," Manish recalls.

Devendra's words shook him deep inside. He realised that not everything was lost. He still had a chance with the 50m pistol event. Though it was not his favourite event, there was still one more opportunity. On the same day, while Manish was trying to regroup for the next challenge, a female pistol shooter offered to accompany them in their tour of the Games Village. Initially, Manish refused the offer. Then she said, "It's ok not to win. Don't put so much pressure on yourself. Only 1% of athletes return with medals, but the Olympics spirit is much more than winning." This further positively impacted Manish. He accompanied other members on the tour of the Games Village, returned from there, and got a nice haircut.

"When I came back, everyone was pleasantly surprised. The common expression was, 'You look different'. I had shed all my negative thoughts and simply wanted to enjoy my remaining time in Tokyo. I had made a firm decision: I wouldn't achieve anything by just lying down in my hotel room. Instead, I resolved to give my best in the upcoming event and not worry about the result," Manish says.

On the day of the event, Manish was in a far better mental state. He had decided to enjoy shooting and have faith in the process and techniques that had yielded results in the past. Everything was falling into place. Manish was in his own league and his own zone. "I didn't check the standings; I was just enjoying every round. I just looked up at the board and found myself leading. The thought of winning the medal didn't even cross my mind. I was determined not to repeat past mistakes; I just wanted to trust the process," he says.

In the finals, two Indian shooters were pitted against each other for silver and gold. Singhraj, who had already won a bronze in the 10m pistol, found himself facing off against his friend Manish. But Manish was in a different zone that day. It was one of those rare occasions when the pistol didn't feel like a foreign element but seemed to be the extension of his body. With his last shot, Manish won the gold while Singhraj settled for silver. It marked a historic moment for the country, with two Indian shooters claiming the top positions in the event.

"As the national flag rose and our anthem echoed, tears of joy and pride filled my eyes. That day, I didn't just win a gold medal; I also learnt an important life lesson. Everything in life reflects the choices we make, and those choices should always reflect our hopes, not our fears," reflects Manish. "One gold medal won't satisfy me. I aim to compete in at least 4-5 Paralympic events, and I am confident I will return with a medal in each edition," asserts Manish.

If "*Yeh dil maange more*" is Manish Narwal's life mantra, then our next hero, Nishad Kumar, is a man with a fighter's heart. While this book recounts the stories of exceptional fighters, Nishad's journey highlights how even the most profound helplessness can be transformed into a powerful weapon for conquering life's toughest challenges.

NISHAD KUMAR

A Fighter's Heart

*"Fighters feel helpless. They have been victims,
and they start victimizing others and then themselves,
and real fighters learn to use it, to harness that aggression."*

—**Sam Sheridan** *in his famous book*
*A Fighter's Heart: One Man's Journey through
the World of Fighting*

Nishad Kumar aspired to join the army, but an injury dashed his dreams of becoming the fighter he had always wanted to be. Feeling helpless and victimized by his circumstances, he withdrew into isolation, unable to see a future beyond military service. He avoided interactions with friends, relatives and well-wishers. However, it was from this place of despair that the true fighter in him learnt to channel his frustration into a powerful drive. Today, Nishad stands as a Paralympic Champion.

"I deeply admire M.S. Dhoni. His leadership, calmness, foresight, and ability to be cool in any situation are truly remarkable," says Nishad. Hailing from a small village in the Una district in Himachal Pradesh, Nishad Kumar brought these qualities of Dhoni, India's most successful cricket captain, to the fore to jump to record books. He won the silver medal

at the Tokyo 2020 Paralympics, setting an Asian record with a jump of 2.06 metres. Nishad's life took a remarkable turn following his "Jump of Glory" at the Tokyo 2020 Games. Before this iconic leap, his life was like so many other sports lovers in India, living a simple life in his village. Though praised for his passion for sports, he often received advice to prioritise his studies.

Nishad's family had limited financial resources. His father worked as a *raj-mistry* (chief mason) and struggled to make ends meet. "My village was a typical Indian village with little to boast about," reminisces Nishad. "I was tall and good in sports, particularly kho-kho and kabaddi. Other children in our area often sought me out for their teams as I was much fitter and better in these games," he says.

"I never imagined taking sports seriously, let alone considering it as a profession; it was all about enjoying games with other kids," Nishad explains. "In our region, the allure of the Indian Army is strong. Many aspire to join for a stable and secure life. So, training rigorously for army selections became a routine," he adds.

It felt only natural for him to join the army, given that his *mama* (maternal uncle) and *nana* (maternal grandfather) were already serving. Even today, his two best friends, serving in the army, playfully remind him about achieving their childhood dreams. Nishad grew up in this environment, cherishing an ambition to wear the army uniform one day. He had an instinct of a fighter within him. But one incident would forever change the course of his life.

"I vividly recall that day. It was a summer afternoon, and I was playing with other kids when a *khiloney-waala* (toy seller) entered our village, carrying clay toys. We all swarmed around him, eager to touch and see his toys. I was perhaps the most mischievous among us. In an attempt to shoo me away, the toy seller falsely claimed that my mother was searching for me and was furious that I was roaming about. Terrified of strict and disciplinarian mother, I hurried home, thinking she must have seen us irritating the toy seller, and so she was angry.

"When I reached my home, I found her busy cutting fodder grass for the animals using an electronic grass cutting machine called *tokka*. When she saw me, she said that though she was not looking for me, now that I was there, I should help her with grass cutting. As we talked, I accidently placed my hand on the machine, and she unknowingly switched it on. In an instant, my wrist was totally cut, and blood began to flow. My father, a contractual labourer involved in railway work, rushed to our aid and took me to the nearby army hospital on a bicycle, as it was the only available means. Everyone around me was crying. Though I was in deep pain, I just kept asking the doctors '*Mein army mein bharti to ho jaoanga na*' (Will I get selected in army now?)," recounts Nishad, his recollection as vivid as if it had happened only yesterday. This incident also highlights Nishad's focus and determination to pursue his dream of joining the army.

Initially, Nishad felt helpless and withdrew from social interactions, becoming somewhat of a recluse. "At first, I was uncomfortable with the pity some people showed me," he remarked. One of his close friends says, "Initially, he struggled to accept that his dream of joining the army was over. He stopped meeting people and felt despondent, especially because the constant reminders of the challenges ahead were distressing." However, after this brief phase, Nishad's outlook began to shift. "As I came to terms with my accident, I gradually returned to my former self and resumed interacting with others as I had before the incident. The only time I felt the absence of my wrist was when I rode a bicycle; the handle's contact with my injured hand caused pain. Yet, with time, even this discomfort subsided, and I grew used to it. Perhaps, being just 10 years old at the time, the incident failed to leave a lasting psychological impact on me. I continued to live as any other child would. My athletic performance never faltered; I remained the best sportsperson in my class. Since I didn't perceive my disability, it was not noticeable to others either," he reflects. Nishad was a true fighter, to the core.

During his early school days, Nishad excelled as a short-distance runner and high jumper. He loved high jump, but there was no coach or senior athlete to guide him further in that sport. Still, he chose high jump over all other sports. Recounting his decision, he shared, "I had absolutely no idea about the techniques or requirements of high jump. Yet, there was a strange pull towards it. When I competed at the school or district levels, I found immense joy in pushing myself higher and higher. I refused to let anyone come close to my achievements. There was a killer instinct in me whenever I used to do high jump. While in other sports, no matter how hard I tried to focus, I never felt the same drive to excel. So, I followed my heart's desire to jump, to leap higher with each attempt."

Nishad started using his frustration to practice hard and improve his performance. He poured his sweat and blood into perfecting his jumps. Gradually, he learnt to channel his frustrations to hone his skills and soar to greater heights.

In 2015, Nishad won a silver medal at the state championship. The following year, he was determined to change the colour of the medal. He represented his state in the National School Games, competing against other regular kids. Until then, Nishad had never heard about the Para Games for people with disabilities. He said, "I was competing at the state level. The previous year, I finished second. But this year, I had practised harder. I began practicing early in the morning, utilised the physical education period for additional practice, and continued training in the evening." His hard work bore fruit. He was successful in winning the gold medal that year.

During the state tournament in the Solan district of Himachal Pradesh, the spectators were captivated by Nishad's performance. Moved by his efforts, they spontaneously started contributing small amounts of Rs 50 or Rs 100 with each jump. By the end of the event, Nishad not only won the gold medal but also collected Rs 3,500 in appreciation from the crowd and other coaches. Nishad used this money to buy his first smartphone, gaining access to YouTube and a huge treasure trove of knowledge about the sport.

Nishad shared the benefits of accessing YouTube, remarking, "When I first gained access to YouTube, I primarily watched high jump techniques demonstrated by international athletes. I was amazed by the level of competition at the global stage. I also realised that if I trained myself differently, I could become a champion, as I had all the qualities needed to become one."

As Nishad delved deeper into the world of high jump, news broke that two Indian high jumpers had won medals at the Rio 2016 Paralympic Games. Mariyappan Thangavelu had jumped into the history books by winning a gold medal, while Varun Bhati won a bronze medal in the same category. Reflecting on this, Nishad stated, "When I watched their videos, I believed I could outperform them. Initially, I was unaware of the para world and its various classifications based on disability. But upon learning about my category, I realised the magnitude of the task ahead. The first step in this direction was to seek guidance from an experienced coach."

It was during this period that Nishad decided to clear his mind of distractions, committing himself fully to sports.

Nishad was never a bright student. He realised that sports was the only field where he could truly shine and excel. But, the absence of proper training facilities or a proficient high jump coach in his vicinity prompted him to make a significant decision—to relocate to Chandigarh. "My *maasi* (mother's sister) lives in Chandigarh. I reached out to her and requested if she could help me find a competent high jump coach," he recalls. "*Maasi's* daughter used to play tennis, and upon discussing my situation with her coach, they identified two promising trainers, Naseem sir and Vikram sir. Both coaches were affiliated with the training centre in Patiala, situated near Chandigarh," he adds.

In June 2017, Nishad met his coaches for the first time. After initial introductions, they inquired about his ultimate goal. "A Paralympic medal," he promptly replied. However, Nishad's technique at the time was based solely on his natural instincts and was outdated. He employed the "scissors technique", locally known as *desi*, without being aware of the modern "Fosbury technique". The Fosbury flop is a jumping style used in the track and field sport of high jump. It was popularised and perfected by the American athlete Dick Fosbury, whose gold medal in the 1968 Summer Olympics in Mexico City brought this technique to attention. The flop became the dominant style of the event ever since then. Before Fosbury, elite jumpers used methods such as the straddle technique, the western roll, the eastern cut-off, or the scissors jump to clear the bar.

When Nishad arrived at the training centre, he was 194 cm tall and could jump 1.75 metres using the scissors technique. As it was June and vacation time, the coaches suggested that he join them at the Tau Devilal Stadium in Panchkula in September.

The tale of Nishad's arrival in Panchkula in September is quite captivating. With a chuckle, Nishad recounts the incident, saying, "When the coaches instructed me to arrive in September with all my belongings, I approached it like a refugee heading to a resettlement camp. I packed everything imaginable—my mattress, bedsheets, utensils, *masalas*, wheat, rice, and even a kerosene gas stove. When I reached the hostel with these items, both the coaches and seniors started laughing at me. I was packed up as if I was relocating to a deserted island. They told me to send everything back."

The initial hurdle for the coaches was to transition Nishad's jumping technique from "scissors" to "Fosbury flop". Despite having used the scissors technique all his life, Nishad showed no reluctance in leaving it. This showed another admirable trait in Nishad—his adaptability.

Nishad shares, "Mutaz Essa Barshim (the gold medallist in the Tokyo 2020 Olympic Games and silver medallist in the 2012 and 2016 Olympics) is my favourite high jumper. Ever since I got a smartphone, I had been watching his videos religiously. I aspired to jump like him. I knew that to even come close to his level, I had to change my technique. So, I placed my trust in my coaches and diligently followed their guidance. But it was not an easy walk. It took me nearly a year to master the Fosbury flop. It's very technical, and if one neglects practice even for a month, years of hard work can go waste."

After months of dedicated practice, Nishad participated in the 18th National Para Athletics Championship in Panchkula in 2018. He was still new to the Fosbury flop technique and unfamiliar with the competitive scene. It was here that he first saw Mariyappan Thangavelu and Coach Satyanarayana.

"I remember seeing Satya sir, and honestly, I was intimidated by him. I wanted to approach him but I felt hesitant to initiate a conversation. While warming up, I tried to talk to Mariyappan, but our communication was limited. Mari doesn't speak much, and we didn't share a common language; I could only speak Punjabi, which made it a bit challenging to connect." Nishad recalls.

There is a popular saying about Satyanarayana: "An eagle can for once miss its prey on the ground, but Satyanarayana' eyes never miss spotting a talented player in the field of para athletics." He is the cornerstone of the para athletics revolution unfolding in the country, known for his keen eye in identifying exceptional talent.

Upon observing Nishad for the first time, Satyanarayana immediately recognised the ingredients of a future champion. Nishad's physique—lean, with long legs and good height—coupled with the progress his coaches were making in honing his technique, convinced Satyanarayana of his potential. "I immediately began mapping out Nishad's future events, aiming to ensure he would be in peak condition for the Paralympics. I also had to focus on his mental preparation. In major events like the Paralympics, it's the mind that ultimately drives the body to achieve its best. Mentally preparing him for the grandest stage in the para world became a crucial aspect of our training regimen," says Satyanarayana, drawing on his seasoned coaching experience.

As everything was moving ahead according to plan, the world was struck by the onset of COVID-19. The Tokyo 2020 Paralympic Games were postponed, bringing all the planning and scheduling of the players to a halt. Adding to the adversity, Nishad got infected with the virus and was in complete isolation for nearly two weeks. However, it was during this challenging period that his coach, support staff, and family members rallied around him, ensuring his physical and mental readiness for the impending major event.

For six months, Nishad remained in Bengaluru, training under the vigilant guidance of Satyanarayana. When the games were finally rescheduled, there was a sigh of relief. "We had a very strong contingent of 54 players, with nearly 30 ranking in the top three within their respective categories. Our contingent comprised a blend of youthful talent and seasoned athletes, all eagerly anticipating the opportunity to shine on the grandest stage in sports. Moreover, perhaps for the first time, there was so much of buzz surrounding the event. We received a grand send-off, complete with a special theme song dedicated to the Paralympics—a first in its own right. Prime Minister Shri Narendra Modi even personally talked to select members of our contingent. Needless to say, we were ecstatic and pumped up," says Nishad. For the fighter in Nishad, the countdown for the final battle had begun.

Nishad recalls very little about the pre-event preparations. Although the Tokyo 2020 Games commenced on 24 August 2021, his event was scheduled for August 29. "I can't even recall the exact date when I won the medal," Nishad admits. "There was nothing particularly special about that day. Satya sir kept things relaxed, and we spent our time joking around in the room. Due to the strict COVID protocols, we were confined to our quarters. I remember arriving at the venue two hours prior to the event and warming up. I was in pretty good rhythm," he adds.

Nishad competed in the T46/47 category, reserved for athletes with a unilateral upper limb impairment resulting in varying degrees of function loss at the shoulder, elbow, and wrist. For some time, this category had been dominated by two American athletes: Roderick Townsend-Roberts and Dallas Wise. Roderick, in particular, is one of the greatest para jumpers in the sport's history. In the Rio 2016 Games, he had won gold medals in both high jump and long jump, a feat unmatched by any other athlete. Before competing in the high jump finals, Roderick had already won a silver medal in the long jump event. But on that particular day, he was in an altogether different zone.

Nishad Kumar began his event with a solid jump of 1.89 metres and never looked back. While Roderick seemed to be in a league of his own that day, competing against his own standards, Nishad found himself in a neck and neck battle with Dallas Wise. Nishad soared to a new Asian record with a 2.06-metre jump, a feat matched by Dallas Wise in his subsequent attempt. However, despite their best efforts, neither athlete could clear the 2.08-metre mark even after three tries. Meanwhile, Roderick had already surpassed this mark, setting a new world record at 2.15 metres. Despite several attempts, he couldn't improve upon it to reach 2.18 metres. Both Nishad Kumar of India and Dallas Wise of the USA were awarded silver medals, with no bronze awarded in the event.

"I could have done better. I thought I had something more left in me. Maybe it was destiny, but I am definitely going to aim higher in the next games," promises Nishad. The fighter in him has already set his next target.

Following his Paralympic silver medal win, life has changed for Nishad, marked by newfound wealth and recognition. Yet, when he returns to his village, he hardly steps out of the house. He has the same set of friends from his school days, some of whom serve in the Indian Army. Despite his achievements, Nishad still harbours a significant fear of disappointing his parents. "*Darta to mein abhi bhi bahut hoon. Ek din yahi darr to gold medal jitwaayega mujhe* (I am still scared of my mother and father. But it's this fear that will keep me grounded and ultimately propel me toward winning the gold medal one day)," he concludes.

Take on tasks that evoke fear in you, for the only way to overcome fear is by conquering it; victory lies beyond fear. In the next chapter, we honour the journey of another fighter, the grandson of a war veteran and a freedom fighter. His grandfather foresaw that despite his disabilities, his grandson would bring pride to the nation. Singhraj Adhana's life is a riveting narrative of how self-belief can triumph over adversity.

SINGHRAJ ADHANA

A Son India is Proud of

We see a person's disability with our eyes. But our interactions tell us that the person has extraordinary powers. Then I thought, in our country, instead of using the word viklang, we should use the word divyang. These are the people who have a limb or several limbs with divine powers, which we don't have.

**—Prime Minister Narendra Modi in his *Mann Ki Baat*
programme**

As we go through the narratives of the real heroes of this book, we come to understand the profound meaning and significance behind the sentiments articulated by Prime Minister Narendra Modi and the path-breaking decision of his government to replace the term *viklang*, which means a disabled person or one with a non-functioning body part, with *divyang*, symbolising someone with a divine body part.

When most people met Singhraj Adhana, our next real-life hero, they saw only his disability. They expressed sympathy and discouraged and demotivated him at every turn. "What could he possibly achieve in life with such a disability?" became the standard remark whenever he appeared. However, it was his grandfather who stood out as a man possessing a rare level of understanding and wisdom. A war veteran who had served in

both World Wars and played a significant role in India's freedom movement, Singhraj's grandfather recognised the promise and potential of his grandson, seeing divine strength in his limbs. Perhaps this conviction drove him to believe that despite the discouragement and neglect from others, his grandson would one day bring pride to the nation. Singhraj Adhana faced every challenge heads-on, ultimately making the entire country proud by securing two medals in the Tokyo Paralympic Games. Let us now delve into the incredible journey of Singhraj Adhana.

Unlike some of the other heroes presented in this book, Singhraj Adhana's journey to success took off later in life. Singhraj began his career as a professional para shooter relatively late. He was born in the Faridabad district of Haryana, which borders Delhi, the capital of India. His father, Prem Singh Adhana, was a farmer, and his mother, Vedvati Singh Adhana, was a homemaker. Unfortunately, the family failed to give him the timely administration of polio drops, leaving him vulnerable to the deadly poliovirus. As a result, both of his legs were severely affected. In fact, they became so weak and contorted that they touched his stomach.

Singhraj hailed from a deeply religious and god-fearing family. His childhood was filled with memories of relatives and friends visiting their home, expressing pity, and offering hollow advice and false assurances. As he was constantly reminded about his disability, the innocent child would often ask, "Mother, when will I be able to walk like the other children?" In response, his mother would fight back tears and reassure him, "Just have faith in yourself and in God; everything will be alright one day." The family sought medical advice, visited shrines and places of worship, and offered prayers in hopes of young Singhraj's recovery. Unfortunately, nothing seemed to help.

"I once read that the mind tends to suppress bad memories and remember only the good ones. That's probably why I have very vague memories about my early childhood. Kids would laugh and tease me when I spoke about walking again one day. My siblings and cousins would play with my toys, knowing I couldn't chase after them," Singhraj reflects with a smile.

Amidst all these challenges, Singhraj had only one wish, dream: to stand on his own legs without any support. His mother always comforted him and urged him to keep the hopes alive and never give up. It was during this phase of his life that Singhraj's *mama ji* (maternal uncle), Girdhari Lal, stepped in as a mentor. He took Singhraj to local doctors and tried to get him treated. Singhraj's early childhood was during the early 1980s, a time when medical science and technology had yet to reach remote parts of the country. Physiotherapy and rehabilitation were either unfamiliar to many or were minimally practiced.

In their relentless pursuit of finding a cure, Singhraj's family sought every possible treatment, including one prescribed by a doctor that still haunts Singhraj. "My parents would vigorously rub a certain type of oil on my body. Afterward, they would lay me down on my stomach on a cot, straighten my legs, and then secure them to a tree or pole to prevent bending. I had to maintain this position for four to five hours every day. The doctor had said that my body needed a lot of sunlight. So, my parents made me lie down under the sun in soaring temperatures of 40–42 degrees Celsius. I cried out in pain, but my parents would remind me that bearing these hardships was necessary if I wanted to stand on my own legs. Despite the unbearable pain, the very thought of standing on own legs kept me going," Singhraj recounts. Fortunately, after enduring a long phase of such trials and errors, things gradually began to improve for him.

When Singhraj turned 10 years old, he accomplished a significant milestone by standing on his legs for the first time in his life, albeit with the aid of crutches. Though his legs were still very weak, he somehow managed to walk with support, bringing immense joy to the family. But Singhraj was not very happy and expressed his dissatisfaction to his family, lamenting, "These crutches ruin my clothes; they tear easily. I don't want to rely on them. I want to walk on my own legs." His family always stood firmly by his side, instilling in him the values of self-belief and faith in the Almighty. Singhraj diligently followed their advice, and within three to four years, he liberated himself from the crutches. He started to walk unassisted. This victory over his disability not only boosted his confidence but also equipped him with the resilience to confront the worst situations in life. "If I can overcome the severe effects of polio, I can overcome anything. It was like a fresh start, a new beginning for me," he reflects. Singhraj Adhana now set his sights on his next major goal.

Inspired by his grandfather's legacy, Singhraj wanted to make a meaningful contribution to his country. His grandfather, Subedar Major Sumera Ram Adhana, had served in both World Wars. For his valour during the Second World War (1939–44), he was honoured with the Indian Order of Merit and the Military Cross by the British Indian Army. After retiring from military service, he actively participated in the freedom struggle movement alongside Netaji Subhas Chandra Bose and played a key role in the unification of princely states under the leadership of Sardar Vallabhbhai Patel.

Singhraj was just 12 or 13 years old when his grandfather passed away in 1991, yet many of his memories from that time remain vivid and continue to inspire him. "I remember clearly how my grandfather interacted with young people, encouraging them to enlist in the army and serve the nation. He firmly believed that military service was the best way to contribute to one's country, as it instilled discipline and dedication. Unfortunately, because of my physical disability, I was a misfit for the army. There were times when I felt disheartened that I couldn't follow in his footsteps. But my grandfather always reassured me, saying that there would come a time when I would indeed make the nation proud," says Singhraj.

After completing his school education, Singhraj explored various job opportunities. It was during this time that he found a job at the Sainik School, which was located near his house.

Sport had never been a part of Singhraj's life due to his disability. However, everything changed suddenly in 2017 when Singhraj, then 35 years old and happily married to Kavita Adhana, found himself spending time at a sports complex in Sector 12, Faridabad, with his two children and nephew for three to four hours daily. "While the kids played, I returned home dissatisfied every day, feeling it was a waste of time just to watch others play," recalls Singhraj.

"One day, the children proposed swimming for its health benefits, which sparked my interest. I decided to give it a try. However, during the first three days, I couldn't use the pool because I found it uncomfortable to undress. With the pool coach's encouragement, I began going late in the evening when nobody else was around. But when I got in the pool, I found that I couldn't even stand in water that was only two feet deep. As soon as I stepped into the pool, my legs felt different. It felt like I was on the verge of taking my own life. I decided not to swim ever again," Singhraj recalls.

After this, Singhraj's nephew Gaurav introduced him to the discipline of shooting. "I visited the shooting range and observed the coach giving tips to young shooters. Most of them were struggling to hit the target. I couldn't help but smile," Singhraj recalls. "The coach asked me why I was smiling. After a brief pause, I gathered my courage and replied, 'The entire process seems simple, and I wonder why the young shooters are not able to hit the target'." The coach then handed me a pistol and asked me to give it a try. I fired five shots. To my surprise, four of them hit the inner 10s. The coach was astonished, and those present there were shocked to learn it was my first time holding a pistol," he adds.

That memorable day marked a turning point for Singhraj. Things began falling in place. Singhraj learnt about para shooting and its rapid growth. Gradually, he started taking the sport seriously with each step forward.

Singhraj remembers 12 January 2017 as the day he began participating in shooting competitions. At 35 years old, he harboured a fierce determination to excel in the sport. He was aware that in professional sports, people are either retired or nearing retirement by his age. He felt compelled to make every day count. Singhraj was eager to learn everything quicker to compensate for lost time, but his initial coach was sceptical of his ability to progress rapidly. In contrast, Singhraj had already set his sights on representing India at the Tokyo 2020 Paralympic Games alongside the rest of the Indian contingent. He realised that the opportunity to excel at such a level was either now or never. For this, he was ready to put every bit of his sweat and blood into the game. Unable to join the army due to his physical disability, Singhraj saw Paralympic sports as a platform where he could compete, excel and bring pride to the nation. He wanted to fulfil his grandfather's dream, and that became his driving force.

"I practised hard for three months, but my coach didn't believe I could achieve my ambitions in such a short time. So, I shifted my training to the Dr Karni Singh Shooting Range. It was there that I met the National Chief Coach J.P. Nautiyal and shared my burning desire with him. Nautiyal Sir smiled and didn't discourage me. He firmly believes in the process. He encouraged me to practice and train diligently. He was confident that with the right direction, nothing could stop me. His words deeply impacted me, and I started putting my heart and soul into shooting. I trained an average for 12 hours daily, often spending double or even triple the time my juniors did on the range. If my coach asked me to do a specific exercise three times, I did it six times," says Singhraj.

Legendary boxer Muhammad Ali famously stated, "The fight is won or lost far away from the witnesses—behind the lines, in the gym, and out there on the road, long before I dance under those lights." Within a year, Singhraj's hard work started showing promising results. He participated in the national para shooting competition held in Kerala, all set to make an instant impression. By then, his coach had also gained confidence in his abilities.

"I won gold and silver medals and was selected for the Indian contingent. Soon after, we were gearing up for an international tournament, and I had received my playing kit adorned with our national flag. I was so proud and happy; tears welled up in my eyes. In that moment, I thought of my grandfather, who had always wished for me to bring honour to our great nation. I couldn't sleep for two days, and I wore the track suit we were given for nearly four days straight. It was a dream come true, achieved in just one year," recalls Singhraj.

J.P Nautiyal, the National Chief Coach of Indian Para

Shooting, became a fan of Singhraj's work ethic, which meant a great deal to Singhraj. Nautiyal, a former army personnel known for his reputation as a tough taskmaster and hard-to-please attitude, emphasised the importance of discipline and dedication in achieving success in any field. "Singhraj has got both these qualities abundantly. His inner drive to excel is so strong that he consistently exceeds expectations. If a routine calls for shooters to do a specific exercise 20 times, he would do it 40 times. If I were to grade him, I would give him 95 out of 100 for his overall approach," remarks Nautiyal.

By the time Singhraj was leaving for the Paralympics, he had amassed an impressive tally of 13 international medals. Despite this success, he remained unsatisfied with his preparation and sought to ensure all bases were covered.

Singhraj's three years of experience at the international level had opened his eyes. By then, he had discerned the difference between a good shooter and a great one. He understood the fine line that separates winners from ultimate champions. Singhraj was now determined to elevate his game to the next level. He began preparing for the worst possible match scenarios, both physically and mentally. There were days when he would spend up to 18 hours training. His body would ache after such intense workouts and rigorous training sessions. He pushed his physical limits by immersing himself in ice baths, followed by hot water, aiming to maximise his endurance and be in a positive frame of mind.

Whenever you speak to podium finishers at the highest level, they often talk about being in "the zone" before a specific competition. Singhraj wanted to be in that zone before the Tokyo Games. However, just as he was stepping into that crucial phase, COVID-19 struck.

The pandemic was a very tough period. All shooting ranges and grounds were closed, leaving Singhraj confined to his home. "I was the only one who had earned a quota in the 50m pistol category. I had no practice for three to four months. Shooting is a sport where even a week of missed practice can set you back for months compared to players in other sports. Some players had the means to build 10m pistol ranges at home to continue practising. But I had nothing. For three months, I was at a standstill, and my training suffered immensely," he recounts.

Faced with this dilemma, Singhraj called his wife and other family members to discuss the situation. Although they had no idea what to do, they pledged their support. He decided to build his own shooting range. "Constructing a 10m range isn't tough, but I aimed for a 50m range. That's when Sainik School came forward and offered their basement. Thus began my mission," remembers Singhraj about that challenging period.

"No gain, no gain". This maxim about the rewards of risk-taking is often heard from motivational speakers and business leaders. Singhraj, with limited resources at his disposal, risked everything to achieve his goal. Perhaps he had faced so much of pain right from childhood that he had no fear of pain anymore. Singhraj sold his wife's jewellery and liquidated the fixed deposits intended for his children. He also disposed of all movable properties. These funds were used to build a 50m shooting range for his Paralympic training.

Adhana was aware that he was past the optimal age and could not afford to waste time preparing for the Olympics. To build the shooting range, a section of the school's structure had to be dismantled. Despite this, his determination persuaded the school administration to grant approval. Another major challenge was to get the necessary manpower during the COVID-19 restrictions. With strict guidelines limiting movement, finding workers was tough. However, Singhraj found a way out.

"I housed all the labourers with me at home. I lived, ate and spent three months with them," Singhraj recounts. "Due to protocols, allowing them to return home daily risked them fleeing to their villages or contracting COVID-19. So, I covered the additional expenses to keep the workforce available for the shooting range," he adds.

Singhraj and his team imported machines and other shooting equipment from Australia, allowing the shooting range to be ready for use in a record time of three months. Another wonderful aspect of the range was that it opened the doors for his competitors to practise. When news spread about the shooting range, built in a record time despite numerous challenges, officials from the sports department came to inspect it. They were amazed and impressed; they marvelled at how one individual's determination had made such a feat possible without any government support. One of the *babus,* who had come to see the range, asked him, "How can you be so certain of winning? What if you don't win a medal and return empty-handed? What if your entire investment goes down the drain?"

Years later, when reflecting on stories of determination and risk-taking in life, Singhraj Adhana's journey in building the shooting range would undoubtedly make a compelling and relevant subject for a film.

As the world cautiously began to reopen after the initial impact of the virus had subsided, the devastating second wave of COVID-19 struck in 2021, proving far more lethal than anticipated. Singhraj, too, got infected with the deadly virus.

"At first, I thought I just needed to be careful and that this phase would pass soon. But the virus attacked my body fiercely. I couldn't even stand on my own legs. I was in complete shock as my worst fear of losing my ability to walk returned. I couldn't speak or eat. My body seemed to no longer obey me; the virus had taken over, and I felt like I was drifting. I lost control over my bowel movement and was completely confined to my bed. The situation turned dire when my oxygen levels dipped to around 50, prompting my family to rush me to the hospital. My condition was critical. When the doctors started treatment, they gave me only 25 per cent chance of survival. But with the grace of God and the prayers of my family, I miraculously pulled through. In the hindsight, I feel God wanted me to go through this final test before making me an ultimate champion in sports. It toughened me mentally to face future challenges," says Singhraj.

"Slowly, I regained strength and started recovering. Even during my recovery, more than my health, I was concerned about missing out on training. Yet, my coaches supported my physical and mental recovery and helped me find my rhythm again at the shooting range," Singhraj refects, as he takes us through one of the most testing phases of his life.

When our shooting contingent arrived in Tokyo, it was the biggest Indian shooting contingent ever in the history of the games. Manish Narwal and Avani Lekhara were in top form, and most followers of Indian Para Sports had high hopes for them. In contrast, Singhraj had fewer backers placing their bets on him. Yet, those who closely followed his progress in training camps and knew of his high scores remained confident in his abilities. The ultimate challenge was to convert his rigorous training and preparation into a medal-winning performance at the Tokyo Paralympics.

Singhraj's first event at the Asaka Shooting Range in Tokyo was the Men's P1 10m air pistol SH1 on 31 August 2021. Among the 27 top shooters from around the world who had qualified for this event, only eight were to advance to the finals. In shooting and other professional sports, the process is crucial, and results always follow.

In the qualification round, Manish Narwal, who was then the reigning world number one and Singhraj's training partner from Faridabad, emerged as the top shooter with a score of 575. Out of the eight shooters who made it to the finals, three were Chinese. Although one Chinese shooter also scored 575, Manish was declared the top scorer due to his higher inner 10 scores. Singhraj stood at sixth position with a score of 566. His qualification for the finals brought him one step closer to realising his dream.

In the finals, unfortunately, Manish Narwal lost his rhythm and concentration, and became the second shooter to bow out of the finals. Meanwhile, Singhraj was holding his fort and was giving the Chinese shooters a run for their money. Singhraj and Chinese shooter Xiaolong Lou were closely competing for the bronze medal. After the sixth round, Singhraj led with a score of 178.1, while Xiaolong was just behind him with score of 177.5. The next two shots would decide who would be eliminated and who would claim the bronze medal. Singhraj maintained his cool and won the bronze medal for his country.

"I was stunned to see Manish Narwal exit so early. He's the world's best and was in tremendous form. But then I realised I couldn't afford to lose focus. During the finals, I found myself in fourth place with the top three positions held by Chinese shooters. I picked up my pistol, recalled my coaches' advice, and aimed for a solid shot. I hit the inner 10 and moved up to third position after that shot. I didn't lose my focus after that," remembers Singhraj.

There was more relief than joy in the Indian camp. The nation held high hopes for this category, considering it as one of the strongest events with proven champions like Manish Narwal and Singhraj performing on the international stage. At one point, everything seemed lost but Singhraj turned things around, securing at least a bronze medal in the 10m pistol event.

More than the colour of the medal, his determination and willpower were lauded by both friends and even some rivals. Newspaper headlines prominently featured Singhraj's incredible achievements and the risks he took to reach the podium. The overarching lesson for him was that if one has got the will and the determination, it's never too late to pursue one's dreams.

"For me, it wasn't just about winning a medal; it was a victory of the enormous belief my family and my coaches had in me. My family was overwhelmed with tears of joy and celebration. Winning a medal within four years of taking up shooting was unimaginable for many shooters and coaches. I dedicated that medal to everyone who believed in me and helped me on my journey," says Singhraj.

Deep down, Singhraj was relieved that all the investments made, including those from his family members towards building the shooting range, had finally paid off. After this famous victory, Prime Minister Narendra Modi personally called Singhraj to extend congratulations. There was extensive media coverage. Yet, Singhraj and the Indian contingent remained focused, knowing that they were still in the midst of competition. Singhraj chose not to indulge in excessive celebration. His teammate and close friend, Manish Narwal, was emotionally shattered and totally devastated after returning empty-handed from an event he had dominated throughout the build-up and into the final round. Moreover, Singhraj had another event scheduled in just two days, and he wanted to be mentally and physically fresh for it.

Singhraj's next event was scheduled for 4 September 2021: the P4 mixed 50m pistol SH1. Before moving ahead in the story, it's pertinent to understand the nature of this event. The P4 mixed 50m Pistol SH1, also known as a "co-ed" or a "mixed" event, features both men and women participants. Singhraj felt optimistic about his chances in this event, as his performance in the 50m shooting category was stronger compared to the 10-metre one. There were 34 participants in this category, each required to fire 60 competition shots within 50 minutes. Buoyed by his earlier success, Singhraj maintained excellent form and finished fourth in the qualification round with a score of 536 points. Manish Narwal also qualified for the finals, finishing seventh with a score of 533 points. It was a proud moment for the Indian camp as both shooters had reached the final stage.

"People may find it hard to believe, but the moment Singhraj qualified for the finals, I knew that he would win a medal. His attitude and approach in finals were exemplary. Moreover, I've noticed recently that lady luck often favours him on such occasions. So, when he reached the finals, I had a strong feeling he would bring home a medal for the country," remarks Chief Coach Nautiyal.

In the finals, Manish had a slow start, with two poor shots of 7.7. In contrast, Singhraj was in the zone straight away, scoring 19.4 after his first two shots. By the fifth shot, both shooters were well within reach of the podium. Singhraj and

Manish were both in the top three with scores of 46.1 and 45.4, respectively. However, Manish's performance faltered in the next two shots, causing him to slip to the sixth spot, while Singhraj held on to the third position after seven shots.

"The final was quite difficult. When I found myself in in third position, I started to meditate and concentrate on the process our coaches had taught us. 'Good, relax, breathe, focus, Okay. And focus on one shot at a time, just one shot, please. Clear the mind of all other thoughts, and allow it to slow down for a moment. And then go again'," explains Singhraj, who was wearing his lucky hat gifted by his wife.

As the elimination rounds progressed, it posed a challenge, especially for Manish. Nevertheless, he remained composed. By the end of his 12th shot, Manish had clawed his way to the fifth position with 104.3 points. Singhraj was consistent enough to hold on to the third position. After the elimination rounds, Singhraj and Manish were closely trailing each other in fourth and fifth positions. During the second elimination stage, the tables turned with the Chinese shooters slipping to fourth and fifth positions, while the Indians, Manish and Singhraj, moved up to third and fourth positions, respectively. In the shootout, Yang was the one to be eliminated, followed by his compatriot Xiaolong two shots later. This set the stage for the podium positions to be contested between the two Indians and Russian shooter Malyshev.

Malyshev, who had been sailing smoothly until then, buckled under pressure. His scores of 6.9 and 8.5 created the window of opportunity that the Indians were looking for to seal the top spots. Eventually, Manish and Singhraj were the last shooters competing for the gold medal.

The entire country had its eyes glued to the television sets. Never before in the country's sporting history had there been a situation where two Indians contested for top two positions in an individual event at the Olympics or Paralympics. Manish bagged the gold while Singhraj secured the silver. The Indian flag flew high at at both first and second positions, and the Indian national anthem was played during the medal ceremony. It was a sight never seen before.

"During my growing years, Delhi's Trade Fair at Pragati Maidan was one of the most anticipated events annually. Students always looked forward to attending, and they often asked me to accompany them. Year after year, I would make excuses to avoid going. Deep down, I feared the possibility of injury that could prevent me from walking again I had somehow managed to stand on my feet after so much hard work and prayers of my parents. The thought of losing them forever due to any mishap terrified me. So, I found reasons to decline their invitations," recounts Singhraj.

"Back home, I would often cry in front of the mirror, questioning the purpose of life if I couldn't even fulfil such simple dreams. Afterward, I would wipe my tears and pray. I aspired to achieve something meaningful that would make my parents and the country proud. I wanted to fulfil my grandfather's wishes. After the Tokyo Games, I got a call from the Chief Minister's Office in Chandigarh inviting me to inaugurate the Trade Festival of Haryana. I just smiled. Dreams do come true," he says.

God listens to prayers and answers them in His own time and way. Singhraj won silver and bronze medals for India in the Tokyo 2020 Paralympics. While his dream of winning the

SINGHRAJ ADHANA

gold medal remained unfulfilled, he is a happy and contented man.

With a wry smile, he says, "I started my journey in shooting at the age of 35. By the age of 39, I had won two Paralympic medals for the country. Though I'll be 42 by the time of the Paris 2024 Paralympics, who knows? Perhaps I'll bring home a gold medal for India." Singhraj now has his sights firmly set on the Paris 2024 Paralympics, where he is aiming for the gold.

Meanwhile, as we move on to our next protagonist in this book, we get to understand the ugly shades of life. The world we live in isn't always just black and white; it's filled with shades of grey as well. In the chapter ahead, we explore the inspiring journey of Sundar Singh Gujar and his quest for "the medal of redemption".

SUNDAR SINGH GURJAR

The Medal of Redemption

"Anybody who believes and experiences their life
and doesn't have shades of grey in it
does not live where I live and is simply not in touch
with the reality of the human condition."

—**Alexis Denisof, American actor**

Throughout our research for this book, we were constantly reminded of this famous quote by Alexis Denisof. The narrative of Sundar Singh Gurjar must be told to bring readers closer to the environment that nurtures real-life heroes, who etch their names into the nation's psyche. Any aspiring athlete inspired by the achievements of these Paralympic heroes should be prepared to confront the "shades of grey" within this environment, until we collectively work to reform it.

Sundar Singh Gurjar's journey is a story of transformation from darkness to light—a tale that deserves to be told. It begins in the small village of Karauli in Rajasthan. Sundar's parents were very poor and struggled to provide a proper shelter for their children while making ends meet. Like any other child in the village, Sundar harboured a passion for sports, particularly wrestling. His father, a *desi* (local) wrestler, competed in neighbourhood *dangals* (wrestling arenas), inspiring Sundar to follow in his footsteps.

However, it was Sundar's sports teacher who recognised his potential and steered him towards athletics. Sundar possessed greater strength and a more robust physique compared to other children his age. In the adjoining area, no one could match his prowess in throwing events like discus, javelin and shot put. He started participating in sub-junior state and national tournaments, quickly making a name for himself. As his talent grew, it became evident that to further enhance his skills, Sundar needed to step out of his village and compete against stronger opponents. With this goal in mind, Sundar made the crucial decision to relocate to Jaipur, the epicentre of sports activities in Rajasthan.

In 2015, Sundar shifted to Jaipur to train under national and international coaches. To minimise travel time, he choose to stay near the Sawai Man Singh Stadium. He got accommodation at the Gurjar Samaj Youth Hostel nearby. Though Sundar had the power and agility of a wrester, he needed to refine his technique for javelin throwing.

However, tragedy struck just a few months into his training, and his life changed forever! "It was a non-practice day, and I was relaxing at the youth hostel," Sundar recalls. "A friend who lived nearby was constructing a shed for his cattle. As I was all alone in the hostel and missing my family, I decided to visit and help out," he remembers of that fateful day.

When Sundar arrived at his friend's house, he found the family busy roofing the shed with steel sheets. "I saw my friend's elderly parents lifting heavy, sharp-edged metal sheets. I insisted they rest and offered to help lift the sheets myself," Sundar recounts. Unfortunately, an accident occurred when one of the heavy sheets slipped from the top and landed on Sundar's left wrist, causing severe bleeding.

"They rushed me to a nearby hospital where the doctor delivered the devastating news: the sheet had severed several crucial nerves in my left hand, and to stop the bleeding, amputation of my wrist was necessary. Reluctantly, I pleaded with the doctors for any alternative, but they reiterated that it was the only option. With time running out and the bleeding failing to stop, we had to make a quick decision. I placed my trust in my family and the medical staff, and went as per their advice," he says tearfully.

After the surgery, Sundar woke to find his left hand had been amputated at the wrist, shattering his dreams of becoming an international athlete. Devastated, he returned home to recover. For three months, he didn't come out of the house or talk to anyone. He didn't know what do to next or how to plan his future.

Sundar was from a rural background where identity is an overriding factor. "We Gurjars take a lot of pride in our physical strength and appearance, and I was no different. I had gone to Jaipur to become an international athlete and came back home with only one hand. You know how people are, always asking me strange questions. The worst part was that most people I met took pity on me. Instead of encouraging me, they used terms like *bichaara* (poor fellow) and *badnaseeb* (unfortunate), and each time, it felt like a blow. I reached a point where I refused to leave my home. Even when I was at home, I asked my family to say I was out of town. People even spread rumours that I had asked the doctor to cut my wrist so I could qualify for para sports. It was so humiliating. My mind was filled with uncontrollable thoughts," says Sundar, while remembering those difficult times in his life.

During our research into the para sports ecosystem, we had in fact come across numerous allegations and counter-allegations of individuals intentionally causing injuries or self-harm to qualify for para sports. While not every allegation may be unfounded, it is heartbreaking for those who have genuinely gone through such traumatic events to then face accusations of deceit. This only adds to their already difficult challenges in life.

There comes a point in life when one must leave certain things behind, open their eyes, and change their perspective. Devendra Jhajharia, a celebrated para athlete, had created waves in the country by winning a gold medal in javelin throw at the Athens 2004 Paralympic Games. His journey from a mud house in Rajasthan's Churu district to Olympic glory has already been covered in this book.

Devendra's coach, Ripudaman Singh Aulakh, also known as R.D. Singh, is a recipient of the prestigious Dronacharya Award and has been instrumental in shaping the careers of numerous athletes. One of R.D. Singh's students, known to Sundar, suggested that he consider para sports. Sundar initially declined his suggestion for two main reasons. First, he felt it was beneath his stature to compete alongside individuals with disabilities; despite losing a wrist, he remained determined to compete against able-bodied athletes. Second, he feared it would validate accusations that he had intentionally injured his wrist to qualify for para sports.

However, Sundar's perspective underwent a profound change when he met R.D. Singh. "When Sundar first came to meet me, the greatest challenge was helping him come to terms with his disability. Whatever had happened to him was beyond his control, but what he could achieve was totally in his hands. There was no doubt about his talent, but mentally, he struggled with low self-belief and confidence," says R.D. Singh about their initial meeting.

During our discussions with established coaches in para sports, one common thread we discovered was that they often had to address two critical areas simultaneously: the first involved physical conditioning and skill development, while the second, arguably more crucial, was mental preparation. These coaches emphasise that a big portion of their success lies in mentally empowering their athletes and instilling a positive mindset about their potential.

In October 2015, Sundar packed his bags and moved to Hanumangarh, a small district in Rajasthan, where R.D. Singh had set up a small hostel for athletes who came from distant places to train under his aegis. Sundar's arrival breathed a new life into R.D. Singh's coaching efforts. With Devendra Jhajharia having moved on after his gold medal win in Athens, R.D. Singh saw in Sundar a student with the potential to surpass Jhajharia's achievements. Over time, Sundar adapted to his new environment and dedicated himself wholeheartedly to training.

Soon, Sundar started achieving remarkable results in state-level tournaments, consistently shattering existing records in his category and even exceeding the world record marks during practice sessions. Just as things were going ahead smoothly, one night Sundar abruptly left R.D. Singh's hostel in Hanumangarh and turned up at Sawai Man Singh Stadium in Jaipur. R.D. Singh was shocked and devastated by this sudden turn of events. He tried to contact Sundar to understand the reason behind his departure. With the Rio 2016 Paralympics looming, changing coaches seemed illogical.

Till date, R.D. Singh maintains that it was a conspiracy. "There were people who didn't want me back in the spotlight. I had discovered and nurtured Devendra into a champion. Now, I was mentoring Sundar, who was ready to dominate the world. But certain middlemen spread malicious falsehoods about me and my coaching for their own gain. They completely misled Sundar. I don't blame Sundar for leaving me, as he was convinced that his career wouldn't flourish under my guidance. It was like a stab in the back," says R.D. Singh.

To this day, Sundar has not disclosed why he left R.D. Singh just before the Rio 2016 Games. "Everything happened so quickly. I prefer not to dwell on those things because there is no point in looking back," says Sundar regarding the incident. Another contentious issue that has shadowed Sundar since he took to para sports is his bitter rivalry with Devendra. Both athletes competed in the F46 category. Close associates of Sundar have accused Devendra of attempting to sabotage Sundar's career right from the outset. In the book, we have come across narratives of some para athletes who, despite being rivals on the field, forged strong bonds off the field and thrived in each other's company. Unfortunately, this has not been the case with Devendra and Sundar.

Meanwhile, Sundar began training under the guidance of Mahavir Prasad Saini, another veteran coach based at Sawai Man Singh Stadium. Saini, renowned for training athletes in the state, oversaw Sundar's preparation as the trials for the Rio 2016 Paralympic Games took place in Sonepat, Haryana. Sundar appeared significantly more prepared and physically fit than Devendra during these trials. While both athletes qualified for the Rio Games, Sundar emerged as the gold medal prospect, given his exceptional qualification throws that surpassed even the existing world records at the time.

The Rio 2016 Olympics did not bring much cheer for the Indian contingent, but the para athletes uplifted the nation's spirits with their outstanding performances, compared to their able-bodied counterparts. However, for Sundar, the Rio Paralympics left him with memories he will never be able to forget. On the day of the F46 category javelin throw event, all the athletes assembled at the warm-up area. India had three participants—Devendra Jhajharia, Rinku Hooda, and Sundar Gurjar. The names of athletes were announced for reporting at the calling area and registration desk.

Devendra and Rinku promptly reported and registered, but for some reason, Sundar failed to do so. When he realised at the warm-up area that the other Indian athletes had already gone for the competition, he rushed to the registration desk. But he was denied entry because he was 52 seconds late. The weight of those 52 seconds would continue to haunt him. All his meticulous planning and preparation for the event went for a toss because of those crucial 52 seconds.

"Even today, when I recall or am reminded of that day, I just want to scream out loud. I neither speak nor understand English. It was my first major international event. No one informed me about a specific reporting time, and I couldn't understand when my name was called. Even my teammates didn't signal or indicate anything. The world knows that I was the best javelin thrower, leading my category for the past few months," says Sundar about that fateful day. The blame for the mishap fell squarely on Coach Mahavir Saini. Despite being present on the ground, he failed to guide his athlete.

"I have experienced a lot in my personal and sporting life, but that one incident will haunt me until I die. Everyone took their frustration out on me. Initially, I was accused of taking Sundar away from R.D. Singh, and now they blamed me for depriving the country a medal. Some even demanded that I put in jail. I wasn't there officially; I had paid for my own tickets and hotel to support my student. No one questioned the officials of the Paralympic Committee of India for their failure. I was made the punching bag," says Coach Mahavir Saini.

Sundar's loss turned out to be Devendra's gain. Devendra won the gold medal and thus became the first Indian athlete to win two gold medals at the Paralympic Games. He had previously won gold at the Athens 2004 Games. After the games, when asked about Sundar's absence, Devendra remarked, "It was shocking for me when I realised that Sundar couldn't report on time. We all were practising in the warm-up area. While Rinku Hooda and I registered ourselves, Sundar was practising a bit farther away from us, so we couldn't signal him. People can blame whoever they want, but ultimately, it's the athlete's responsibility to be aware of these things."

Sundar returned to India totally devastated and shattered. He went to his home in Rajasthan and confined himself to his room, swearing never to touch a javelin or set foot on the ground again. His family and friends empathised with his pain, agony, and disappointment. But everyone started worrying when Sundar started exhibiting signs of depression.

Unable to endure two successive setbacks, Sundar started having thoughts of suicide. "I wanted to end my life. What was the point of living now? I had raised the hopes of my parents, relatives, friends, my community and the entire country. I kept asking myself, *Ye mere saath kyun hua*? (Why did this happen to me?) If I had come last after giving my best, I would have accepted it. But being in the warm-up area and unable to compete was something I couldn't bear. I just wanted to silence all these thoughts, and the only way seemed to be ending my life. There were days when I came very close," Sundar recalls, reflecting on the darkest period of his life.

However, it was during this time that Coach Mahavir Saini stepped in to support his protégé. "I never left him alone, not even for a minute. Sometimes he would shout at me to go away, but I never did. For me, it wasn't about sports anymore; his life was at stake. He was on the brink of a nervous breakdown. I took him to several counsellors who held sessions with him. I introduced him to motivational speakers who encouraged him to accept life as it came. Sports was nowhere in the picture. First, there is life, then everything else," explains Coach Mahavir Saini, while talking about that critical phase in Sundar's life.

It took nearly six to eight months for Sundar to come out from that phase. Redemption lay not in giving up but in achieving his unfulfilled dream. When he returned to the ground, he did so with even greater fervour and determination.

After the Rio fiasco, Sundar made a triumphant return at the 2017 Fazza IPC Athletics Grand Prix held in Dubai. He scripted history by winning three gold medals across different events: javelin throw in the F46 category, discus throw in T44–46 category, and shot put in the T44–46 category. This achievement was unprecedented and a feat never achieved by anyone before in the Indian athletics landscape.

Continuing his stellar performance, Sundar secured another gold medal at the 2017 World Para Athletics Championships in the F46 category of javelin throw with a throw of 60.36 metres. This victory made him the second Indian athlete to claim gold at this prestigious tournament. At the 2018 Asian Para Games in Indonesia, Sundar added to his accolades with a silver medal in the javelin F46 category and a bronze in the discus-throw F46 category.

However, competing in multiple events began to take a toll on Sundar's body, particularly his shoulder, which endured maximum stress. In early 2019, Sundar faced a severe shoulder injury that confined him to home. The injury was so severe that he could not lift his arm.

It was time to take a tough decision regarding his career. Sundar decided to leave discus and shot put events and concentrate exclusively on javelin. After recovering from his injury, he staged a remarkable comeback at the 2019 World Para Athletics Championships, clinching a gold medal with the season's best throw of 61.22 metres. He was in peak form and ready for the Tokyo Paralympics when the COVID-19 pandemic brought the world to a standstill.

The news of the Paralympics' postponement evoked a sense of déjà vu reminiscent of 2016 for Sundar. "I wondered, *why do the Paralympics keep slipping away from me*? In 2016, I couldn't compete, and now again, there's uncertainty about the games' schedule. The pervasive gloom that gripped the world made me feel even more disheartened. I started thinking these games would never happen, and I'd have to wait till the Paris 2024 Games. Sometimes, I questioned whether I'd ever get the chance to participate in these games at all. Will the ghost of the Rio Games haunt me for the rest of my life?" Sundar reflects, remembering those lockdown days.

When the lockdown was suddenly announced, Sundar found himself stranded at the Sawai Man Singh Stadium. In hindsight, this situation turned out to be a blessing in disguise. While other trainees at the hostels had returned home before the nationwide lockdown in March 2020, Gurjar made a deliberate choice to stay and continue training alone within stadium walls.

"As soon as I learnt about the impeding nationwide lockdown, I requested permission to remain and train there.

I didn't have the necessary equipment or space at home for training. I moved in there on 18 March and didn't step out of the stadium for four months. During this time, my friend Ahmet Singh Gurjar helped me with my diet and other needs. Initially, I stayed in touch with my coach Mahavir Prasad Saini via video calls. Eventually, he started coming to the stadium daily to oversee my training. I consider myself fortunate to have had the opportunity to continue training here, which undoubtedly gave me the much-needed advantage over my competitors," says Sundar.

The Tokyo Games were finally scheduled for August–September 2021. By the time Sundar's event commenced on 30 August 2021, Neeraj Chopra had become the country's biggest sporting sensation. His Olympic gold medal in javelin throw had taken the sport and the athlete to unprecedented levels of popularity, rarely witnessed in India. This inspired para athletes, particularly javelin throwers, to give their best performances.

However, Sundar started the event nervously. Athletes like Sumit Antil and Sandeep Chaudhary, who trained with him, vouch for his strength and power. "I've personally measured his throws during practice sessions, and they have consistently reached nearly 70 metres. But under pressure, Sundar tends to falter because he lacks mental strength," remarks Sumit Antil.

On Sundar's competition day, being the first athlete on the start list gave him an advantage and alleviated the pressure. His throw of 62.26 metres significantly boosted his confidence. Meanwhile, Sri Lanka's Herath Mudiyanselage was in a different league on that day. He was leading the pack right from his first throw. But after that first throw, Sundar began to lag behind. Devendra, with a throw of 64.35 metres, and Cuba's

Varona Gonzalez, with a throw of 63.30 metres, were leading alongside Herath, who had set a world record at 67.79 metres.

"After the first round, I found myself in second place, and all the memories of Rio started flooding back. I wasn't thinking clearly. When I fouled my fourth throw, it hit me that I might leave empty-handed. That's when I knew I had to regroup," says Sundar, remembering the event.

Sundar's fifth throw measured 64.01 metres, which secured him the third position. Devendra had won silver, while Herath took home the gold medal with a world record performance. The entire country erupted in joy. Finally, Sundar's moment of redemption had come. Celebration and satisfaction filled his small village in Karauli, Rajasthan. The man who was on the verge of ending his life fought back valiantly and won a bronze medal for the country.

"This wasn't Sundar's best performance; it simply lifted a weight off his shoulders. He wasn't just competing against other athletes but also wrestling with his inner demons. Now that this burden is lifted, the world will see what Sundar can accomplish in the Paris 2024 Games," says Coach Mahavir Saini, expressing pride and relief. The coach-athlete duo now aims for gold, which they have dubbed the "Medal of Redemption". Sundar has got his eyes firmly set on the Paris 2024 Paralympics.

In the upcoming chapter, we visit the life and journey of another gem from Vadnagar in Gujarat, Bhavina Patel.

BHAVINA PATEL

The Paralympic Gem from Vadnagar

"I haven't a clue about the biology or the psychology involved when a person dissolves into tears, but it's fascinating to note what turns them on. There are wives who can cascade over a late husband or a burned dinner, and equally pour tears of joy over a new bonnet or a renovated bathroom. A while ago I took a ship back from Europe. Amid the tumbling confetti ... I found myself misty-eyed watching a young lady waving a tearful farewell to her boyfriend on the dock. I couldn't figure out if I was crying at her plight, or in delight that he wasn't coming along with us."

—**Malcolm S. Forbes,** *American entrepreneur and publisher of Forbes magazine*

Over the years, both athletes and sports journalists have developed a peculiar fascination for tears of joy. Whether it was the legendary Sachin Tendulkar shedding tears after India's historic victory in the 2011 World Cup or more recently, Lionel Messi tearing up following Argentina's triumph in the 2022 FIFA World Cup, I've found myself moved to tears alongside these sporting icons. As a passionate sports enthusiast, I've cherished witnessing such emotional moments. However, none has touched me as deeply as when Bhavina Patel, the first Indian table tennis player to

win a Paralympic medal, cried after her remarkable victory. That moment will undoubtedly remain etched in my memory for as long as I live on this beautiful planet.

In 2022, I got the opportunity to visit Vadnagar in Gujarat. As we roamed through its streets, it felt like several eras were converging in the city's atmosphere. One can feel the weight of thousands of years of history embedded in the city's environment, with its fascinating pottery fragments, textiles, ornaments, and other tools, each enriching the essence of the place. Vadnagar is mentioned in the *Puranas* and in the writings of the Chinese traveller Hiuen Tsang. Throughout history, the town has produced numerous luminaries, from Gujarat's greatest poets like Dayaram and Narasinh Mehta, to renowned figures such as novelist Govardhanram Tripathi and musician Kaumudi Munshi.

One of our country's towering political leaders, Narendra Modi, also hails from Vadnagar. On 6 November 1986, another gem was born there—Bhavina Patel. She was born in Sundhiya, a small village in Vadnagar Taluka, Mehsana district. Bhavina's father, Hasmukhbhai, owned a small grocery shop, where villagers could get their daily necessities. The family had enough resources to meet their basic needs. Life was pleasant until tragedy struck Bhavina at the age of 12 months when she was diagnosed with poliomyelitis.

In the 1980s, many parts of the country, especially rural areas, were without advanced medical facilities. Furthermore, the prevailing mindset in these regions often linked certain diseases to past wrongdoings or *karma*. Some believed that polio, in particular, was a consequence of immoral acts in previous lives, and one must endure penance to cleanse their soul.

Bhavina's parents consulted many doctors and diligently followed every medical advice given. However, over time, the strength in her legs deteriorated to the point where she could no longer stand without support. After exploring various options without success, Hasmukhbhai took Bhavina to Andhra Pradesh for surgery as a final resort, which unfortunately did not yield positive results either.

"We did everything that we could," says Hasmukhbhai, who shares a special bond with his daughter. "I dedicated myself entirely to her. I searched every temple, every hospital, and every place where there was even a glimmer of hope for relief, hoping to find a cure for my daughter. But ultimately, nothing worked, and she ended up relying on crutches. I lost faith in divine powers. I had no explanation for why my little girl was suffering. In the end, I had no option but to accept our circumstances," he adds, tears welling in his eyes.

Finally, the family came to terms with their situation, and Bhavina accepted her fate. Crutches and sticks became her constant companions. While the joyful noise of her friends playing outside reached her ears, she remained confined within the four walls of her home. Despite the virus weakening her legs, it could not dampen her spirit. Bhavina continued to be the most cheerful member of the house. She engaged her father in lengthy conversations about managing his shop and being more organised. Bhavina loved the smell of spices and eagerly joined her mother in the kitchen during cooking. She developed a keen interest in cooking herself and experimented with different dishes.

When her younger sister was born, Bhavina found a new companion in the house. However, as she matured and became more aware of the world, one concern disturbed her deeply.

Her parents' lives revolved around her, and she began to feel like a burden on them. "Although I used to take care of myself and handle most things independently, I had a few limitations because of my disability. During my growing years, I noticed that everything in the household centred on me. My parents adjusted their schedules according to my needs. Since my school was quite far, they arranged someone to drop me off and pick me up. On rainy days, my father would carry me in his arms. Sometimes, when the locality was flooded, he would lift me onto his shoulders and take me to school. I started feeling like a big burden on my family," remembers Bhavina.

Meanwhile, her parents were determined to ensure her education was completed at any cost, willing to go to any extent to make it happen. Despite their best efforts, there were days when Bhavina had to miss classes. With urgent household and business matters demanding their attention, there were days when they couldn't devote all their time to Bhavina. As Bhavina progressed to higher classes, her absences began affecting her academic performance. It was during this time that her childhood friend Pinki stepped in to help. After school, Pinki would rush to Bhavina's house and brief her on the day's school activities and lessons taught by the teachers.

Bhavina was very good in mathematics and science and showed a natural inclination towards technical subjects. As she grew older, she developed a passion for playing chess. Gradually, she began winning against all the members of her house. She became the top chess player in her school. She started participating in state- and national-level chess tournaments. Her success in chess also had a positive influence on her academic performance. The sport improved her concentration and ultimately resulted in her improved grades. Playing chess also helped in shaping her strong personality.

In Gujarat, Navratri holds a special significance among the various festivals. During this festival, different communities come together to participate in the traditional dance form known as *garba*. *Garba* involves rhythmic clapping and synchronised movements in a circular pattern accompanied by music. Despite her disability, Bhavina actively joined in the *garba* and Navratri celebrations, dancing and moving with the group while in her wheelchair.

There used to be special *garba* competitions for differently-abled individuals, and Bhavina consistently won prizes in the wheelchair *garba* category each time she participated. "Oh, life without *garba* is unthinkable for boys and girls in Gujarat. I am a typical Gujarati girl, where *garba* is a big part of our growing-up years. I love dressing up in *chaniya-choli* and preparing for the dance. I have to be cautious because the crowds can be huge and overwhelming at times. But my friends always took care of me. Despite my disability limiting my movements, it never dampened my spirits. I often sang along with the band playing *garba* songs," recalls Bhavina, he face lighting up with a huge smile. Bhavina loved singing, and she admits that if she had not been an accomplished table tennis player, she would have pursued singing as a career.

As Bhavina grew older, her parents began to worry about her future. "*What would she do for a living? How would she survive in this tough world? Who would marry her? What did the future hold for her?* These were some of the questions that troubled me and my wife a lot. There were nights when we believed that the Almighty would take care of everything, but there were also times when we felt helpless and saw no way out," says Hasmukhbhai.

After completing her school education, Bhavina aspired to become a teacher. She was confident in her ability to connect with children and inspire them. However, she was rejected in the interview, without receiving a clear explanation. She later got to know that concerns about undue attention toward a disabled teacher played a role in her rejection.

It was during this challenging phase that Hasmukhbhai came across an advertisement from the Blind People's Association (BPA) in Ahmedabad. As one of India's largest non-governmental organisations dedicated to serving individuals with disabilities, BPA offered various educational courses. Bhavina decided to move to Ahmedabad, about 100 km from her village, to pursue one of these courses. She was eager to explore the world of computers and technology, recognising India's emerging role in information technology.

In addition to its educational programmes, BPA was also known for fostering holistic development through sports and other activities. Although Bhavina initially excelled in chess, she was encouraged to pursue a physically demanding sport, given the importance of physical fitness for someone using a wheelchair. This is how Bhavina's journey with table tennis began.

"A few of my friends played table tennis, and inspired by them, I initially started playing the game just for fun," Bhavina recalls. "But soon, I started liking the game so much that I wanted to play table tennis all day long. I had to learn the sport from the scratch, and in the beginning, it was difficult just to keep the ball on the table. However, I began to enjoy it immensely. First, it gave me the much-needed physical exercise for my upper body, and secondly, like chess, it's a tactical game. These two primary aspects are what drew me to table tennis," she adds.

From then on, playing table tennis became as integral to Bhavina's routine as her academics. Within a couple of months, she made major progress in the sport. Bhavina had enrolled in the Industrial Training (ITI) curriculum course, which spanned three years, and she was determined to make the most of it. During this time, Bhavina caught the attention of Tejal Lakhia, head of the department where Bhavina was enrolled.

"She was a very cheerful girl who loved to sing and constantly motivated those around her. Whatever the situation, she always wore a smile. But her greatest strength was her exceptional mental strength. She was punctual for her classes, only missing them when she could not get off her bed. Table tennis practices were in the evenings, and she was the first to arrive and the last to leave. However, during our time at BPA, none of us could have imagined that we were nurturing a future Paralympic medallist," says Lakhia.

Despite her diligence, Bhavina faced numerous challenges. There were no formal coaches available, so she learned through trial and error. After three years of rigorous self-practice, she entered her first National Championship and won a bronze medal. This achievement, attained without proper coaching or planned training, gave her the confidence to pursue sports professionally.

It was during this period that Bhavina met Coach Lalan Doshi. Doshi used to visit BPA to coach para table tennis players. The moment he saw Bhavina playing, he recognised her immense potential. When he heard stories about her determination and strong willpower, he decided to become her mentor. Thus began a partnership that would shape her future career.

"Bhavina had trained all by herself and was quite raw. She would come, play, and leave, impressing everyone with her self-taught skills. However, there was much to refine. Concepts such as reflexes, muscle memory, and strength training were unfamiliar to her. So, we decided to adopt a systematic and scientific approach, addressing all aspects of the game," explains Doshi about his initial days with Bhavina.

Under the careful guidance of her coach, Bhavina's game started improving in leaps and bounds. She began competing in more local tournaments and winning more prizes. With every win, her confidence in the game and her self-belief skyrocketed. However, her primary challenge lay in securing the financial support necessary to sustain her passion. While she managed with odd jobs to support herself, the additional expenses associated with professional table tennis were substantial.

"When facing physical and mental challenges, positivity and exercise can often help," Bhavina reflects. "But financial struggles are different. It is a burden you can't easily share or ask for help with. You cannot do anything. Income sources were limited, making it difficult to finance tournament expenses. My bat alone costs between Rs 25,000 and Rs 30,000, and the rubbers are also costly. For major tournaments, I couldn't compromise on equipment. Given the wear and tear from playing on tables and in a wheelchair, bats needed frequent replacement every couple of months. It was not easy for a middle-class family. These were difficult times, and I never wanted to burden my parents, who were already working hard to keep the house running," she adds.

Due to these financial constraints, Bhavina's opportunities to participate in international tournaments were limited. This lack of exposure meant she rarely faced top-ranked players and had fewer chances to test her skills against the best in the world. It was a major impediment in taking her game to a world-class level.

Though Bhavina was India's top contender in para table tennis at the 2010 Commonwealth Games, she lost in the quarter-finals. She later competed in the 2013 Asian Para Table Tennis Championships in Beijing, where she won a bronze medal—a great achievement given the competitive field dominated by Chinese players.

Bhavina had also qualified for the Rio 2016 Paralympic Games. However, due to some technical issues, her entry was not processed by the Table Tennis Federation of India. She refuses to discuss about this period and wishes to put it behind her. Yet, she acknowledges this setback as one of the lowest points in her life, particularly lamenting her inability to fulfil her Olympic dream despite her father's efforts, who even took a loan to cover the expenses. She could not participate in the games, yet the pressure of the loan remained. Close acquaintances reveal that it was a point in her career, where she even contemplated quitting sports.

"I request not to dwell on that particular episode," Bhavina insists. "The 2016 Games were a source of great stress and led me into depression. I struggled to focus, even on yoga, with so much going on my mind. At times, I considered giving up everything. But, to be honest, I had no choice but to carry on with my training and hard work," she reflects on that challenging phase. This is where her husband, Nikul Patel, stepped in.

The story of Bhavina and Nikul meeting each other could be a captivating movie plot. They first connected through common friends who would gather occasionally. During one of these meetings, they exchanged phone numbers and began communicating more frequently. They shared passion for sports and fitness quickly solidified their bond. Nikul, a club-level cricketer, understood the emotional upheavals that athletes face during their journey. Nikul was shortlisted for the Indian team for the 2002 ICC Under-19 Cricket World Cup, alongside Parthiv Patel, the team captain, and others such as Irfan Pathan and Stuart Binny, who also represented the country.

"People used to ask me why I was marrying someone with a disability," recalls Nikul. "But whenever I looked at Bhavina, I saw a passionate, kind-hearted person. She is incredibly caring and is the glue that binds our family," he adds.

"I've seen her endure many challenges due to inadequate facilities for persons with disabilities," Nikul elaborates. "She navigates bus changes, relies on autorickshaws, and resorts to staircases when lifts are absent. Her determination and resilience are what drew me to her."

Initially, there was resistance from Nikul's family. It was the case of people judging her without knowing her. However, after their marriage, Bhavina won everyone over and became the darling of the family.

"He is not just my husband but also my mental coach, motivator, and strongest support system," Bhavina says of Nikul. "At home, he manages everything, ensuring I never miss a practice session. As a sportsman himself, he understands my journey and sacrifices. Whether I'm having a good day or facing challenges, he keeps me grounded and encourages me not to give up. When I travel for competitions, he fulfils multiple roles as my trainer, coach, nutritionist and companion, all rolled into one. We are each other's best company," she adds, grateful about Nikul's influence her life. It was his company that made her forget the disappointment of the 2016 Paralympics and move ahead in life.

Putting the disappointment of Rio 2016 behind her, Bhavina intensified her efforts to pursue her goals. Financial constraints were always there, but after the success of our para athletes in the Rio 2016 Paralympics, more support started pouring in from different quarters.

"Her dedication and hard work reflected in her game. To me, hard work means striving for something even when your mind is telling you to give up, and achieving it nonetheless. Bhavina has perfected this," Coach Lalan Doshi reflects. "Professional sports demand many sacrifices, especially for differently-abled athletes who face unique challenges. She adheres strictly to a diet, sacrificing spicy and sweet foods to maintain her weight. After physiotherapy sessions, her body pains every day. There are days when she can barely hold a bat due to blisters and calluses from eight hours of daily practice. Despite these challenges, she wakes up every day, gets back to her training, and refuses to compromise. I've have never seen such dedication in anyone else," says Doshi concludes, speaking highly of his favourite student.

Bhavina's determination and hard work started reaping rich dividends. In 2011, she won a silver medal at the Para Table Tennis Thailand Open. This was followed by another silver at the Asian Regional Championship in 2013. Her success continued with a medal at the 2018 Asian Para Games. In 2019, she reached the peak of her career when she won her first gold medal in singles at the International Para Table Tennis Championship in Bangkok, Thailand, swiftly followed by a gold medal in doubles.

Subsequently, Bhavina qualified for the Tokyo 2020 Paralympics, moving a step closer to her ultimate goal. Before Rio, she had represented India internationally 29 times, where she won 5 gold, 14 silver, and 8 bronze medals. However, as she prepared for the Tokyo Games, the outbreak of COVID-19 brought the world to a halt.

"Every morning, I prayed to the Almighty not to cancel the games," she recalls. "This was the second time that I was close to competing in the Paralympics, and I was determined not to miss it again, no matter what. I had given my all this time, and I had no resources left to go through the grind again," she says.

"So, during the initial weeks of the lockdown, I kept on troubling God with my prayers," says Bhavina with a smile. Her prayers were answered when the games were not cancelled but postponed by a year. Bhavina turned this situation to her advantage by focussing on improving the weaker aspects of her game.

Nikul brought home a club-level table tennis table, but finding space for it was a challenge. They decided to clear a small storeroom to accommodate the table. However, the room was so small that even with the table and Bhavina's wheelchair, there was barely enough room for her practice partner. Nikul found a solution by acquiring a robot that feeds balls to players during practice sessions. After thorough research, he managed to procure a second-hand robot in good condition with assistance from the sports ministry.

Together with her coach, Bhavina worked on various aspects of her game, including analysing videos of foreign players, refining her reflexes, mastering tricks and techniques, and perfecting her services. This focused training helped her to better understand her opponents' strategies and implement countermeasures during crucial matches. As the process of qualification for the games was complete, Bhavina knew who her opponents would be. She did a video analysis of her opponents and devised specific strategies for each.

"Now when I look back, the lockdown period was a big boon for me. I practised for nearly 9–10 hours a day, and addressed many weaknesses in my game. When not exercising or training, I was studying my opponents' game through videos, strategizing on how to overcome them," reflects Bhavina on her training regimen during the lockdown period.

When the contingent of 54 athletes arrived in Japan, few had heard of Bhavina Patel, and even fewer expected anything remarkable from her. In fact, when the Paralympic Committee of India identified potential medal winners, Bhavina's chances were considered quite modest. Strict COVID-19 restrictions limited practice sessions to just 90 minutes, which was a matter of great concern for most athletes.

The TT tables in Tokyo had a greater bounce than what Bhavina was accustomed to during her training. Moreover, due to the lockdown, there had been a considerable gap since she last played on similar tables before the Tokyo Games began. It was here that her mental toughness and meticulous preparation for the event helped her to navigate through the challenge. Bhavina maintained regular contact with her Coach Lalan Doshi, sending him practice videos and discussing strategies, which helped her to regain her rhythm gradually.

As her event approached, Bhavina faced another challenge. Just days before her first match, she fell seriously ill with a high fever of 103 degrees. "I knew immediately that I needed to get tested for COVID-19. If I had tested positive, my dreams of winning India's first-ever medal in the sport would have been shattered before the event even began. I was anxious, but Nikul kept reassuring me not to worry. After testing negative, he interpreted it as a positive sign from above, affirming that I was on the verge of creating history. His words greatly boosted my confidence," she recounts. With no coaches accompanying Bhavina during matches, Nikul's presence alone provided her with the belief and encouragement she needed to compete at her best.

Bhavina, seeded 12th, found herself in a group that included top-seeded Chinese player Zhou Ying and 9th-seeded Megan Shackleton of Great Britain, among others. Only two out of the three paddlers would qualify for the knockout stage. Bhavina's first match against Zhou Ying lasted less than 20 minutes, ending in a decisive defeat of 11-3, 11-9, and 11-2. This left Bhavina in a do-or-die situation for her match against Shackleton, where every aspect of her game was put to the test.

After winning a hard-fought first game 11-7, Bhavina faced a setback in the second, losing narrowly at 9-11. The third game was a tense battle, with Bhavina holding her nerves to clinch it 17-15. Shackleton gave her everything in the fourth game. Yet Bhavina kept her calm, winning crucial points to take the game to 13-11 and securing her place in the knockout stage.

Next, Bhavina was pitched against 8th-ranked Joyce de Oliveira of Brazil in the Round of 16. She demonstrated the same great game temperament and won important moments to win the match at 12-10, 13-11, and 11-6 to advance to the quarter-finals. In the quarter-finals, Bhavina had to climb a mountain named Borislava Perić-Ranković, a gold medallist at the Rio 2016 Games. It was clear to everyone that Bhavina had to play out of her skin against the world No. 2 Serbian in order to progress to the semi-finals.

In this edition of the games, advancing to the semi-finals ensured at least a bronze medal by default due to the unique rule where both semi-final losers automatically received bronze medals without a match for third place.

To everyone's surprise, Bhavina dominated the quarter-final match from start to finish. She dictated terms against the defending champion and won the match in straight games 11-5, 11-6, and 11-7 in just 18 minutes. With this, she was assured of at least a bronze medal. Tears welled in her eyes, and these tears will forever be remembered by sports writers like us. Every tear symbolised the unwavering will, determination, and resolve of this gem from Vadnagar. Vadnagar has produced gems across various fields, from poets Dayaram and Narasinh Mehta, novelist Govardhanram Tripathi, and musician Kaumudi Munshi, to Narendra Modi, and now Bhavina Patel.

Bhavina scripted history, marking India's first-ever medal in table tennis at the Paralympics. While the country had started celebrating, Bhavina had her eyes fixed on the semi-finals. She was not content with just a medal; she wanted the gold. The dominance of Chinese players in the para table tennis is such that defeating them is considered the most difficult, if not impossible, task. In a thrilling semi-final clash, Bhavina achieved the impossible by stunning China's Zhang Miao, ranked third in the world and silver medallist at the Rio 2016

Paralympics, in a hard-fought battle. The match lasted 34 minutes and concluded with scores of 7-11, 11-7, 11-4, 9-11, and 11-8, securing her spot in the finals.

Immediately after the victory, she said, "It is the first time that an Indian player had defeated a Chinese opponent. It is an immense achievement for me. Many used to say beating a Chinese player was impossible. But today, I have proved that nothing is impossible in this world. Everything is possible if you want to do it."

In the final match, Bhavina faced Zhou Ying once again, who had defeated her in a group match lasting only 18 minutes. Zhou Ying is one of China's most decorated para paddlers, boasting of five Paralympic gold medals. She had won two medals in both singles and team events during the 2008 and 2012 Paralympic Games. While she missed the singles podium in Rio 2016 Games, she secured glory in the team event. Zhou Ying is also a six-time World Championship medallist, a 14-time Asian Championship medallist, and a five-time Asian Games gold medal winner. Bhavina could not match Zhou Ying's prowess and skills in the finals, losing 11-7, 11-5, and 11-6 and settling for the silver medal.

Life changed for Bhavina after securing the historic medal. She had never spoken to Sachin Tendulkar, her idol and inspiration whom she dreamed of meeting. Shortly after receiving her medal, she received a call from the Indian cricket legend. It was an emotional moment that brought tears of joy. Remembering the moment, Bhavina says, "Yes, definitely. I had never spoken to Sachin Tendulkar *ji*. He is my role model and inspiration. How do I start off? What should I say? I couldn't gather my thoughts. I had tears in my eyes. I was overwhelmed with emotions and did not know how to handle the moment. I told him, 'Sir, you are my inspiration, and I am learning a lot from you.' He responded, 'No, right now, you have become an inspiration and a role model for the whole world.'"

The God of cricket was spot-on. "I received a call from the Prime Minister of the country, Narendra Modi sir. I feel special now. After winning the medal, the government announced a cash reward. I am being treated as someone special. So, life has really started changing," Bhavina said even before her return to the country. She credits all her achievements to the love of her life and her life partner, Nikul. She says, "I want to tell the world that I consider Nikul to be my greatest mentor in life. Since the day I first met him, he has always stood by me. Although he was a budding cricketer with little knowledge about table tennis, he invested time and effort to learn the nuances of my sport. Nikul has reached a level now where we plan strategies together, and he always helps me with some wonderful inputs about my opponents."

"After the major disappointment of the Rio 2016 Paralympics, he played a major role in helping me overcome the lowest point in my life and plan my qualification for the Tokyo Paralympics. Together, we meticulously planned how to secure my qualification. He has also served as my physiotherapist at numerous events, ensuring I received the necessary massages when I felt stiff before crucial matches. Whenever I am confused about my sport, I turn to him. He knows how to motivate me and explain things in detail. His strength lies in analysing the strengths and weaknesses of my major opponents, which is of great help to me. Above all, whenever I feel down, *Nikul ghazab ke inspiring examples le aata hai* from other sports and fields that cheers me up again," she adds.

Responding to this, Nikul exclaims, "I am over the moon, because my wife has done India proud! Despite the applause she receives today, her journey was never easy. In Ahmedabad, I have seen her travelling 50 km daily for her training. Along the way, she had to change buses and travel in shared autos. She did this for a solid 18 months without ever complaining about it. I have seen her represent the country in tournaments where no other Indian had qualified. There were venues where she had to manoeuvre her wheelchair on her own for more than a kilometre. Despite all these challenges, after winning medals, she would sometimes tell me, '*Mujhe receive karne koi nahi aaya*' (no one came to receive me). What sets her apart is the fact that despite everything, she never gave up and continued inspiring everyone around her. I am honoured that she considers me as her best *guru,* but it's her own hard work, focus, and determination that have helped her in creating history. She has always been very focused on her goals. In fact, after we left for Tokyo, she didn't speak to her parents until after the finals!"

When Bhavina arrived at the Ahmedabad airport, she was greeted with a grand welcome. There were drumrolls, loud cheers, dances, and hoardings which read, "India's pride Bhavina Patel". Tears welled up in her eyes once again. This was the first time in her career that she had received such a tremendous reception. People from around the world wanted to catch a glimpse of the woman whose indomitable spirit had made an unprecedented accomplishment possible.

In the next chapter, our focus shifts to Yogesh Kathunia, whose achievement is a living example of the impact a mother's prayer can have on one's journey in life.

YOGESH KATHUNIYA

The Power of a Mother's Prayers

"The king upon his throne has no higher work than has the mother. The mother is queen of her household"

—**Ellen G. White** in *Adventist Home*

Many great individuals throughout history have written extensively about how their mothers' prayers have shaped their lives. For instance, former American President Abraham Lincoln once said, "I remember my mother's prayers, and they have always followed me. They have clung to me all my life."

Ezra Taft Benson, former United States Secretary of Agriculture and religious leader, reflected, "God does hear and answer prayers ... From childhood, at my mother's knee, where I first learned to pray ... I know without question that it's possible for men and women to reach out in humility and tap that unseen power."

American lecturer and author Dale Carnegie remarked, "During all those years of struggle and heartache, my mother never worried. She took all her troubles to God in prayers."

Yogesh Kathuniya's inspiring journey is yet another testament to the innate strength and power of a mother's prayers.

When Meena Devi and her husband Gyanchand Kathuniya welcomed their baby boy on 3 March 1997, the first thing Meena Devi said was, "Let's name him Yogesh, as he is born on a Monday." In Indian tradition, Monday is associated with Lord Shiva, the God of destruction of the universe. As a devoted follower of Lord Shiva, Meena Devi chose this name for her son to honour her revered deity and to signify the beginning of a new chapter. Since Gyanchand was serving in the Indian Army, Yogesh's early childhood was spent in various locations across the country, depending on his father's postings.

In 2006, Gyanchand was stationed in Chandigarh, while his family had travelled to Bahadurgarh in Haryana to spend time with relatives. Yogesh was nine years old then and was enjoying his summer vacation with his cousins and friends when, one evening, he suddenly fainted and collapsed. Initially, the other children thought it might be a prank, but as Yogesh remained unresponsive for a few minutes, panic spread among them. The children quickly went to inform Yogesh's family that he had fainted while playing.

The family initially suspected heatstroke or dehydration and administered water, lemonade and ORS (Oral Rehydration Salt). However, Yogesh's condition did not improve. His fever escalated, and he could barely speak.

The situation worsened when Yogesh was unable to stand on his own. Realising that his illness might be more serious than initially thought, the family sent an urgent SOS to Gyanchand in Chandigarh.

When Gyanchand reached home, he was shocked to find his son lying in bed in such a distressed state. He immediately took Yogesh to the army hospital, where he was diagnosed with Guillain-Barre Syndrome (GBS). GBS is a rare and severe autoimmune condition that affects the peripheral nervous system, which includes all the nerves outside the brain and spinal cord.

The autoimmune disease causes the immune system to mistakenly attack and destroy specific groups of healthy cells. This damage prevents the nerves from sending sensory information, such as touch, to the spinal cord and brain, resulting in numbness. Furthermore, the brain and spinal cord struggle to transmit signals back to the body, leading to muscle weakness. After a thorough check-up, the doctors informed the Kathuniya family that Yogesh may have to spend the rest of his life on a wheelchair. The family was devastated, unable to come to terms what the medical experts were saying.

"How could this happen to us?" was the first question they asked.

Meena Devi recalls, "Yogesh was too young to grasp what was happening, but his questions deeply troubled us. The virus had begun affecting his body, transforming him from a lively and active child into a wheelchair-bound boy. It was very hard for us to explain what was happening to him."

Yogesh cried and wanted to run away from the hospital. He yearned to run and play as he had before. It was an emotionally devastating and challenging period for the Kathuniya family.

After a while, Gyanchand had to return to work, leaving Meena Devi alone with Yogesh at the hospital. For two years, Yogesh was treated at the Chandigarh Army Hospital, with his mother by his side throughout.

Yogesh fondly recalls, "My mother learned all the physiotherapy exercises and how to perform them correctly to keep my muscles strong. She became my personal trainer. While the nurses would spend half an hour each morning and evening on my physiotherapy, my mother made sure I did exercises at regular intervals throughout the day."

Irrespective of what the doctors said, Meena Devi refused to accept defeat against the virus. She had a strong belief that Lord Shiva would take care of her problems. At the same time, she was aware that God favours those who put in their own effort. Meena Devi believed that a miracle would happen only if she devoted herself fully to her son's recovery.

The doctors and medical staff did their best and eventually discharged Yogesh from the hospital. Returning to Bahadurgarh, Yogesh was still in a wheelchair and his condition showed no immediate signs of improvement. The family knew that two valuable years of Yogesh's education had been lost, and it was crucial for him to return to school.

Yogesh's elder sister Pooja, who was in the same school, took on the responsibility of bringing her younger brother to school in his wheelchair every day. "Those were difficult and painful days. My friends and the neighbourhood girls who had previously walked with me to school began avoiding us. They said they were ashamed to be seen with a boy in a wheelchair. I often heard other students making insensitive remarks about Yogesh. I used to engage Yogesh in some conversation or the other on our way to school so that he doesn't listen to these hurtful comments," Pooja recalls.

When Yogesh's condition didn't show any further signs of improvement, his mother's prayers and devotion to Lord Shiva grew even more intense. Alongside medical treatment, she began seeking remedies beyond conventional science. Some family elders suggested exorcism as they feared that some evil eye might have cursed her son's life.

"I found myself in a constant struggle with Lord Shiva," Meena Devi recounts. "Indian mythology describes Shiva as the hardest deity to please, yet He is averse to no one. Be it a demon or a God, everyone is welcome in His kingdom. I took Yogesh to every temple where exorcism was performed. I even went for a 20-day self-penance in a village in Rajasthan where we had to live on our own without anyone's help. I wanted to try everything for my child. While other parents were able to gift their children sports equipment, all I could provide for Yogesh was a wheelchair. A mother can never endure seeing her child suffer," says Meena Devi with tears in her eyes.

But a mother's prayers cannot be ignored for long. Yogesh's strength began to return to his legs, and a day came when he could stand on his own. It is still rare for someone suffering from the deadly Guillain-Barre syndrome to achieve such a feat. Initially, he needed some support to stand. The entire family rejoiced as if celebrating his second birth. Though his legs would never be the same and he would walk with a limp, the fact that Yogesh would no longer need a wheelchair was a tremendous achievement.

"My Lord fulfilled my wish and showered His blessings on Yogesh. I was certain that Lord Shiva must have had some special plans for him. That day, I vowed to keep a fast every Monday (the day dedicated to Lord Shiva), for the rest of my life," Meena Devi reveals.

Yogesh, who had always been sharp-minded and good in his studies before the virus struck, now wanted to concentrate fully on his education. With his legs still weak, sports then were no longer an option. He scored good marks and secured admission to the prestigious Kirori Mal College (KMC) in Delhi.

"I don't have fond memories of my school days. I was mocked and called various names. But college life was a completely different experience. By then, we had become more mature and had a better understanding of life. My fun-loving and jovial nature made it easy for me to make new friends. We constantly motivated each other," Yogesh says with his characteristic smile.

In college, Yogesh began to make up for all the fun and mischief he had missed during his school years due to illness. He even contested the student elections at KMC. "We were actually supporting a friend for the joint secretary's post. But seeing the kind of response I was getting from the students, the panel decided to switch gears and asked me to run for the position instead. I never thought I'd win, but the girls in the college had a very positive image of me. In college elections, if the girls support you, the boys' votes automatically follow. I ended up winning by a considerable margin," Yogesh recalls with a smile.

So what issues did he raise while campaigning? "Oh, they were quite silly. We promised a grand college fest and a new water tank," he chuckles.

But then how did sports make a comeback in his life?

Yogesh had won bronze and silver medals in his first and second grades at school. He still had those medals hanging at home, but he had resigned himself to the fact that he would never be able to run again. He never imagined he would ever set foot in a stadium again.

India's success in the Rio 2016 Paralympic Games marked a transformative moment for para sports in the country. The love, admiration, accolades, and celebrations for the Rio 2016 medal winners ignited what is known as the "trigger effect" in sports. In 2017, while Yogesh was enjoying his college life, he and his friends visited the university grounds one day and saw athletes training. One of his close friends, Sachin Yadav, suggested that Yogesh consider rekindling his interest in sports, proposing that para sports could be a great option for him.

"When I first went to the field, I saw a discus lying there. I had never touched a discus before. That day, I picked it up and threw it. The way it left my hand gave me an amazing feeling. That was the beginning of my para sports journey," Yogesh recalls.

On that day, sports made a dramatic comeback in his life. Though he initially practised the discus throw on his own, he soon realised the need for a professional coach to guide him through the nuances of the sport and to navigate the complexities of para sports.

Before finding a coach, Yogesh had to first convince his parents. His mother was fully supportive, but his father was hesitant and apprehensive. He was aware that, with weak legs, there was a risk of back injuries or even slip-disc issues for discus throwers. His father had not forgotten the difficult years when Yogesh had been confined to a wheelchair. However, Yogesh's excitement and determination eventually won his father over. How could he not allow his son to pursue his dream?

After securing his parents' support, Yogesh began his search for a coach. "I don't want to get into the complexities of the coaching world and how it affects your growth in para sports, but I initially had some disappointing experiences with coaches. Then someone recommended Naval Singh, and my life changed completely," Yogesh recalls.

People advised Yogesh to think twice before approaching Naval Singh, a Dronacharya awardee and known for his tough demeanour. But Yogesh had made up his mind that he wanted to train under Naval Singh.

"When Yogesh came to me, he was quite soft. He had long arms and a natural talent for discus release. But I had to make him tough, both physically and mentally. He was always willing to do whatever I asked and never questioned my methods. Sometimes I can be eccentric, but that's because my goal is to get an Olympic medal. If you aim for the highest, then there are no shortcuts. The training has to be the toughest," says Naval Singh.

"One day, after the morning practice, Coach *Sa'ab* said, 'Come at 2, and we'll resume our session.' I was puzzled because it was May and very hot during the day. I said, 'Sir, it will be extremely hot at 2 p.m.' The coach looked at me and replied, 'I'm not talking about p.m., I'm talking about 2 a.m.' That's how rigorous Coach Naval's training was," says Yogesh. The coach's intense and rigorous training, combined with Yogesh's hard work, began to show results. He competed in the Nationals and performed exceptionally well. He won a gold medal at the Grand Prix tournament and qualified for the 2018 Jakarta Asian Games. "When I qualified for the 2018 Asian Games, my parents were really excited. No one expected me to reach this milestone so quickly. When I was given my ceremonial and playing kits, there were tears in everyone's eyes. I had worn blazers before, but this one had 'INDIA' emblazoned on it, along with our Tricolour. I can't express what that moment felt like," Yogesh recalls.

The 2018 Jakarta Asian Games were Yogesh's first major tournament, and it was a significant challenge for him as an emerging athlete competing against established names at the Asian level. Despite not winning a medal and finishing in fourth place, the experience boosted his confidence immensely. "I told myself that all I needed to do was work harder, and I could surpass them. Even though I didn't win a medal, my confidence soared after the Asian Games," he says.

However, one mistake Yogesh made was trying to pursue discus, javelin, and shot put simultaneously. This put a lot of pressure on his body, leading to frequent injuries. "Yogesh was good in all three disciplines, so as a coach, I thought that if he became stronger, he might be able to compete in all three events and bring more accolades to the country. But his body couldn't handle the demands of all three. We eventually decided to focus solely on his favourite event, discus throw," recalls Naval Singh.

From that point on, Yogesh dedicated all his focus, efforts, and training to discus throw. In 2019, he participated in the World Championships in Dubai, which are on a par with the Paralympics in terms of competition level. This was a golden chance for Yogesh to make his mark on the world stage. He threw the discus 42.51 metres and won a bronze medal—a remarkable achievement for both him and his Coach Naval Singh. This success also qualified Yogesh for the Tokyo 2020 Paralympic Games.

"Winning the World Championship medal brought many changes. There was significant media coverage. While I had always had the support of my family and friends, I started receiving support from various new quarters across the country. People in my area began to realise that one of their own had become a world champion," says Yogesh.

With the Tokyo Paralympic Games as their ultimate goal, Yogesh and his team began meticulous planning and training. However, the COVID-19 pandemic disrupted the preparations and introduced uncertainty about whether the event would proceed as planned. Yogesh's parents also contracted the virus. While his mother was asymptomatic, his father's health was severely affected.

"It was a very tough period. All training centres, gyms, and sports grounds were closed. We couldn't travel or move freely. The country's lockdown had brought everyone's lives to a standstill. I had mentally and physically prepared for the Tokyo 2020 Games, but now they were postponed. We didn't even know if the games would happen at all. There was frequent discussion that if even major sports like cricket were affected, para sports would likely be neglected. The atmosphere was filled with negativity. I even considered quitting the games," Yogesh recalls.

This was the phase when Yogesh turned to online gaming, spending hours each day immersed in virtual worlds. It became an obsession and addiction, but in hindsight, this distraction helped him push negative thoughts to the background. Though his physical training did suffer during lockdown, Yogesh was mentally refreshed and eager to return to his sport.

So when the lockdown was gradually eased for international athletes, Yogesh's mind was clear of negativity. He wasn't bogged down by overthinking his discus throw. It was then that the new dates for the Tokyo Olympic and Paralympic Games were announced. It was a huge relief for all athletes, including Yogesh, who had invested years of hard work and dedication into their training.

"Neeraj Chopra's gold medal at the Olympics had made the entire country proud. Until then, India's Olympic results had been underwhelming, but Neeraj's victory lifted the nation's spirits and set a positive tone for the upcoming Paralympic Games," Yogesh explains.

In total, 54 athletes had qualified for the Tokyo 2020 Paralympic Games. This was the largest contingent India had ever sent to the para games. Prime Minister Narendra Modi added a personal touch by engaging with the athletes and extending his best wishes before their departure to Tokyo. There was a palpable excitement in the air around para sports, as everyone recognised that while the Rio 2016 Games had laid the groundwork, the Tokyo 2020 Games were poised to build on that foundation with even greater achievements.

"I remember that day vividly. I woke up at 2 a.m. and couldn't get back to sleep. It was such a big day. As I lay in bed, my mind was going through the entire process. I was reminiscing about the good times and trying to stick to the routine that had brought me success before. I had thrown 45.58 metres in the selection trials. I knew that if everything went well, I could win a medal. But my goal was to break the world record of 46.68 metres set by a Brazilian athlete in 2018, and I was confident I could do it," he says, taking us back to that day.

In the list of eight competitors, Yogesh was assigned the third spot. Each player had six attempts, and Yogesh had devised a strategy: he would take risks with his first three throws and play it safe with the remaining three if needed. On his first throw, he gave it his all, but his hips raised and it was given a foul. After this, Yogesh became a little nervous and decided to play it safe, aiming to secure at least some distance in his name on the scoreboard. His second throw landed at 42.84 metres, putting him in second place after two throws. However, Yogesh was disappointed with this distance, as he had consistently thrown over 44 metres during practice.

In his next two attempts, Yogesh pushed himself but both resulted in fouls, with the issues being similar to his first foul. By this time, Leonardo Diaz Aldana of Cuba had thrown 43.36 metres and moved into second place, while Konstantinos Tzounis of Greece had achieved 42.86 metres and was in third. After four throws, Yogesh had only one valid attempt and was in fourth place.

Regaining his composure, Yogesh then threw 43.55 metres, propelling him into second place. Batista dos Santos from Brazil had been leading from the start, and his fifth throw of 45.25 metres solidified his lead. On his sixth and final throw, Yogesh pushed himself further and achieved a distance of 44.38 metres, which was also his season's best. This final throw secured him the silver medal and made history for the country.

"It was a sigh of relief. If you look at my reaction after the sixth and final throw, you'll see I was a bit disappointed. I felt I could have easily broken the world record and won gold for India. Nonetheless, it was a great moment. Four years of hard work and perseverance from everyone had paid off," said Yogesh.

The entire town of Bahadurgarh erupted with joy. Yogesh's modest home was overwhelmed with local, national, and international media. His grandfather was occupied with interviews, his face beaming with pride and happiness over his grandson's achievements. However, the person who was the happiest was his mother Meena Devi. Her tears flowed continuously for two days, as she felt her Lord Shiva had given her much more than she had ever expected. Destiny had put Yogesh on wheelchair, but his mother had lifted him onto the podium.

"*Mere paas Maa hai, Gold to mein lekar hi aaonga*" (I have my mother with me. I will definitely get the gold) are the words Yogesh now carries with him as he sets his sights on the Paris 2024 Paralympics. Indeed, *Maa ki praarthana se badhkar kuch nahin* (nothing is more powerful than a mother's prayer)!

After the power of a mother's love, it's time to explore how education can complement sports. As we continue our journey in this book, the next chapter introduces our hero, Harvinder Singh—the smiling professor.

HARVINDER SINGH

The Smiling Professor

*"Padhoge likhoge, banoge nawab, kheloge kudoge, banoge
kharab (Education, and not sports, will provide you
with the means of living)."*

—A popular saying

While we were growing up, our parents and teachers fervently preached this adage, emphasising the value of education over sports. However, in the new India, it's time to update this adage to reflect a more balanced view: *Padhayee aur khelkood dono hai jaruree. Padhoge to badhoge; kheloge to khiloge* (Both studies and sports are equally important. If you study, you will advance in life; if you play, you will blossom).

Tennis legend Mahesh Bhupathi summarised the situation perfectly when he said that Indian parents push their kids into education with the same intensity that parents in Australia push theirs into sports.

Times are changing, and more Indian parents are now encouraging their children to pursue sports. In today's evolving India, professional sports have become a lucrative career path. Even those in other professions are recognising the value of

sports in maintaining physical fitness and enhancing their overall performance.

Likewise, professional athletes are increasingly acknowledging the importance of academics in gaining a deeper understanding of their sport. One such sporting icon of our time is Paralympics medallist Harvinder Singh. Due to his exemplary demeanour, he is affectionately known as "The Smiling Professor."

On the morning of 25 February 1991, in the remote village of Gull Cheeka, near Ajitnagar town in the Kaithal district of Haryana, a new day dawned like any other. Harvinder Singh was born on that day to Paramjeet Singh and Harbhajan Kaur, a farming couple with a modest financial background. Life was progressing smoothly for the family until Harvinder was 15 months old. At that time, he caught a high fever and was diagnosed with dengue. As the fever did not subside, he was treated with high doses of medication. Unfortunately, the incorrect medication led to severe side effects that began affecting his lower body, particularly his legs.

The family was devastated when they realised that their baby would not be able to walk or run like other children of his age. Harvinder's mother was heartbroken, and she wept day and night, struggling to come to terms with the situation. Despite the initial gloom, the Singh family gradually accepted their circumstances and embraced it as their destiny. They chose to move forward with their lives, making a conscious effort to ensure that Harvinder did not feel that anything was amiss. They were determined that this adversity would not hinder his growth and development.

There is a unique beauty in childhood, where the concerns that trouble adults are often met with the carefree laughter of youth. Harvinder grew up alongside the other kids in his village and attended the local primary school. What made him stand out as a child was his remarkable aptitude for academics. His concentration and focus were exceptional, and he would not rest until he had solved any problem that arose in his studies.

Although Harvinder was an introverted child, he kept himself busy with his multitasking abilities. "As a kid, Harry was very good at juggling various activities. He never turned down an opportunity, whether it was playing with friends or joining in their mischief, while still managing to complete his homework and score good marks. Though we provided him with the best we could, there were always limitations, but he never complained. He was more mature than other children of his age, and as he grew older, he started keeping to himself," recalls Harvinder's father.

Looking at his academic progress, it became clear that the local primary schooling in the village wouldn't be sufficient for Harvinder. His potential for higher studies was evident, so with a heavy heart, his family agreed to let him move to Punjab University in Patiala, nearly 100 km from their village. It was here that Harvinder's life was destined to change forever.

"In my village or nearby, we never knew that archery was a sport. We always thought it was used only as a weapon in wars," Harvinder recalls. "It wasn't until I arrived in Patiala for my graduation that I first saw archers practising. That's when I realised that archery was also a sport. I had a natural attraction to bows and arrows because, as kids, we used to watch television serials like the *Ramayana* and the *Mahabharata*. I also felt a sense of calmness in the game, which appealed to me. My interest was further piqued when I watched archery at the London 2012 Olympic Games. I spent hours observing the archers practice, fascinated by how different the sport was in real life compared to what I had imagined as a child," he adds.

Inspired by this newfound passion, Harvinder Singh decided to seriously pursue archery.

Jeewan Jyot Singh "Teja" was the first coach to introduce Harvinder Singh to the basics of archery. Harvinder began with compound archery, which uses more advanced bows. He worked hard with full dedication and purpose, but the results were disappointing, leading him to contemplate quitting.

"I was disheartened by the results. After three years of giving my all, there was nothing to show for it. I didn't understand what was going wrong, but my friends and coaches encouraged me to persist. I'm deeply grateful to them for their support," Harvinder recalls.

Instead of quitting, Harvinder decided to switch from compound archery to recurve archery. This change had an immediate positive effect, and he began to see significant improvements. The arrival of Coach Gaurav Sharma in Harvinder's life proved to be a major turning point.

Harvinder never missed a practice session and focused on addressing his weaknesses. His hard work paid off as he started winning medals at the national level. This success instilled confidence in local coaches, who began to believe that Harvinder could build a career in the sport he had initially pursued as a secondary interest.

Harvinder made his first major appearance at the 2016 National Para Archery Championship in Rohtak, Haryana, where he clinched a bronze medal. The following year, he secured seventh place at his first Para Archery World Championships, a result that further solidified his coach's belief in his potential. Just as it seemed his career was on the verge of taking off, Harvinder faced a major setback in his personal life.

Just days before the 2018 Para Asian Games, Harvinder lost his mother. For an athlete on the brink of peak performance, this was a tremendous blow. Harvinder, however, took the personal setback in his stride and astonished everyone by winning a gold medal in Jakarta.

"It was one of the most difficult phases of my life; I lost my mother 20 days before the games. But I remained focused, kept my motivation intact, and gave it my all. Although I had worked hard, the gold medal was a surprise, and it was dedicated to my mother," Harvinder said in an interview published on the Tokyo 2020 Paralympics website in June 2020.

After this remarkable achievement, Harvinder made a decision that revealed a different facet of his personality.

"When I won the Asian gold medal, my PhD supervisor asked if I wanted to continue with my studies. He assumed that, having achieved a medal, I might not be concerned about my future. I told him that I definitely wanted to continue with my studies. Not only was it enhancing my knowledge, but it was also benefiting my archery. When you study, you have to do a lot of research and experiment with various methods to solve problems. I applied these skills to improve my scores and overall performance in archery. So, my education didn't hinder my game; in fact, it complemented it," Harvinder explains, discussing why he never quit higher education.

In my professional journey, I have had the opportunity to

speak with some of the most successful cricketers such as K. Srikkanth, Javagal Srinath, Anil Kumble, Rahul Dravid, and V.V.S. Laxman. One key aspect that sets them apart is their emphasis on the role of education. They have often talked about how their academic pursuits not only improved their performance on the field but also contributed to their overall well-being. Their success in academics provided them with stability during both the highs and lows of their careers.

After his gold medal performance at the Para Asian Games, Harvinder had a disappointing outing at the Fazza Para Archery Championships in Dubai. Despite this disappointment, he rallied to secure ninth place at the Para Archery World Championships, which earned him a spot at the Tokyo 2020 Paralympics.

However, the onset of the COVID-19 pandemic and the ensuing lockdown brought unprecedented challenges. During this period, when the very survival of human beings was at stake, Harvinder Singh faced multiple difficulties.

"We were instructed to leave the sports facilities and return home when the lockdown was first announced. None of us had ever heard of or faced a situation like this before. We were all deeply concerned about our own safety and that of our families, so we went back to be with them. Then came the news that the Olympics and Paralympics had been postponed indefinitely. Personally, I was very disappointed and low after the announcement. However, nothing was more important than the lives of people. So, like many other athletes, I had to take this in my stride. For a few days, I practiced indoors with whatever objects I could find around the house. Once the restrictions eased, I retrieved my archery gear from Patiala and resumed my practice at home," says Harvinder.

By April, the fields lay empty, and the uncertainty caused by the restrictions meant no one knew when the next crop would be sown. Harvinder asked his family to set up targets in the fields so he could resume his practice during the lockdown. Sports camps restarted in October 2020, allowing him to return to Patiala and resume his routine. However, the country was soon hit by a severe second wave of COVID-19, bringing everything to a standstill once more.

"I didn't waste much time during the second wave," Harvinder recalls. "The situation was even more alarming with the increasing number of deaths and widespread panic. I packed my bag and headed back to my village. This time too, it was that time of the year where the fields were empty, so I set up temporary targets once again. This time, I was joined by two young boys from the village who showed an interest in archery. They became my practice partners, and I began teaching them the intricacies of the sport. Having the company of the kids was enjoyable and made the practice sessions more fun," says Harvinder with a smile.

Harvinder practised in the fields both morning and afternoon. In the evenings, he would have the boys use mobile phone flashlights to illuminate the targets, allowing him to practice shooting in the dark. Reflecting on it, Harvinder acknowledges that this unconventional night practice subsequently helped him to get the medal for the country.

"My semi-final and final matches were held at night during the Tokyo Games. If I hadn't practised with mobile torch lights in the field, I don't think I would have been as well-prepared for those night events," confesses Harvinder.

Finally, along with the rest of the Indian contingent, Harvinder reached Tokyo. A total of 31 archers qualified for

I admire M.S. Dhoni. I too try to be as cool as MSD before my event.

NISHAD KUMAR

SINGHRAJ ADHANA

I aspired to achieve something meaningful to make my parents and country proud, while fulfilling my grandfather's wishes.

I thought of ending my life but realised redemption lay not in quitting but in fulfilling my uncompleted dream.

SUNDAR SINGH GURJAR

BHAVINA PATEL

I have proved that nothing is impossible in this world. Everything is possible if you want to do it.

When I first saw a discus in the field, I threw it and felt an incredible thrill; thus began my para sports journey.

YOGESH KATHUNIYA

HARVINDER SINGH

I was the first Indian to achieve a podium finish in Paralympic archery. My achievement will inspire future contenders.

When you pursue a passion that you enjoy, favourable results often follow.

SUHAS L.Y.

PRAVEEN KUMAR | *It was a significant moment for my family and me when I fully dedicated myself to sports; it was the wisest decision I made.*

More than anything, I was delighted with how I was performing. I cleared all four heights on my first attempt.

SHARAD KUMAR

MANOJ SARKAR

When you excel in a sport, children don't discriminate against you; in fact, they respect you more.

Pranav Soorma

Rudransh Khandelwal

Thulasimathi Murugesan

EMERGING ATHLETES

Simran Sharma

Mona Agarwal

Sheetal Devi

EMERGING ATHLETES

the individual recurve event at the Tokyo Paralympics. During the ranking rounds, each archer shoots 72 arrows, and they are seeded based on their scores. The single highest-ranked archer from these rounds would advance directly to the round of 16.

Archery is a sport where external factors play a major role on the performance, and even a slight breeze or wind can disrupt an archer's preparation and strategy. Tokyo's weather presented a significant challenge, as it fluctuated between bright, sunny, and windy conditions on 27 August 2021 during the qualification round.

After shooting 72 arrows, Harvinder was ranked 21st with a score of 600. His performance included 14 arrows hitting the 10-point mark, with 6 of those being bull's-eyes.

"It was very sunny and windy on the day of qualification. It was tough not just for me, but for all the archers to hit the target under such conditions. The 21st rank that I got was my lowest rank in qualification till date in international tournaments. However, I didn't let it deter me as I always believe that whatever happens, it happens for a reason. I refused to let the pressure affect me," says Harvinder remembering the tough qualification day.

While the qualification day had been sunny and windy, the day of the competition brought a persistent light drizzle from the morning, presenting a new set of challenges for the archers. Harvinder's first match was against Italy's Stefano Travisani, who ranked 12th after the qualification round.

Harvinder began with great momentum, winning the first two ends and taking a 4-0 lead. However, he lost his rhythm, allowing Travisani to come back in the match. Harvinder lost the third end, drew the fourth, and lost the fifth. After five ends, the scores were tied at 5-5, pushing the match to a tie-breaker shot.

In the tie-breaker, Harvinder maintained his composure and shot a perfect 10, while Stefano managed only a 7. Harvinder and the entire Indian contingent were relieved by his victory.

Harvinder Singh, a Sikh who always competes wearing a turban, faced an additional challenge due to the persistent rain. His turban became soaked, and he didn't have a spare one in his kit bag. With only a five-hour gap between his first and second matches, there was no time to return to the Games Village and change into dry clothes.

Harvinder had lunch and took a nap at the temporary facilities provided at the venue. However, since the venue was air-conditioned and he was wearing wet clothes and a wet turban, he began to develop a fever, with his body temperature rising slowly.

"I didn't allow my fluctuating body temperature affect my mindset. Since my mind was strong, my body started fighting the fever. I stayed completely focused on my next match, confident that if I didn't worry about the fever, it wouldn't impact my performance," says Harvinder about his small battle with the fever.

Harvinder's next opponent was Bato Tsydendorzheiv of Russia, who was in an exceptional form on that day. Tsydendorzheiv had finished 5th in the qualification round and had already delivered a strong performance in his previous match. As it was the round of 16, the pressure was intense. Despite Harvinder's mental strength, the five-hour gap and his rising fever began to affect his concentration. He lost the first two ends, trailing 0-4.

At this point, Harvinder feared his journey at the Tokyo Games might end here. However, he made a remarkable comeback, winning the next two ends to level the score at 4-4. The final end was a tie, with both archers scoring 28 each, sending the match into a tie-breaker.

In the tie-breaker, it was Tsydendorzheiv who succumbed to the pressure, scoring a 7, while Harvinder managed to score an 8. With this narrow victory, Harvinder advanced to the quarter-finals, marking another significant milestone in his journey.

Harvinder was now just one step away from winning a medal, but his fever continued to worsen. By the time the results were announced, he was shivering and feeling quite unwell. Although he wanted to take some medicine, his coach advised against it. Harvinder was thus battling on two fronts: preparing for his next opponent while grappling with fever and fatigue.

In the quarter-finals, Harvinder faced Maik Szarszewski of Germany. Determined not to drag the match out, he secured a victory in just four ends, with a score of 6-2. The rain and his fever seemed to have little impact on his performance, and his concentration improved with each passing match.

In the crucial semi-final match, Harvinder was set to compete against Kevin Mather from the USA, who had defeated the top-ranked archer in the tournament and was eager to face the Indian opponent. Before the start of the semi-final, the weather shifted once again: the rain stopped, but the wind began to blow unpredictably, varying between strong gusts and gentle breezes.

Harvinder says, "It was very difficult to gauge the impact of the wind on my arrows. Some arrows hit the target perfectly, unaffected by the wind, while others veered off course even with just a slight breeze. It was very tough to calculate and I erred. I needed a 10 to tie the score, but I only managed an 8, which led to my loss in the semi-final."

Archery is one event that has been associated with the Paralympic Games right from the beginning, yet no Indian athlete had managed to reach the podium until Harvinder's journey. The semi-final loss, despite being close, raised concerns about whether he would experience the familiar feeling of "so-near-and-yet-so-far". Though disappointed, Harvinder was not heartbroken after the loss. He understood that sometimes, despite one's best efforts, external conditions can be overwhelming and beyond control. He still had one last opportunity to bring honour to himself and his country in the bronze medal match. So he channelled all his energy and focus into this final battle, fully aware that this was his moment to shine.

Harvinder's bronze medal match was against South Korea's Kim Min Su, who had suffered a setback after leading 5-1 in his semi-final against China's Zhao. Kim, determined to redeem himself, entered the match with renewed vigour and was considered one of the favourites to win.

Harvinder won the first end with a score of 26-24, but Kim Min Su responded strongly, taking the second end with a high score of 29-27. Harvinder came back in the third end with a 28-25 victory, and the fourth end ended in a tie at 25-25. Before going to the last end, Harvinder was leading 5-3 and needed just a tie to secure the bronze medal.

However, the pressure of the moment affected Harvinder's performance. "I would have won the medal in the fourth set itself. I just needed an eight to score. But my mind got cluttered with all kinds of anxious thoughts. It was about winning the bronze medal, jumping around, how I would react, and how my life would change after winning the bronze medal. After all, no Indian before me had won a Paralympic medal in archery. Till the time I was releasing the arrow, my mind was unstable. As a result, my arrow missed the target completely. I hit a seven, which I rarely do even on my worst days," Harvinder recalls.

This mental lapse allowed Kim Min Su to come back, and the scores were tied after the fifth end. The match went to a tie-breaker, with everything riding on a single arrow. However, this time, Harvinder was alert and approached the final shot with clarity and resolve. Like Arjun of the *Mahabharata*, he honed his concentration solely on the target.

"I just went into that zone and I was lucky that I slipped into it comfortably. For me, the rest of the world did not exist for those 30 seconds. I was in a deep zone where I just loaded the arrow, locked it, and released it. During the entire process, my mind was so calm that I could hear my heartbeat and my breath very clearly. I was able to hit the target and win the medal, but I just couldn't celebrate it the way I had imagined because I was still in that zone of calmness. I had never been in this zone before. It was surreal," Harvinder recalls.

He reflected on the gravity of the moment, saying, "Out of the five matches that I played, three went to a tie-breaker, which meant that the entire outcome of my nine years of training and hard work came down to that one shot. So, one had to be really calm and composed during those crucial moments. I won't say I was totally elated, but, yes, I think I did reasonably well. After I won the bronze medal by hitting a 10, my expressions were very normal because I was still in that zone of complete focus, and coming out of it and feeling everything again took at least 10-15 minutes more."

After the medal victory, a great frenzy of celebrations erupted. Harvinder shared a small celebration with his teammates and then took part in the medal ceremony. The euphoria continued as Prime Minister Narendra Modi personally called to congratulate him over the phone. The celebrations carried on until 4 in the morning. Despite the joyous occasion, Harvinder admitted that it hadn't fully sunk in yet.

It was only when he was alone in his room that the reality began to set in. "After me, Indians can aim for the podium finish in archery at the Paralympics. I was the first to achieve this. For now, I am alone up there, but my achievement will serve as an inspiration for others in the future," reflects Harvinder.

Archery and shooting are perhaps two sports where even the well-laid predictions can go awry. While thorough preparation and training can significantly reduce the chances of uncertainty, the outcomes on the final day remain largely impossible to predict. Despite the effort and practice invested, success often comes down to a few critical moments.

"I can't promise anything about the results in Paris 2024, but one thing I can promise is my complete dedication, hard work, and commitment towards the event," Harvinder asserts. The person who had considered quitting archery in 2016 had now become the sole Indian to win a medal in Paralympic archery.

As he wraps up the conversation, one final question arises: What would Harvinder have become if he had quit archery in 2016? "Don't worry sir, I had cleared my UGC-NET exam in 2016, so I would have ended up becoming a lecturer," says Harvinder with a smile! Rightly said, the smiling professor!

As we reach the final stages of our journey in the book, it's time to turn the spotlight onto Suhas Y.L., another remarkable figure in the world of para sports. Suhas is not only notable for his achievements on the court but also for being the first Indian Administrative Service (IAS) officer to win a medal at the Paralympics.

SUHAS L.Y.

The Civil Servant Who Smashed his Way to Paralympic History

"When I was a young man just out of the law school and eager to get on with my life, on whim I briefly put aside my reading preference for fiction and history and bought one of those how-to books: 'How to Get Control of Your Time and Your Life' by Alan Lakein. The book's main point was the necessity of listing, short-, medium- and long-term goals, then categorising them in the order of importance, with the A group being the most important, the B group next and C the last and then listing under each goals the specific activities designed to achieve them."

—The opening lines of former US President Bill Clinton's autobiography *My Life*

Author Alan Lakein, whose books have influenced millions, including Bill Clinton, is credited with several quotes, the most famous being: "Time = Life. Therefore, waste your time and waste your life, or master your time and master your life." Our next real-life hero, Suhas L.Y., has mastered this mantra to perfection. Suhas's life journey mirrors Lakein's question, "What is the best use of my time right now?" At various crucial stages in his life, Suhas has sought to answer this question in his own way, and has achieved phenomenal

success across diverse fields. Here is an attempt to unravel the journey of Suhas, an Indian Administrative Service (IAS) officer who has won a Paralympic medal for the country.

Suhas Lalinakere Yathiraj, popularly known as Suhas L.Y., was born to L.K. Yathiraj and Jayashree C.S. in the Hassan district of Karnataka. He completed his early schooling in Dudda. As his father was a government servant, Suhas had to move frequently, travelling with him during his various postings.

In his blog, Suhas writes,

My dreams were different. My initial days were spent in Dudda, a remote village in Mandya district where my father was posted. I used to travel to Shivalli, a nearby village, for Kannada-medium school by bullock carts. My dream then was to play in paddy fields and fly in an airplane. As I was from a village and studied in Kannada medium, I was denied admission for Class 5 in an English medium school in Tiptur, a taluka in Karnataka. Similar denial was repeated at Shimoga, my hometown for the same reason (in spite of good previous academic records). Finally, when I got into an English medium in 8th standard, the first English class seemed as a strange Italian movie! I could pull it off somehow, as I was lucky to have good guidance and enough opportunities, with the support of my father who had more confidence in me than I had in myself. This paragraph is not at all written to boast about my past achievements (because I know many people who have come out of far more tougher situations to do a lot more), but to give some confidence to people who might have faced similar situations and to tell the world that sadly such things do happen even today.

In the same blog, Suhas beautifully narrates the significant gap between the two worlds of rural and urban life:

There is a tremendous gap in the quality of teaching, access to resources between a city like Bangalore and a village like Agumbe. So the amount and types of skills differ between a Bangalore boy and an Agumbe boy (though born with same chromosomal abilities/IQ). While the former (with the help of coaching, knowledge of English, etc.) can reach up to the position of CEO of a company, the latter's skills become only good enough for a low-paying industrial job or for a job in agriculture. Please note, I am not envying the former but only empathizing the latter. One question arises: when a person fails, we blame him or her, but do we anytime blame the system that played its part? Two, successful people should be thankful first and proud next. Warren Buffet asserted that if he were born in Congo or Rwanda, he probably wouldn't be as successful as he is today. His investment capabilities were more than useful in a capitalist country like America, he but would have needed different capabilities to succeed in Rwanda! When the second richest person makes such an admission, I can stop going to others to confirm the same.

Perhaps, it was the desire to bridge the gap between the two Indias that led Suhas to forgo a lucrative opportunity abroad with an MNC and instead pursue the challenging path of the IAS exam. We will explore this aspect of his life further as we proceed.

Born with a disability, Suhas received rock-solid support from his parents, especially his father, which helped him remain unaffected by his congenital one-legged disability. Suhas says, "For me, disability is a state of mind that you need to overcome. The way society treats you is often unfair, and that's where the real challenge lies. How do you motivate yourself and maintain your confidence when faced with adverse comments or when things don't go as planned? If you can overcome this mental hurdle early in life, the rest of the challenges will be easier to handle."

Suhas adds, "I owe a great deal to my parents. I was never given any special treatment from the start. My parents encouraged me to play with my schoolmates and participate in inter-school races—opportunities that many parents of children with special needs might not provide. I believe that stigma often starts at home, and the strengths needed to lead a normal life also begin there. My father encouraged me to interact with able-bodied individuals, as they are the ones with whom we coexist in society. He was my role model and always set goals that seemed beyond my reach. However, these 'out-of-bounds' targets pushed me to stretch my limits, leading to the achievement of various milestones."

Suhas excelled in school and cracked both medical and engineering entrance exams after Class 12. While his family wanted him to pursue admission at Bangalore Medical College, Suhas was determined to follow in his father's footsteps and become an engineer. This conflicting desire was distressing for him, but with his father's support, he was able to navigate through it.

Suhas recalls, "When we came home, the whole family was celebrating. However, the next day, my father noticed that I wasn't as happy as everyone else. He realised that, despite securing a medical seat, I was more inclined towards engineering. He called me aside and said, 'While we all want you to become a doctor, you want to be an engineer.' Just like in the popular Hindi film *Dilwale Dulhania Le Jayenge*, where Simran's father encourages her to move forward and live her life as she wishes (*Ja Simran, jee le apni zindagi*), my father told me, '*Jaa jee le apni zindagi*' (go and live your life)."

After this, Suhas's father arranged for career counselling, which led him to pursue engineering. He was subsequently admitted to the National Institute of Technology, Surathkal, Karnataka, where he pursued a degree in computer science and engineering, and topped his batch. From that point, the sky was the limit for Suhas. Like many in his position, he could have pursued an MBA from a prestigious international institution and secured a high-paying job at an MNC. However, Suhas had different aspirations. He had to make a choice between a predictable path and one filled with uncertainty. Ultimately, he sought answers in life's questions in his own way and decided to embark on a career in public service.

Suhas writes in his blog,

As my father was a government servant, he had many times mentioned to me about IAS being a wonderful option. I had, in fact, seen how government service provides an opportunity to interact with people and contribute to public life. I had, however, also seen many disadvantages of that—low salaries, more constraints, etc. All I knew (or had heard, to be more correct) about the exam then was that it was tough, and tougher for those with the science background. Candidates preparing for these exams had to work very hard, sacrifice sleep to be able to cover the vast course, compete with 0.4 million people write it, and approximately only 500 people would make it through, so the level of uncertainty and risk was Himalayan.

Further, in the blog, he writes,

Now the time had arrived. I had to decide between accepting and rejecting the MNC offer. I decided to ask myself, what did I want to do in my life? After 20 years, if I look back, which career path would give me better satisfaction? The answer was, I wanted to serve this society, wanted to change many things in this society, work among the people. One practical means to satisfy these desires was to join the civil services. (I know all of you may not agree with this.) The decision was taken. I rejected the MNC offer. Then I set all my energies on "Mission IAS Exam".

Aside from a lack of interest, many people shy away from taking the civil services exam (commonly known as the "IAS exam") due to several reasons: First, there is a perception of professional hazards such as limited autonomy in these roles. Secondly, not everyone is willing to invest valuable years of their youth into something with uncertain rewards, often resulting in little more than "best of luck" from peers and a vast amount of knowledge gained through extensive study. For someone who can secure a monthly salary of Rs 30,000 in a private job, the idea of "one bird in hand being better than two in the bush" is compelling, especially knowing that thousands of others are also vying for the same opportunity.

Suhas writes in his blog,

Out of approximately 4 lakh candidates, nearly 500 make it to the final list; the rest 3,99,500 fail in the attempt. Accepting failure is more difficult than accepting success. However, a majority have the difficult task cut out. With so much of uncertainty hovering around, to overcome the fear of failure, I told myself that, after 20 years, I should not regret of having not done something which I wanted to do. If I try and fail, that's more acceptable than to have not made any effort towards my dream. After all, the journey of chasing dreams is not a bad one. (I read *"The Alchemist"* and saw the film *Lakshya* to reassure myself!) Even if I fail in my journey, I would end up becoming a better person with all the knowledge that I would have gathered with attempts in civil services exam. Any day, a career in software industry would assure me my bread. For now, other things in life can wait. In simple words, "Suhas, follow your dreams", was my conscience call.

Following this decision, Suhas, along with a few friends, started working towards achieving his aim. Once he committed himself, he spared no effort. Balancing work and preparation was challenging at first, but he gradually mastered the art. Ultimately, 10 November 2006 became a pivotal day in his life—this was the last day of his IAS exam.

In his blog, he writes,

I had to write answers for 6 hours that day. The night before, I did not get sleep for more than an hour and as I was about to leave my house for the exam, I started feeling sleepy, discomfort crept in to my head. Mr Fear was staring at me. Before entering the exam hall, to keep my "body" awake I took two wet kerchiefs, and to keep my "mind" awake I took the ideals of freedom fighters, and many great people who had fought greater odds and had come out with flying colours. I thought to myself, this is the day, this is the hour that could change my destiny. It did. I got selected to the Indian Administrative Service (IAS). Among all the papers, I got the highest score in the paper I wrote that day. If you cross Mr Fear, you will see Ms Victory. Believe me, she is beautiful. The lady is worth fighting for, and worth waiting for.

Later in his blog, Suhas beautifully sums up his journey to Mussoorie, writing: "Life takes us to places, gives us successes, failures, joys, sorrows, etc. It has certainly done that for me, from Shimoga to Stuttgart and from Mandya to Mussoorie. The same society that once denied me opportunities has given me a chance to reach the higher echelons of administration.

It has done the same for many others. In the 'journey of life', we have to seek answers to two questions: What do you want to do in life? How do you want to do it? This quest shapes the choices we make and the decisions we take. I believe there is no one 'best' journey. As I begin my journey to Mussoorie (where the training academy is located), I still pinch myself to confirm that I am indeed an IAS officer—I'm not just sleeping (dreaming)!"

Having secured the Uttar Pradesh cadre, Suhas faced a fresh set of challenges. Those who have observed Suhas closely in the Uttar Pradesh bureaucracy talk about his initial struggles, ranging from adjusting to a new language and culture to earning acceptance in the corridors of power. Despite these hurdles, Suhas made a significant impact and quickly became a favourite among the influential in the state. He built a reputation as a doer. As the Azamgarh district collector, he harnessed technology to address malnutrition, a pressing issue in the state. When Suhas assumed charge of the district in 2015, Uttar Pradesh already initiated the "State Nutrition Mission" programme. He further advanced this effort by introducing the "Weight at a Glance" (*Kuposhan Ka Darpan*) app to combat malnutrition more effectively.

With this app, *Anganwadi* workers (community health workers) could easily track a child's physical and mental growth and determine malnutrition status based on World Health Organization guidelines. Previously, these workers had to navigate a lengthy and cumbersome 100-page growth chart to assess nourishment levels.

In 2016, while serving as the District Magistrate of Azamgarh, Suhas was honoured with the 'Yash Bharati Award', the highest civilian accolade from the Akhilesh Yadav government.

Simultaneously, Azamgarh, a constituency of Samajwadi Party leader Mulayam Singh Yadav at the time, received recognition from the Modi government for its outstanding implementation of the Pradhan Mantri Jan Dhan Yojana. Suhas was credited with opening eight lakh accounts under the scheme.

In 2019, as the Yogi Adityanath government prepared for the multi-crore Kumbh Mela, Suhas, the District Magistrate then, organised a meeting of the Uttar Pradesh cabinet on the banks of the Sangam. After the meeting, all ministers of the cabinet took a ceremonial dip in the holy waters.

In this book, we have discussed how COVID-19 halted the world and disrupted the preparations of the Paralympic athletes. For Suhas, the challenges were different as he was tasked with leading the battle against the pandemic in one of the country's most difficult districts.

Suhas was on a break from government service when Uttar Pradesh Chief Minister Yogi Adityanath summoned him to handle the COVID-19 crisis in Noida, which had become a major hotspot by then. The chief minister was outraged by the previous DM's mismanagement, and the city was in turmoil. Suhas arrived within hours of the order. On his first day, he immediately sealed a company where 16 employees had tested positive for COVID-19 and filed an FIR for the company's failure to disclose its staff's travel history. This decisive action sent a clear message: comply with regulations or face severe repercussions.

Under Suhas's leadership, 300 surveillance teams, comprising 900 officials, were established to manage containment zones, and the Delhi-Noida border was completely shut down. These measures proved effective, and Noida soon became a model for crisis management. But how did this accomplished administrator also become a Paralympic medal winner?

Suhas has had a fascination with sports since childhood. During his college years, he played cricket and badminton with great enthusiasm. However, a significant turning point came when he transitioned from being an avid player to a professional sportsperson.

In an interview with *The Times of India*, Suhas said, "As a child, I used to watch my father playing ball badminton, a sport predominantly played in South India. I was captivated by it. After joining the IAS, I played badminton just for my passion. In 2016, while serving as the district collector in Azamgarh, I had the opportunity to inaugurate a badminton tournament. I participated in a few matches and defeated some able-bodied state-level players. A few coaches present at the event encouraged me to pursue the sport seriously."

Gaurav Khanna, the coach of the Para badminton team, was also present at the tournament. Known for his keen eye for talent, Khanna was the one who initially encouraged Suhas to seriously consider pursuing Para badminton. At first, Suhas hesitated, concerned about balancing the demands of his hectic schedule with the commitment required for professional sports. However, after five months, Suhas reached out to Khanna and decided to take the plunge into para sports. Suhas recalls, "At the Beijing Asian Championship in 2016, I entered as an unseeded player and won a gold medal. This was a major turning point." He won the gold medal by defeating Hary Susanto of Indonesia in the finals. He, thus, became the first Indian bureaucrat to win a professional international badminton championship.

This victory likely bolstered his self-belief to compete and excel in the sport. Following his win in Beijing, Suhas secured gold medals at the Japan Open and the Turkish Open the next year. He then earned a bronze medal at the Asian Para Games in Jakarta in 2018. These achievements set the stage for his participation in the Tokyo 2020 Paralympics, where badminton was included for the first time.

The 38-year-old made history by becoming the first IAS officer to win a medal at the Tokyo Paralympics. He achieved this milestone by securing a silver medal in the men's singles SL4 category, losing only to the top-seeded world champion Lucas Mazur of France with scores of 21-15, 21-15, 21-15. In the semi-final, Suhas had defeated Indonesia's Fredy Setiawan in straight sets. His achievement was particularly remarkable as he managed to train effectively despite his demanding role leading the COVID-19 management team in Noida.

The entire nation celebrated this unique sporting hero, with Prime Minister Narendra Modi praising his accomplishments. The Prime Minister's tweet read, "A fantastic confluence of service and sports! @dmgbnagar Suhas Yathiraj has captured the imagination of our entire nation with his exceptional sporting performance. Congratulations to him on winning the Silver medal in Badminton. Best wishes to him for his future endeavours."

When asked about this, Suhas said in an interview, "Prime Minister Narendra Modi was incredibly supportive of all the athletes, medallists, and participants. The way he received us when we returned from Tokyo and encouraged us before we left for the Paralympics was truly exemplary. One of his inspirational remarks that particularly motivated me was, 'Play your natural game. Don't worry who the opponent is'."

Suhas's wife, Ritu, a provincial civil services officer, has been a pillar of support throughout his journey. Reflecting on his achievement, she told reporters, "He managed both his duties as District Magistrate and his sports career with complete dedication. That's why both his professional and athletic results were exceptional. During the COVID-19 crisis, he worked tirelessly, often around the clock, which allowed him to connect with more people. His commitment to practice was immense—no holidays, no Sundays, no festivals. I don't watch his matches; I prefer to pray while he plays. I did the same during this competition."

In professional sports, where competition is intense and dedication is crucial, a common question from experts and sports journalists was: How did Suhas manage his time so effectively?

In the lead-up to the Tokyo 2020 Paralympic Games, Suhas maintained a rigorous schedule. He woke up at 6 a.m. and began his office duties by 8.30 a.m., which included inspections, video conferences, and reviewing files. This kept him busy throughout the day. After returning home at night, Suhas devoted time to his practice sessions, starting around 10 p.m.

Suhas described badminton as a form of meditation for him: "I don't think about anything—neither the past nor the future—while playing. I just enjoy myself on the court. When you pursue a passion that you enjoy, favourable results often follow. Choose a job or activity that makes you happy. Create your own opportunities and fortunes."

His passion for his job motivates him to devote the final two hours of each day to pursue his sport. In the process, he has no qualms about sacrificing leisure activities like watching movies or attending social gatherings. This commitment leads to another natural question: Is the IAS officer from the Uttar Pradesh cadre, who won a Paralympic medal, now setting his sights on the Paris 2024 Paralympics?

In response to this, Suhas remarks, "Destiny has led me here. I am disciplined in life and confident that positive outcomes will follow. Winning a Paralympic medal is a source of immense pride and joy for the country. While I don't want to plan too far ahead, a Paralympic gold would be a great achievement. Since Paralympic silver is not gold, there is still a step I have not conquered. So that is definitely there in the back of the mind. As our honourable Prime Minister Narendra Modiji says, *aag lagee rahnee chahiye ander* (there should be fire within), so that fire is definitely there." If we apply Alan Lakein's philosophy to Suhas's journey, it is clear that he has mastered his time and, in doing so, has become the master of his own life.

In the chapter ahead, we will meet our hero Praveen Kumar, who, after getting knocked down multiple times in his life, has mastered the art of standing up again and raising the bar further.

PRAVEEN KUMAR

Scripting History on Debut

*"A winner is that person who gets up one
more time than she is knocked down."*

—**Mia Hamm**

After 17 years of an illustrious career in professional sports, including two World Championships, two Olympic gold medals, and unparalleled success as a marketing icon, Mia Hamm retired from professional soccer in 2004. Known for her inspirational quotes, Hamm's above quote echo the journey of Indian Paralympic medallist Praveen Kumar.

Like Hamm, Praveen Kumar faced multiple setbacks, but he persevered and ultimately stood on the podium, having risen one more time than he was knocked down. Praveen believes that his journey had just begun after the Tokyo Games. His future plans are guided by another of Hamm's inspirational quotes: "Celebrate what you have accomplished, but raise the bar a little higher each time you succeed."

It was a chilly morning in northern India when a young mother, Nirdoshi Devi, with a her baby in her arms, stood waiting for a bus near Jewar, a small town about 100 km from the national capital of India. She was on her way to Agra, a

city famous for the magnificent Taj Mahal. However, Nirdoshi Devi's journey was not for sightseeing; she was travelling to Agra in the hope of a miracle for her one-year-old son, Praveen Kumar. Born with a congenital impairment affecting the bones connecting his hip to his left leg, Praveen struggled with a limp while walking.

In many parts of rural India, disability is still viewed as a curse from a past life, and Nirdoshi Devi was on her way to Agra to see a godman believed to have the power to remove such a curse. As she waited for the bus on the highway, two *sadhus* passed by and, upon noticing the young boy and his feet, suddenly stopped. One of the sadhus remarked, "*Iske to sonay ke paanv hain*" (he has feet of gold). He told her not to view the disability as a curse but as a sign that the Almighty had destined a change in her family's fortunes. Intriguing as it may sound, the *sadhu*'s words proved to be true later on.

Nirdoshi Devi's husband, Amarpal, was a small-scale farmer, and the couple struggled to make ends meet. They lived in Govindgarh, a village in Gautam Buddha Nagar district of Uttar Pradesh. Despite being only 100 km from New Delhi, the village lacked basic amenities. When their son, Praveen, was born on 15 May 2003, they were overjoyed, as the birth of a boy is often celebrated more in some parts of the country. For the first few months, everything seemed normal. However, as Praveen began to stand with support and take his first steps, his parents noticed an issue with his left leg. Further medical examinations revealed that he was born with a congenital impairment affecting the bones connecting his hip to his left leg.

Amarpal didn't have the resources to afford treatment for his son. After some initial consultations and efforts, he had no option but to accept it as their fate. Sometimes, acceptance can alleviate a great deal of pain, and that was the case for Amarpal and his family. Other than the problem in his leg, Praveen grew up as a healthy child with a strong interest in physical activities. He loved spending time outdoors with friends, playing various sports. Children often overlook what might trouble adults, and Praveen's peers did not see him as different. In fact, he was an active participant in most of the games and teams formed within his peer group.

"The thought that I had a disability never crossed my mind because there was nothing that others could do that I couldn't. In fact, I was better than most of my friends when it came to physical activities. This really boosted my confidence during my growing-up years," says Praveen with a spark in his eyes.

One day, as Praveen's uncle was returning from the fields, he saw many kids hanging upside down from a tree. "This is common in the villages," he recalled, "but when I saw Praveen hanging upside down like a monkey on one of the branches, I was really worried. I rushed over and scolded everyone, especially Praveen, fearing he might hurt himself due to his weak leg and make his parents' lives even more difficult. They all came down, but as soon as I left, I saw everyone back up in the tree with Praveen hanging upside down again. At the time, I frowned, but today, I laugh at myself for not recognising the diamond we had amongst us."

"I faced this a lot. Just because I had one weak leg didn't mean I was any less than anyone else," Praveen says with a hint of frustration. "But many people looked at me with sympathy. My parents always worried that I would hurt myself while playing with other kids. Even though I never saw myself as any different from others and my teammates never thought of me as lesser, my parents and other elders in the village constantly reminded me of my weak leg. They urged me to be extra careful and not consider myself the same as the other kids," he adds.

Praveen was a very good volleyball player and widely regarded as the best in his village. His skills were so impressive that teams from nearby villages sought him out to join their ranks. One key reason for his success was his remarkable jumping ability. Nimble on his feet and fearless in his movements, Praveen could jump so high that his performance at the net was a delight to watch. His physical agility left people in awe, and they encouraged him to participate in more local tournaments.

"We were very happy when people praised our son, saying, 'Your son is such a good player!' This was especially true after his village team won several competitions. Over time, our apprehensions about his physical disability faded. We began to believe that he was no less than anyone else and realised that we didn't need to constantly worry about his well-being," says Praveen's mother.

When Praveen was in the ninth grade, he decided to participate in the school's Sports Day for the first time, eager to test his skills against other students. The winners would have the chance to represent the school in further competitions. Unsure of which event to enter, Praveen knew he wouldn't fare well in running events against able-bodied students. Someone suggested he try the high jump, as his disability might not significantly impact his performance in that event.

However, when Praveen went to register, the physical education (PE) teacher refused to enrol him. "Who will take responsibility if anything happens to you or if you injure yourself? This is a tough sport, and we can't risk players with disabilities like you," the teacher said. Even though Praveen and his peers tried to persuade the teacher, he remained firm in his refusal.

Heartbroken, Praveen confided in his father about the issue. His father took the matter up with the school administration, which promised to review the situation. On the day of the event, Praveen, accompanied by his parents, returned to convince the game in-charge to reconsider. Despite their efforts, the official initially remained firm in his refusal. However, after persistent intervention by the school manager and with Praveen's parents signing an indemnity bond, he was finally allowed to participate at the very last moment.

By then, Praveen's event was about to start, and his name was added to the scoring sheet at the last minute. As he was getting ready with excitement, little did he know that another challenge was about to unfold.

"I was shocked when other participants came together to object to my participation in the event. Many of them had played volleyball and cricket with or against me, so they knew I wasn't a pushover. They protested my late entry, arguing that a disabled player shouldn't compete with able-bodied athletes. Some even claimed that my disability meant I had been given extra powers by God, making me unfit to compete against them. One participant said that even if they won, people would laugh at them for defeating a disabled boy. I was so angry that I felt like hitting someone that day," Praveen recalls.

But then, the game in-charge came to my defence and reprimanded the other participants for their behaviour. I was both happy and sad. I was saddened by the discrimination I faced because of my disability, but I was also pleased that the able-bodied players were afraid to compete with me," he adds.

Praveen not only won that event but also won over the PE teacher who had initially refused to let him compete. Impressed by his performance, the teacher invited him to participate in the Cluster Games. The Central Board of Secondary Education (CBSE) organises sports events at the cluster, zonal, and national levels for its affiliated schools each year, with separate categories for boys and girls in various age groups.

The following year, Praveen secured third place in high jump at the Cluster Games. This achievement boosted his self-belief and confidence, taking them to new heights.

"Though there was some controversy over the results at the Cluster Games, as we thought he had secured second place, the final result showed him in third," says Praveen's father, Amarpal. "This performance and the result dispelled any fears Praveen had about being less than any other athlete. The Cluster Games are significant for gauging one's abilities, and Praveen excelled," he adds.

This newfound confidence led Praveen to regularly win medals at various tournaments and events in his age category. He was even selected for the Khelo India Games but struggled to make a significant impact at such a large platform due to his lack of preparation for the event at that time.

For nearly four to five years, Praveen was not introduced to the world of para sports. Although he had heard about Mariyappan Thangavelu making history by winning a gold medal at the Rio 2016 Paralympics, no one suggested that he consider participating in para games. Deep down, Praveen was reluctant to focus solely on para sports, believing he could make a significant impact in regular athletic events. During this period, he competed exclusively against able-bodied students and consistently outperformed them. However, he lacked a dedicated high jump coach or mentor to guide him.

At a district-level competition in Noida, Praveen crossed paths with Ashok Saini, a local athletics coach. After observing Praveen's first jump, Saini immediately recognised his exceptional talent. He advised Praveen to reach out to Coach Satyapal Singh, who had been instrumental in the development and promotion of para sports in India for over a decade. Satyapal Singh, honoured with the prestigious Dronacharya Award in Para Athletics for 2012, was renowned for his relentless work in the field. Destiny seemed to have chosen the perfect mentor for Praveen.

Saini contacted Satyapal to inform him about Praveen's performance and potential. Intrigued, Satyapal invited Praveen to Jawaharlal Nehru (JLN) Stadium, where he was training other para athletes. A few days later, Praveen visited JLN Stadium and was awestruck by the number of athletes training there.

Praveen met Coach Satyapal, who took him to the high jump area. After a brief conversation to make Praveen comfortable, Satyapal asked him to attempt a few jumps. This was not to evaluate his skill but to gauge how he had developed without formal coaching. Praveen managed to clear a height of 1.75 metres from just a few steps, which was phenomenal. Satyapal realised he had discovered a raw talent with the potential to shine on a national level. From that moment, he decided to move Praveen's base from Jewar to New Delhi and took full responsibility for his training and development.

"I still remember the day. It was 17 October 2018, when I moved in with the coach. I didn't know what the future held for me but I had complete trust in my coach. Our first aim was to improve my technique and the second target was to get a classification depending on the disability. It was a big moment for me and my family when I decided to dedicate myself totally to sports and it was the wisest decision that I could have made in my life," remembers Praveen about the day he shifted to Delhi.

Classification of athletes according to their disability is crucial in para sports. Following a thorough physical and medical evaluation by experts, athletes are assigned to a category in which they will compete against others with similar impairments. This system was established by the International Paralympic Committee (IPC) and stems from a 2003 initiative to address "the overall objective to support and co-ordinate the ongoing development of accurate, reliable, consistent and credible sport focused classification systems and their implementation".

Based on his experience, Coach Satyapal initially thought that Praveen's disability would place him in the T42 category. The T42 classification applies to athletes with single above-the-knee amputations or comparable disabilities, specifically for track and field events.

The world record for the T42 category high jump is 1.96 metres, set by Arnold Boldt of Canada in 1980. Coach Satyapal was confident that with Praveen Kumar's talent, he could surpass this mark. For a year, the coach and Praveen worked diligently on refining his technique.

"It was very difficult to change Praveen's technique," says Coach Satyapal. "He had developed his own method over the years, known as the Standing Technique or Scissors

Technique, where you simply run and jump. However, this approach is not successful at the international level. Here, we need to adopt the famous Fosbury Flop, which requires a completely different style. Transitioning from one technique to another involved a lot of unlearning and hard work for both of us," he adds.

After a year of intensive training, Praveen was ready to compete at the international level in 2019. However, before he could do so, he needed to undergo classification into the appropriate category. The classification process generally involves four stages: The first stage of classification is a health examination. This is often done on the site at a sports training facility or competition. The second stage is observation in practice, the third stage is observation in competition and the last stage is assigning the athlete to a specific classification.

During the observation phase, athletes may be asked to demonstrate their abilities in various athletic activities, such as running or jumping. This comprehensive evaluation helps in assigning the athlete to the most suitable classification for their events.

After completing the classification process, Praveen and his team were stunned to find that he had been assigned to the T44 category, rather than the expected T42. The T44 classification is designated for athletes with a "single below-knee amputation or those who can walk with moderately reduced function in one or both legs". For general understanding, Praveen's disability was not considered as serious and hence he was given a much stronger category. This reclassification was unexpected and disheartening! The coach and Praveen felt their dreams were shattered, as they had prepared to compete against athletes in the T42 category, which was significantly different in terms of competition.

"I was shocked and very disappointed. With my knowledge and experience, I had anticipated that Praveen would be classified in the T42 category. However, because his one leg is very strong, the impact of the disability in the other leg was less pronounced. But that doesn't take away the fact that his one leg is very weak," says Coach Satyapal.

Praveen was devastated by the unexpected classification. "I locked myself in a room and cried endlessly," he reflects. "With every tear, it felt like my dreams were being washed away. I had dark thoughts and felt overwhelmed, even considering to ending my life. My only mistake was becoming so strong and fit that my disability seemed less severe than it truly was," he adds.

The day after his reclassification, Praveen faced his event in the new T44 category without having had the chance to practice. He was grappling with thoughts of giving up, primarily because the performance standards in the T44 category were significantly higher. While the world record for the T42 category was 1.96 metres, the world record for T44 was 2.19 metres. At that time, Praveen was around the 1.85-metre mark. In high jump, where every centimetre matters, improving such a distance seemed almost impossible.

Praveen had little interest in practising for the competition. On the day of the event, rather than jumping straight into training, Coach Satyapal took a different approach and asked Praveen to join him for a walk. As they strolled together, Satyapal shared a crucial lesson: rather than running away from his struggles, Praveen needed to confront them head-on. This conversation marked a turning point for Praveen.

"My coach didn't console me," Praveen recalls. "Instead, he asked me to trust him and give him one year of my life wholeheartedly. For one year, he said, 'forget you are anyone's son or a brother or a friend or anything. Just eat, sleep, practice, and repeat.' I was amazed with the confidence my sir had in me. On that day, we made a pact: for the next one year, the rest of the world would cease to exist for us and we would give our heart and soul to high jump," Praveen adds.

For the next year, Praveen and Coach Satyapal were relentless in their pursuit. Their goal was not to win a medal but to qualify for the Tokyo Paralympics. They dedicated eight hours a day—four hours in the morning and four in the evening—to rigorous training. Their regimen included not only physical exercises but also a strong focus on mental fitness and strategic goal-setting. High jump traditionally favours taller athletes, but Praveen, at 5.5 feet, was equally dynamic.

His training was so thorough that not a single day was missed, regardless of the weather conditions. If it rained outside, he had his training indoors. Praveen recalls one particularly gruelling day when exhaustion and pain almost led him to skip a practice session. When he hesitated, Coach Satyapal's urgency was palpable. "My coach called up and yelled, *'Tu aa raha hai ya main aaon?'* (Are you coming or should I come?). Such was the fear of the coach that I just rushed to the ground," says Praveen.

After a year of intense preparation, Praveen competed in an international event and cleared a 1.90-metre jump, achieving the Minimum Qualification Score (MQS) required for the Tokyo 2020 Para Games. Although he placed fourth overall, qualifying for the Paralympics was a significant victory for both Praveen and Coach Satyapal. In just one year of intense training and unwavering dedication, they had reached their target of making it to the Paralympics.

Just as everything seemed to be falling into place, the COVID-19 pandemic brought the world to a standstill. With all sports facilities closed, Praveen's training was severely disrupted. High jump, being a highly technical sport, requires consistent practice to maintain form and technique. Even a short break can introduce technical issues and hinder performance. Realising this, Coach Satyapal made a crucial decision: he sent Praveen back to his village, where he had access to open spaces for practice.

Praveen adhered to his coach's instructions diligently, making the most of the open fields to keep up his training. When it was confirmed that the Paralympics would be rescheduled to 2021 and restrictions began to ease, Praveen returned to Delhi. There, he and Coach Satyapal resumed their rigorous training regimen, preparing intensively for the rescheduled games.

By the time Praveen arrived in Tokyo for the Paralympics, his performance had reached impressive levels. He was consistently clearing heights of around 2 to 2.05 metres, which bolstered his confidence and gave him hope for a potential medal. However, the anticipation and pressure before the event were overwhelming. As 3 September 2021 approached, Praveen was plagued by sleepless nights and heightened anxiety, his mind bombarded with various thoughts.

On the day of his event, it was a fine evening in Tokyo, but Praveen's heart was racing with nerves. There were seven competitors in his event. The competition was fierce as the high jump event progressed. The first height was set at 1.83 metres, which Praveen cleared effortlessly. However, the Venezuelan high jumper retired at this stage, leaving six competitors in the race. The bar was then raised to 1.88 metres, which Praveen also cleared on his first attempt.

The next height was set at 1.93 metres. While Praveen chose to pass this height, it proved too challenging for three other high jumpers, who failed to clear it and were eliminated from the competition. With only three jumpers remaining, Praveen's medal was secured if he could clear the next height of 1.97 metres. He achieved this on his first attempt, guaranteeing himself a medal.

The current champions, Maciej Lepiato of Poland and Jonathan Broom-Edwards of Great Britain, were also performing well. Praveen's first attempt at 2.01 metres was unsuccessful, but he managed to clear it on his second attempt. As the bar was raised to 2.07 metres, Lepiato, the defending gold medallist from the Rio Games, was unable to clear it and bowed out, leaving Praveen assured of at least a silver medal. Praveen cleared this height on his second attempt, while Broom-Edwards succeeded on his third. The final height was set at 2.10 metres. Praveen made three attempts but could not clear this mark. Broom-Edwards, on the other hand, cleared the mark on his second attempt, securing the gold medal.

Despite not securing the gold, Praveen had made his country proud and etched his name into the annals of history.

When asked by this author about his final jump and what went wrong, Praveen responded with a mischievous smile: "*Bhaiya*, you know I don't get things without struggle in life. It's good that I didn't get everything in my first games. Now this has given me a target for the Paris 2024 Paralympics, and I promise you today in advance, I will get the gold there."

What confidence! The entire country will be rallying behind this young champion as he aims for gold in Paris.

India's real journey in the Paralympics has just begun, and it has miles to go from here. As we conclude our series on India's Paralympic heroes, we turn our focus to two more remarkable athletes: Sharad Kumar and Manoj Sarkar, whose strength and success are rooted in the power of belief.

SHARAD KUMAR AND MANOJ SARKAR

The Power of Belief

"You are what you believe in.
You become that which you believe you can become."

—Bhagavad Gita

Man is shaped by his beliefs. As he believes, so is he. Belief serves as the cornerstone of our lives, moulding our thoughts and guiding our actions toward our ultimate outcomes. As we explore the stories of the real-life heroes covered in this book, we come to appreciate the immense power of their self-belief. This is particularly evident in the final chapter, which features two remarkable individuals: Sharad Kumar and Manoj Sarkar. It is their unwavering belief that has empowered them to overcome every challenge they have faced.

We began this book by tracing the history of the World Paralympic Movement. India is taking promising steps towards becoming a leader in this movement. While the potential is there, the journey is still long. This leads us to a lesson from the Bhagavad Gita that has deeply influenced the life of Paralympian Sharad Kumar. The essence of this teaching is: "You have the right to work, but for the sake of work only. You have no right

to the fruits of work. Desire for the fruits of work must never be your motive in working. Work done with anxiety about results is far inferior to the work done without such anxiety, in the calm of self-surrender. Seek refuge in the knowledge of Brahma. Those who work selfishly for results are miserable."

To emerge as a leader in the Paralympic Movement, India must consistently embrace this spirit of selfless dedication in the years to come.

Sharad Kumar was born in Kodarkatta Purantola, a small village in Motipur, Muzaffarpur district, Bihar. From this modest origin, he ascended to become the world's leading high jumper. His early life story reflects the sacrifices and determination of many Bihari parents from humble backgrounds who, despite their limitations and poverty, dream of seeing their children achieve great heights. It is this courage that has propelled many Biharis from modest beginnings to become esteemed figures in multinational companies, premier global educational institutions, academia, bureaucracy, media, and the judiciary.

Sharad Kumar's parents, Surendra Kumar and Kumkum Devi, stretched their resources to ensure their son received a quality education, first at St. Paul's School in Darjeeling, then at Kirori Mal College (KMC) in Delhi University, and finally at Jawaharlal Nehru University in Delhi. The strong foundation provided by these dedicated parents and esteemed institutions was instrumental in shaping his character and resilience. This preparation became his greatest asset as he faced the dual challenges of living with a disability and contending with allegations and penalties related to doping, ultimately rising as a successful Paralympic champion.

Sharad was only two years old when he was administered a faulty polio vaccine during a local health drive, which resulted in permanent paralysis of his left leg. This devastating blow was nearly unbearable for his parents. However, Surendra Kumar and Kumkum Devi realised that staying in Motihari would severely limit Sharad's opportunities. They also feared that the local environment would stifle his potential.

Surendra Kumar recognised early on that education was the key to empowering Sharad and his other children. He was determined to ensure his kids had opportunities far beyond what was typical for those growing up in their surroundings. So, he decided to send them to a boarding school in Darjeeling.

Sharad reflects on this decision, saying, "I never understood why my father sent all of us to boarding school in Darjeeling until I was older. It was only then that I realised it was for our benefit. My father's boss was an educated man whose children also attended boarding schools in Darjeeling. When these children came home for vacations, they were always smartly dressed and spoke fluent English. My father wanted us to be like them. So he requested his boss to help with our admission. Despite not being able to afford the fees, my father was determined to push beyond his limits. He borrowed money from his boss and promised to work extra to repay it."

In addition to his strong desire for his children's success, there was also a pressing need behind his decision. Surendra Kumar was deeply concerned about the safety and security of his family, given the unstable law and order situation in Bihar at the time.

"In my school, no one discriminated against me because of my disability. In fact, I was always worried about our financial status. Most of the other kids came from affluent families. But my school was a wonderful place. My teachers emphasised that we were all equal there, and our success depended on how well we performed. No one judged me by looking at my family background. I really enjoyed my time there," Sharad recalls of his school days.

Sharad was an active student, and was part of the table tennis team. However, when it came to sports, his younger brother often garnered all the attention from their parents. His brother excelled in sports and had won numerous trophies and certificates, while Sharad was expected to focus more on academics. Sharad, however, harboured a desire to excel in sports like his brother. Little did he know that this sibling rivalry would become one of the driving forces that propelled him to achieve podium finishes at the Paralympics later on in his life.

"I didn't choose high jump; it was high jump that chose me. In my school, we either participated in marathons or joined athletics. While most of the kids competed in one of these events, I was assigned to work at the high jump event. My role was to reposition the bar if any athlete dislodged it during their jump. After the event, when everyone had left, and no one was around to try the high jump, I decided to give it a go myself. To my surprise, I successfully cleared the bar. Even the other kids who had been there were amazed at my agility and strength. I shared this achievement with my brother, telling him how I had managed to jump higher than anyone else. He was pleasantly surprised and encouraged me to participate in inter-house games and other school competitions," Sharad shares.

In about a year, Sharad set a new school record for the high jump. When his teachers recognised his talent, they briefly discussed the possibility of the Paralympic Games with him.

However, Sharad didn't take it seriously at that time. His primary goal was to advance his parents' dream of enrolling him in another prestigious educational institution. He saw sports as a means to achieve this, hoping to secure admission to Modern School, Delhi, for his 11th and 12th grades, and then to one of Delhi University's prestigious colleges.

Sharad's excellence in sports earned him admission to KMC. Professor Bhim Singh, the then principal, supported him wholeheartedly, even allowing him to skip some classes to focus on his training and tournaments. His first two years at college were enjoyable, with his training going well and his sights set on international events.

However, just as things seemed to be on track, there came news that almost destroyed his sporting dreams: Sharad's sample tested positive for a banned substance, leading to a two-year ban from professional sports. Due to this, he could not compete in the London 2012 Paralympics, a blow that shattered him internally. Sharad was convinced that this was a case of sabotage; he suspected that one of the para athletes training with him had contaminated his supplements during the practice sessions.

"I was certain that it was a plot against me, with something being added to my supplements. I was devastated when I learned about the doping charges. The thought of fighting a doping case and missing the London Paralympics was deeply humiliating. Proving my innocence to the committee seemed almost impossible, and the ban felt inevitable. Those two years were a nightmare, but they also made me tougher. They taught me about the additional challenges of being a sportsperson in India," Sharad reflects.

Eventually, Sharad's two-year ban from professional sports came to an end. He made a remarkable comeback at the 2014 Asian Para Games, where he set a new Asian record with a jump of 1.80 metres. With this achievement, he emerged as one of the leading contenders for medals at the Rio 2016 Paralympics. However, he had to wait longer for his success. At the Rio Games, he finished a disappointing sixth, while his friends and training partners, Mariyappan and Varun, won gold and bronze medals, respectively.

Despite this setback, Sharad was determined to come back stronger. He delivered a spectacular performance at the 2018 Asian Para Games, clearing 1.90 metres to set a new record and achieve a personal best. Nevertheless, Sharad wasn't content to rest on his laurels. He was determined to leave no stone unturned in his preparation for the Tokyo 2020 Paralympics. To this end, he decided to train in Ukraine under the expert guidance of Evgeny Nikitin. However, training in Ukraine for five years proved to be a tough task.

The Sports Authority of India had invested in Sharad and placed their trust in him, and he was acutely aware of this responsibility. He was determined to put every sweat and effort into his training. Being alone in a foreign country was very tough; Sharad found himself cut off from the rest of the world, living out of a small room while training relentlessly. To cover his expenses, he began taking classes on investing in the stock market. His master's degree in Economics from JNU helped. This provided a mental and financial cushion as he prepared for his "Mission Paralympics".

Unfortunately, the arrival of COVID-19 brought everything to a grinding halt. "I wanted to give everything I had. I was training so hard for this one event, and then it got postponed after coming so close. I knew there was nothing anyone could do, but I started to feel like destiny was plotting against me. I began to doubt whether a Paralympic medal was ever meant for me. This thought troubled me deeply and caused anxiety attacks. Life had been unfair, and I had to find the strength to motivate myself for another 15 months of hard work. My practice was the only part of my day that I looked forward to, but even that was halted due to COVID-19," Sharad recalls, reflecting on the lockdown period.

Eventually, the trials were held, and Sharad qualified for the Tokyo Paralympics.

Just before he was set to leave for Tokyo, Sharad experienced a severe fever. Fortunately, he recovered just in time to make the trip. Due to COVID-19 restrictions, athletes were allowed to arrive in Tokyo only 72 hours before their events and had to depart within 48 hours after completing them.

"The Paralympics is more than just a competition for me; it feels like a homecoming. In the Games Village, there's no judgment based on disability, because everyone shares a similar experience in some way or the other. When I'm in India, especially in public places, I sometimes need to be cautious about my walk. I wear trousers to avoid drawing attention to my legs. But at the Para Games, I could simply be myself, walking around in shorts and slippers. No one makes you feel self-conscious about your disability," says Sharad.

We should absorb this mindset of inclusiveness from the spirit and atmosphere of the Paralympic village. Though Sharad was there in the world of para sports since 2008, he had never won a Paralympic medal, unlike many of his friends and counterparts. In 2012, Girisha had secured a silver medal at the London Paralympics, and at the Rio 2016 Para Games, Mariyappan and Varun had also won medals. For Sharad, it had been a long wait.

Just as the anticipation for a medal seemed within reach, another hurdle arose. Two days before the event, during a warm-up session, Sharad landed awkwardly, tearing his meniscus and experiencing terrible pain. He couldn't walk properly and was on the verge of pulling out of the event. It was at this critical juncture that his coach imparted another valuable life lesson.

"I was disheartened, and my coach questioned why I was thinking about the result," Sharad recounts. "He said, 'You're contradicting your own thought process and perception. You want to relish this moment, yet you're cluttering your thoughts by obsessing over the medal. Forget about the medal, forget about the result, just enjoy the process and savour the environment.' My coach often tells us, 'You and other differently-abled athletes are not just athletes; you are artists. It's not merely athletic prowess to jump with two normal hands or legs. But when someone with one limb achieves it, it becomes an art—something that astounds and inspires many. So, don't fret about the medal; just go out there and perform your art,'" he adds.

"On the night before the event, I nearly broke down. I had trained rigorously and prepared myself in the best possible way. Spending five years training in Ukraine, I had set my sights on breaking the world record. However, just two days prior, this injury occurred, and I contemplated withdrawing from the event," he added.

"I always carry the Bhagavad Gita with me. My father knew this. That night, he advised me to read it. Even though he knew I always had it with me, it was the first time he had given me such advice. There, I read about how Lord Krishna advises Arjuna to simply perform his duty and forget about everything else, as the result is beyond our control," Sharad remarks.

The verse from the Bhagavad Gita, "*You have the right to your actions, but never to the fruits of its work; Let not the fruits of action be thy motive nor let thy attachment be to inaction*," profoundly affected Sharad. It dispelled his negative thoughts, calmed his mind, and brought clarity. Now, his focus was solely on giving his all, clearing the high jump bar at six different heights. He began mentally strategizing and preparing himself, confident that his body would effortlessly execute what his mind had planned.

Sharad approached the ground with the mindset of an artist ready to showcase his skill. The sight of the stadium filled with an enthusiastic audience infused him with positivity and energy that made him forget all his pain. "I was amazed by the entire atmosphere. I believe the body responds to that. In life's biggest moments, the body seems to react differently. I think my body released some chemicals that made me feel less pain," says Sharad, remembering the electric atmosphere of the Tokyo athletics stadium.

As the event began, a light drizzle started, presenting challenges for athletes in the T63 category who have weak legs, making them cautious about their balance. The wet track conditions were particularly unsuitable for high jump. For Sharad, with pain in his one knee, things couldn't have gone worse; yet he remained resolutely positive and focused on delivering his performance.

In the T63 category, nine athletes, including the favourite Mariyappan Thangavelu, participated. The initial jump height was set at 1.45 metres, which all top jumpers, including

Mariyappan and Sharad, opted to skip. Passing a jump indicates confidence in clearing it easily. It was only at 1.73 metres that both Indian jumpers attempted their first jumps, successfully clearing it on their initial tries. Meanwhile, Sam Grewe of the United States faltered in his first attempt but managed to clear the height on his second try.

Sharad continued to perform well, clearing heights of 1.77 metres and 1.80 metres without difficulty. With only four athletes remaining in the fray, the competition intensified.

By then, the rain too had intensified, soaking the athletes' socks with few spare pairs available. The bar was set at 1.83 metres, and Sharad, along with Mariyappan and Sam, cleared it on their first attempts. However, Lukasz Maciej Mamczarz of Poland struggled at this height, failing to clear it despite three attempts, securing medals for the remaining three athletes.

"More than anything, I was delighted with how I was performing. I cleared all four heights on my first attempt. My body seemed to move effortlessly, guided by muscle memory and years of dedicated practice," says Sharad, recalling the moment he realised he had secured a medal.

The bar was then raised to 1.86 metres. Small puddles were now forming on the track and the rain was just not stopping. The organisers didn't halt the event, but the conditions were far from ideal for high jump. Like the other athletes, Sharad found it challenging to control his steps and was apprehensive about slipping on the wet surface.

Sharad struggled at 1.86 metres, unable to clear the bar in any of his three attempts. Even though Mariyappan failed in his first two attempts at 1.86 metres, he successfully cleared it on his third try. Mariyappan and Sharad won a silver and bronze, respectively.

"To be honest, winning the Paralympic medal brought more relief than joy. There was immense pressure on me to achieve it, mostly self-imposed. While I had previously won Asian medals and World Championships which I cherished more, the desire for this particular medal had given me a lot of stress and I felt a great sense of relief when I finally achieved it," reflects Sharad, recalling the moment he realised he had secured the bronze medal.

Sharad understood that day the timeless wisdom of the Bhagavad Gita, which never fails those who grasp its essence. It is this wisdom that future Indian para athletes should embrace to propel India towards its goal of becoming a formidable Paralympic nation.

Like Sharad Kumar, another Indian Paralympic champion, Manoj Sarkar, reflects, "Sometimes, the greatest journey begins with the smallest of the targets."

Manoj was born to Maninder Sarkar and Jamuna Sarkar in Rudrapur, a small town in Uttarakhand, where he grew up in a joint family with many cousins. The family faced severe financial hardships, struggling to make ends meet and lacking even a proper roof over their heads. Manoj was just one year old when he contracted a severe fever that led to a polio infection affecting his entire left leg. Despite their best efforts, his parents could not find a cure, leaving Manoj with Post-Polio Residual Paralysis (PPRP), which permanently weakened his right leg. Though shocked, his parents had no choice but to move forward in life.

Manoj grew up in an environment filled with passionate sports enthusiasts. They used to play many sports, but badminton was their favourite. The sport was played with great competitiveness and adherence to rules. Manoj vividly recalls his childhood days spent watching his elders play badminton.

"Badminton was mostly played in winter when the air was calmer. We never knew it was an indoor sport because we always saw it being played outside. We would bring blankets from home and sit for hours, watching and cheering on the players. In our society, badminton was the biggest sport, and excelling in it earned a lot of respect among our peers. Back then, I had no idea it was played at international levels or that there were tournaments at district, state, and national levels. I simply wanted to excel because it gave me a lot of pride," reminisces Manoj.

Manoj couldn't afford the equipment needed for badminton. Other children who had their own rackets and shuttles monopolized most of the play and practice time. Manoj had to wait patiently until they grew tired or lost interest before he could join in.

"Every day, I'd go home and ask my parents for a racket. But for a family where food and shelter were the main priorities, a badminton racket was considered a luxury," Manoj recalls.

During a festival, one of Manoj's cousins received badminton rackets as a gift from his parents, which left Manoj feeling even more miserable. He cried for two days and refused to eat until his parents got him a racket. His mother was deeply moved. At that time, the family lived in an area where the production of *beedi* (a type of cheap strong cigarette made from tobacco rolled in *tendu* leaf) was booming. Manufacturers used to hire local residents to bundle and pack *beedis*. Manoj's mother worked for a few days and earned Rs 10, which she gave to him to buy a racket.

Manoj was over the moon but made a silly mistake. "The moment my mother gave me Rs 10, I rushed to buy a racket. But, instead of buying a new racket, I bought another boy's racket, thinking that his skill would transfer to me along with the racket," Manoj recalls with a smile.

"My mother had the biggest influence on me. She always instilled two principles in me: first, to be a good human being regardless of the circumstances, and second, that rivalry can be a positive force if you channel it into improving yourself," says Manoj.

With the racket gifted by his mother, Manoj wanted to beat all his cousins and peers to become the best. In his area, badminton was mostly played seasonally, but Manoj continued to practice and play throughout the year while other kids switched to cricket.

"To be honest, with my disability, playing other sports was not feasible. In badminton, everything happens within a small area of the court. Fitness is crucial but not everything. With good game sense and maturity, one can triumph over opponents. That's how it was for me—I excelled even among able-bodied kids. It was like I owned my part of the badminton court. So, when you excel in a sport, children don't discriminate against you; in fact, they respect you more," Manoj explains, reflecting on why he opted for badminton.

When Manoj was in the sixth grade, he wanted to participate in the trials for district-level tournaments and school selection trials. However, his sports teacher stopped him, fearing it might aggravate his pain. Other children informed the teacher about Manoj's talent and proficiency in the game, putting the teacher in a dilemma. He contemplated how to accommodate Manoj, a disabled student, during the trials without causing delays for others if he were to select him.

Disheartened by the discrimination and being barred from participating, Manoj returned home crestfallen. However, during the trials, he learnt that badminton was a global sport and realised he could potentially represent his country if he devoted himself to it. Finally, in 2007, during his 11th-grade year, Manoj seized the opportunity to represent his school.

"I was sitting in the classroom when I saw two students passing by with badminton rackets. Something inside me just clicked, and I ran out of the class. My teacher shouted after me, asking how I dared to leave the class like that. But in that moment, nothing else mattered to me. The students informed me about the school badminton selection trials, and I pleaded with them to lend me their rackets. If I went home to fetch mine, I knew I would miss the trials. They agreed, and with that borrowed racket, I went on to defeat all the players in the selection trial. When the Principal of the school heard about this, he was astonished at how a boy with a weak leg could outperform other able-bodied kids. It was truly a memorable moment for me," shares Manoj.

Not only did Manoj secure a spot on the school team, but he also went on to represent his district at the state-level tournament.

When Manoj began representing his university at inter-university meets, badminton coach D.K. Sen took notice of his game. Impressed by Manoj's skill development and exceptional game sense, D.K. Sen, father of Lakhsya Sen, a prominent figure in Indian badminton, advised Manoj to consider taking up para sports. Until then, Manoj had not even heard of para sports. D.K. Sen believed that if Manoj entered para sports, he could not only represent the country but also excel and win medals at the highest levels. D.K. Sen provided Manoj with Gaurav Khanna's mobile number and encouraged him to speak with him. Gaurav Khanna, a Dronacharya Award recipient, is one of the pioneers of para badminton in the country and has dedicated his life to coaching para athletes.

Manoj made his debut at the Para National Games in 2011, where he clinched gold medals in both the singles and doubles categories. However, he was left out of the team for the World Championships due to being a first-time national champion, while other players with more experience were selected instead. This highlighted the complexities of para badminton for Manoj. However, the entire Indian team was unable to participate in the World Championships that year.

In 2012, Manoj triumphed once again in both singles and doubles at the Para National Games. This time, his performance earned him a spot on the team for the World Championships in Paris, France. Yet, another major hurdle awaited him.

"I was informed that I would need to cover my own expenses. The total cost for the World Championships amounted to Rs 1.15 lakh, which was far beyond my means. Go Sports, my sponsor at the time, agreed to contribute Rs 50,000. Initially, they provided only Rs 30,000. It was once again my mother who came to my rescue. She mortgaged our house so that I could gather the necessary funds for the World Championships. She was so confident that I would win a medal, repay the mortgage, and reclaim our home," says Manoj, explaining the obstacles that he had to face in his early career. By 2014, Manoj had won 8-10 international medals, but was still struggling for financial support from the government or other sources.

In 2014, Manoj achieved a significant milestone by winning the silver medal at the Asian Championships. This victory brought substantial relief as he received Rs 10 lakh from the Central government and Rs 1 lakh from the state government. Manoj wisely utilised this award money to fund his international tours. However, within two years, he found himself struggling once more to sustain his career. It was during this challenging period that the government's Top of Podium Scheme (TOPS) came to his rescue.

"I didn't even know what the Arjuna Award was. I don't mean to disrespect the award, but that was the level of my knowledge back then. I was at the peak of my game in 2015 and 2016. Mentally and physically, I was in the best state of mind. I applied for the Arjuna Award for the first time in 2016 and then again in 2017, but I didn't get it. I finally received the Arjuna Award in 2018. To be honest, I was not at my best that year. It is one of the biggest sporting awards of the country, and I was very happy to receive it. I had dreamt of taking both my parents to some big award function. In 2017, my father passed away, but I was very glad to take my mother to the Rashtrapati Bhavan," says Manoj.

The award coincided with the announcement that badminton would be included in the Tokyo 2020 Paralympics, marking its debut in the history of the games.

India fielded one of the strongest contingents and had high hopes for five medals across various categories in the Tokyo

2020 Paralympics. Manoj competed in the SL3 category and was selected for the singles event. Pramod Bhagat was seeded no. 1, while Daniel Bethell from Great Britain held the no. 2 ranking. Manoj was placed in Group A alongside Pramod and Ukraine's Oleksandr. The top two players from each group would advance to the semi-finals.

In his group matches, Manoj lost his first match to Pramod with a score of 21-10, 21-23, and 21-9. He bounced back in his second match with a victory, winning 21-16, 21-9. With one win out of two matches, Manoj qualified for the semi-finals where he faced Bethell. Unfortunately, Manoj struggled under pressure, leading to a one-sided match that ended 21-8, 21-9 in favour of Bethell.

Manoj was deeply upset with himself. He returned to the hotel room, unwilling to talk to anyone. At that moment, his wife Sona called him, and he snapped back at her. Understanding his mood, Sona remained composed and suggested, "Why not channel the same anger you're showing now into your bronze medal match?"

This suggestion struck a chord with Manoj. He quickly put aside his semi-final loss and focused on preparing for his bronze medal match against Daisuke Fujihara of Japan. "I stepped onto the court a lot of anger. I was determined to play aggressively and demonstrate to the world what I had been practicing all my life. However, my coach advised me against making unforced errors due to aggression. The first game was tense, coming down to the wire at 22-20. However, I was adamant not to repeat my errors. Fuelled by confidence and energy after winning the first game, I dominated the second with a score of 21-13. This win not only secured the bronze medal but also brought me immense satisfaction," says Manoj, his pride evident.

From a 10-rupee racket to a bronze medal at the Para Games, Manoj's journey has been a roller-coaster ride that will inspire generations to come.

Meanwhile, the grand superstructure of the future Indian Paralympic Movement will be built upon the solid foundation laid by generations of Indian para athletes—from Murlikant Petkar to Manoj Sarkar.

This may be the final chapter of the book, but the journey is far from over. The road now leads to Paris 2024.

ACKNOWLEDGEMENTS

My 15-year-old daughter Manvi harbours a dream of writing and getting published. Whenever she approaches me with her hungry quest to find her own path, two simple questions invariably accompany her inquiry: "What inspires one to write a book?" And as I get drawn into the profound display of a child's mind, pat comes the accompaniment "how does one choose what to write about?"

Explaining here feels slightly easier than baring it all to my daughter. After all, a book is akin to raising a child. It involves conceiving an idea, nurturing it slowly and steadily, with the hope of leaving behind a lasting legacy—an imprint that points to eternity.

I echo this sentiment, particularly in light of my previous works aimed at capturing the underlying narratives of their time. My earlier books, *Dressing Room: The Inside Story, The IPL Story: Cricket, Glamour and Big Money,* and *She Dared: Women in Indian Sports,* weren't bereft of the essence of their times.

Having hefted newsrooms first as a sports editor and later as and a sports broadcaster, I consistently pushed boundaries, striving to add depth and value to each topic. For me, it was crucial to ensure the content are not merely a collection of parts held together by a catchy title. Perhaps, it's this drive to go beyond mere flashy book covers that led me to embark on my current narrative – *Crossing the Barriers: The Paralympic Legends of India.*

Over the past decade, I have been deeply involved in guiding various stakeholders of differently-abled sporting institutions and associations across India.

The Cricket Association for the Blind in India (CABI), the Wheelchair Cricket India Association, the Special Olympics Bharat, and the Paralympic Committee of India (PCI), were huge eye-openers for me, highlighting the critical imperative to advocate for differently-abled sports.

With a leader as inspiring as the honourable Indian Prime Minister Shri Narendra Modi, who, over the last past decade and during his tenure as the Chief Minister of Gujarat, has created an ecosystem to propel the growth of para sports through his policies and actions, I found no need to seek intellectual stimulation elsewhere.

The decision to nominate Devendra Jhajharia, one of India's most celebrated Paralympians, as a candidate for the 2024 Lok Sabha elections in Rajasthan's Churu constituency will go down in history as a testament to the nation's recognition of one of its true champions.

This day will be etched in memory as the moment when the narrative of para athletic progress shattered the symbolic glass ceiling, boldly entering the arena of popular yet demanding political terrain.

The early years of my impressionable childhood had everything any other kid from a middle-class Indian family would have. However, it also had the numbing, choking grief of losing my three-year-old sister, Sahara to polio when I was only five years old.

Sahara remains vivid in my memory, forever etched in a golden aura of innocence that even the relentless passage of time cannot fade. Much of this cherished recollection has been crafted by my mother, Mridula Devi. Although Sahara left us years ago, my mother has remained my biggest *sahara* (support) in all my endeavours.

During the formative years, it's the bonds of love and innocence that shape every child, and mine was no exception. Growing up in Bhagalpur, Bihar, at my maternal grandparents' home alongside my cousin Renuka Dubey was enlightening. Dr Renuka Dubey, fondly known as "Happy", battled against the malaise of polio since childhood. Yet, like a resilient oak, she never flinched, carving out a life full of grace. I have always admired her strength and determination.

In my family, two exceptional storytellers—Chameli Devi, my *nani* (maternal granny) and Seedha Devi, my *daadi* (paternal granny)—likely sowed the seeds of narration in its purest form. My *nana*, the late Harendra Prasad, was the first to teach me how to craft words from ideas. Moreover, my father, Umakant Dubey, introduced me to the world of newsprint— broadsheets, magazines, and the fascinating world of sports. My *tau* (paternal uncle), the late Prof. Muchkund Dubey, a former foreign secretary, and *mama* (maternal uncle), Pramod Dubey, were always there to pass on invaluable life lessons. With all that cushioning, it's no surprise that I found my calling as a writer. This book was an idea that had been waiting to be expressed.

When my family was impacted by COVID-19, Manvi was deeply involved in assisting a specially-abled child as his writer to write his board exams. This compassionate act itself served as a powerful catalyst to embark on this current endeavour—a tome that will shed light on the unsung heroes of para sports, often overlooked in the journey of discovering everything else.

A team of people—my only team, my family—kept me going as I sat down to put pen to paper, undertaking perhaps the most critical narrative I will ever craft. My better half, Tripti, my children, Manvi and Kabir, my younger brother, Anubhav, and his wife, Rajni, along with my niece, Aadya, and nephew, Nihit, balanced everything for me, never allowing me to lose sight of what truly matters.

My co-author, Mahavir Rawat, has been a rock throughout this project, helping us bring this book to fruition. Mahavir, a former colleague from my *NDTV* days, has been an invaluable partner in uncovering the authentic narratives of para athletes that were once buried in time.

I would like to express my gratitude to Gurusharan Singh, former Secretary General of the Paralympic Committee of India, undeniably the foremost authority on para sports in the country. I also extend my thanks to Prafulla Ketkar, editor of *The Organiser* magazine, and Mallika Nadda, President of Special Olympics Bharat, for supporting me in this project. Furthermore, I am grateful to my friend and co-author of my previous book, Sanjeeb Mukherjea, for chipping in wherever needed.

My colleagues at Prasar Bharati Sports have always been at the forefront in fulfilling the public broadcaster's mission of covering and promoting para sports across the country, serving as a tremendous source of inspiration. I would like to extend special gratitude to my colleagues, Omprakash Kharakwal and Amitesh Srivastava, for their invaluable assistance with this particular project. I also want to acknowledge the significant contribution of officials from the Sports Authority of India (SAI) for selecting DD Sports as the broadcast partner for the inaugural Khelo India Para Games.

My special thanks to my friends, Samarendra Singh and Rajnish Singh, as well as my cousin, Amit Tripathy, for always being there as pillars of strength and for offering constructive criticism when needed.

A special acknowledgement is owed to Ramesh Kumar, Co-Founder of NAAD Wellness, for his support in conducting the essential research for the project.

Lastly, I want to express my appreciation for the major contribution of my publisher, Konark Publishers, spearheaded by K.P.R. Nair, Managing Director, and Jiza Joy, Coordinating Editor. First, for agreeing to publish the book on this subject, and secondly, for their relentless pursuit of perfection across various aspects related to the book.

The primary objective of this book will, however, remain unfulfilled unless we all unite to play our part in realising the vision of our Honourable Prime Minister Narendra Modi for a truly inclusive India. It is crucial that the differently abled are integrated into our growth story, especially as our great nation commemorates 100 years of its independence in 2047.

Jai Hind!

PARALYMPIC FACTOIDS

- ❖ The Paralympic Games began in 1948 at a military hospital in North London.

- ❖ Neurologist Sir Ludwig Gutmann, in order to speed up the recovery of his paraplegic patients, most of whom were World War II veterans, conceived the idea of organising sports competitions alongside the London Olympics.

- ❖ The first official Paralympic Games were held in 1960 and were known as "The Stoke Mandeville Games", named after the hospital where they originated.

- ❖ The Paralympics Games always take place about two weeks after the Olympic Games.

- ❖ Since 1988, the Olympic and Paralympic Games have been held in the same city and at the same venues.

- ❖ The prefix "para" in Paralympic means 'alongside' in Greek, reflecting the Games' objective to exist alongside the Olympic Games.

- ❖ The Paralympic Games initially featured only wheelchair athletes. After the 1976 Games, the scope expanded to include competitors with various disabilities like amputees, cerebral palsy, visual impairments, spinal cord injuries, and intellectual disabilities.

- ❖ The Paralympic Games symbol consists of three waves called "Agitos", meaning "I move" in Latin.

- Two sports exclusive to the Paralympic Games are boccia and goalball.

- Since the London 2012 Paralympic Games, guides in para athletics and para triathlon, as well as pilots in para cycling and para triathlon, are also awarded medals.

- Each Paralympic sport has its classification system to ensure fair and equal competition.

- Only three disciplines are open to athletes with intellectual disabilities: para athletics, para swimming and para table tennis.

- The hoop in wheelchair basketball is set at 3.05 metres from the ground, the same as in the Olympic Games.

- Wheelchair tennis players are allowed two bounces of the ball. The second bounce is permitted even if it lands out of bounds.

- Balls used in blind football and goalball contain bells that make noise when rolling, helping players locate them.

- Blind football players are blindfolded to ensure fair and equal competition for all.

- Para athletics athletes in the T12 (visual impairment) categories can choose to run with or without a guide.

- In para archery, athletes unable to use a conventional bow due to their disability may use assistive devices that reduce the force required to draw the bow.

- Wheelchair rugby is played with a round ball indoors.

- Swimming at the Paralympic Games is open to athletes with all types of disabilities.

- Para badminton and para taekwondo made their Paralympic debuts in Tokyo 2020.

- Para cyclists compete on four types of bicycles: classic bikes, tandems, handbikes, and tricycles.

- Brazil has won every blind football tournament at the Paralympic Games since the sport's debut.

- There are 11 disability classifications in para table tennis.

- Para powerlifting is the only weightlifting discipline at the Paralympic Games.

- In para archery, athletes who cannot use their arms may shoot with their feet.

- The 2024 Summer Paralympics will include 22 sports and 549 events.

- The Olympic and Paralympic gold medal is made of silver.

- The Tokyo 2020 Olympic medals were made entirely from recycled electronics.

- The International Paralympic Committee is the global governing body for the Paralympic Games.

- South African distance swimmer Natalie Du Toit carried the flag at the 2008 Paralympics and Summer Olympics opening ceremonies, making her the first athlete to do so in the same year.

- At the Seoul 1988 Paralympic Games, American swimmer Trischa Zorn achieved an incredible feat by winning 10 gold medals in 10 events and setting 10 world records. She is the most decorated Paralympian of all time, with a whopping

55 medals to her name, which includes 41 gold, 9 silver, and 5 bronze.

❖ The only recorded death in competition at the Paralympics was Bahman Golbarnezhad, a 48-year-old Iranian cyclist who died from cardiac arrest following a crash at the Rio 2016 Paralympics.

❖ The USA has topped the Para athletics medal table at nine Paralympic Games, more than any other country.

❖ China topped the Para athletics medal table on five occasions in a row, including Tokyo 2020 where the Asian country won 27 golds, 13 silvers, and 11 bronze medals.

❖ Wheelchair rugby was once called 'Murderball'.

ABOUT THE AUTHORS

ABHISHEK DUBEY is one of India's leading sports journalists and broadcast professionals with over 25 years of experience covering national and international sports. He began his career in sports journalism at a young age and has since led cross-functional teams at prominent organisations such as *NDTV* and *CNN-News18* (formerly *IBN7* and *CNN-IBN*), to name a few. Abhishek has reported major global events from ground zero, including the inaugural T20 World Championship in South Africa (2007), T20 World Championship in London (2009), ICC Cricket World Cup (2011), and London 2012 Olympics, among others.

A regular columnist for leading dailies and news magazines, Abhishek has authored three critically acclaimed books *Dressing Room: The Inside Story, The IPL Story: Cricket, Glamour and Big Money,* and *She Dared: Women in Indian Sports.*

His expertise lies in overseeing coverage and broadcast of grassroots initiatives in Indian sports like Indigenous Games Festivals in Aizawl and Imphal, Khelo India Youth Games, Khelo India University Games, Khelo India Para Games, Khelo India Winter Games and National Games. He is actively involved in promoting sports for differently-abled athletes and supporting sports leagues across the country.

Abhishek is currently serving as Channel Manager at Prasar Bharati Sports, India's public broadcaster. For his contributions to the field of sports, he was honoured with the prestigious

Media Awards in 2022. Abhishek is committed to his lifelong goal of contributing his bit to positioning India as formidable nation in both the Paralympic and Olympic Games.

 **MAHAVIR RAWAT,** a former sports journalist who is now an anchor, commentator, and author, has embarked on a new chapter in his career by exploring the world of Paralympic athletes and their life journeys.

Drawing on his experience and empathy from his time as a reporter at *NDTV*, Mahavir masterfully crafts a compelling narrative that highlights the indomitable spirit of Paralympic athletes. Through the pages of this book, he sheds light on their extraordinary journeys, illuminating their triumphs and challenges.

His narrative aims to inspire and educate readers, fostering a deeper appreciation for inclusivity in sports.